BAYTRIPPER
CHESAPEAKE BAY
Travel Guide

Volume II
Western Shore

WHITEY SCHMIDT

MARIAN ★ HARTNETT ★ PRESS

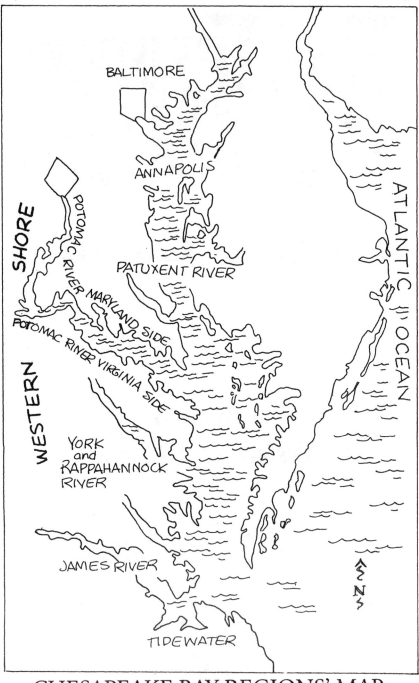

CHESAPEAKE BAY REGIONS' MAP

BAYTRIPPER
CHESAPEAKE BAY

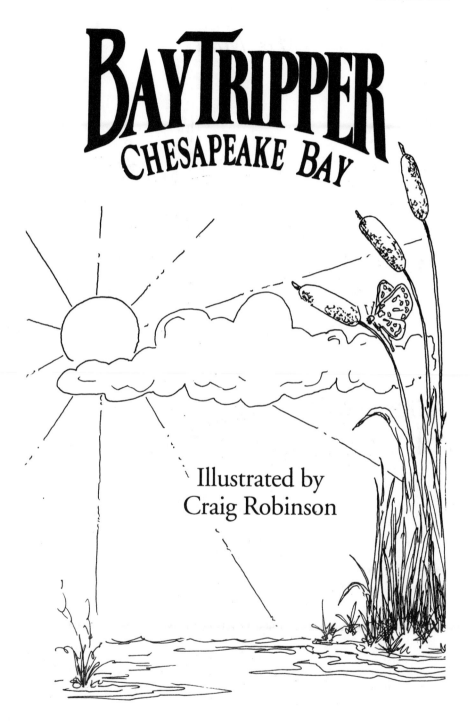

Illustrated by
Craig Robinson

For Matt

Printed in the
United States of America
First Printing 1995
ISBN 0-9613008-2-5

Library of Congress Catalog Number 95-75814
Copyright 1995 by Marian Hartnett Press
Box 51 Friendship Road
Friendship, Maryland 20758

CONTENTS

CONTENTS

CONTENTS

Introduction/Western Shore

Whether you're exploring the Chesapeake Bay region for the first time or returning for another visit, you're in for a treat. I've lived on the banks of the Chesapeake Bay all of my life, and I love it here. About 10 years ago, I moved to a beautiful area approximately 25 miles outside of Annapolis. Where else could I walk a few steps from my home and watch 44 swans meandering off shore? The natural beauty outside my window is ever changing with eagles, osprey, and otters, as well as migrating Canadian geese in the winter. And at the same time, I am only an hour away from Washington, D.C., and all it has to offer.

And there is another reason why I love it here—the fresh crab. Crab cakes and seafood are specialties around the Bay as are wonderful views to dine by. As a restaurant critic, I've sampled the offerings of many of the varied restaurants in the region. All of my books are about the Chesapeake Bay area, and most feature its unique cuisine.

As I worked on my first book, *The Official Crab Eater's Guide*, I spent 5 years traveling the highways and back roads around the Bay. Along the way, I'd spot a museum or an historic site I'd want to return to some day. I started compiling these gems of information, and it wasn't long before I'd collected boxes of material. That background formed the basis for this book.

Falling in love with the Chesapeake Bay is easy, especially if you know the secret hideaways. That's what this book is all about—secrets. I know the Bay as well as anyone, and I've explored its nooks and crannies. The Baytripper travel guides are your guides to unique places. We've got what it takes to make your next trip a pleasure.

Enjoying the outdoors is a major pastime here. You'll find scenic creeks, rivers and marshes. There are a number of nature preserves. Battle Creek Cypress Swamp, located near Broomes Island, Maryland, is a haunting, 100-acre sanctuary that is home to North America's largest northerly stand of bald cypress trees. A boardwalk winds through the swamp, and a visitors center features exhibits of birds, reptiles, and other resident creatures.

Local festivals regularly celebrate life by the Bay. The popular Pork, Peanut, and Pine Festival, held mid-July in Surry, Virginia, is an event not to be missed. Artists and artisans abound at this annual get-together. Baytrippers will want to come just for the food. Pit-cooked barbecue, corn bread, ham biscuits, pigs feet, peanut brittle, peanut pie, and peanut soup are just some of the rewards.

Inside you'll find listings for boat trips of all types, from ferry rides to charter fishing and crabbing excursions to sailing lessons or tours of city harbors. You could climb aboard the Woodwind Schooner near Annapolis for a 2-hour sail into the Bay. Along the way, you'd pass picturesque lighthouses, grand estates, historic sites, and more.

I've pointed out places to see in the special cities along your tour which starts with Norfolk, in Tidewater, Virginia, and ends with Elkton, Maryland. You may want to enjoy one or all of the following. Many people lunch at Baltimore's renovated Inner Harbor when exploring its boutiques and markets. However, within walking distance is Baltimore's Little Italy with its award-winning restaurants. You'll certainly want to stop at the Smithsonian Institution if you visit Washington, D.C., but there's also the Museum of the Confederacy in Richmond, Virginia, for all of you history buffs. And let's not forget Williamsburg, Virginia. The famous restoration offers an authentic glimpse of life in Colonial America. Guided tours of the Governor's Palace and the James River Plantations are a stone's throw away. Nearby is the Busch Gardens "Old Country" Family Theme Park.

These are just a few of my favorites. Skim the pages and select your own. You're about to discover a region packed with something for everyone—just follow the water!

HOW TO USE THIS BOOK

For ease of use, *Baytripper* is divided into two volumes. Volume I, the Eastern Shore, explores the towns from Chesapeake City, Maryland, in the north to Cape Charles, Virginia, in the south. Volume II, the Western Shore, covers the region from Norfolk, Virginia, in the south, to Elkton, Maryland, in the North.

Each chapter begins with a map of the area indicating the locations of the towns that dot the roads, fields, rivers, and creeks. Introducing each town is a description painting a broad picture of the historic, geographic, economic, and other factors that contribute to it's individual character.

You can begin your circle tour of the historic Chesapeake Bay region at any point along the 800-mile route. Those living in neighboring areas might choose a town that is closest to them. Continue clockwise or counterclockwise around the circle tour, seeing something new and doing something different each mile. There is no need to backtrack. You can stay on the main highways between the attractions or you can branch off on the back roads and chart your own route to discovery. Create your own unique experience using the *Baytripper* travel guides, moving at your own pace, emphasizing the things you want to see and do.

DISCLAIMER

While every care has been taken to ensure the accuracy of the information in this guide, the passage of time will always bring change, and consequently the publisher cannot accept responsibility for errors that may occur. The prudent Baytripper will avoid inconvenience by calling ahead.

CREDIT CARDS ARE ABBREVIATED AS FOLLOWS:

AE - American Express
CB - Carte Blanche
D   - Discover Card
DC - Diner's Club
MC - Master Card
V   - Visa

TIDEWATER
Norfolk to Suffolk

Follow the water....

- Norfolk
- Portsmouth
- Suffolk

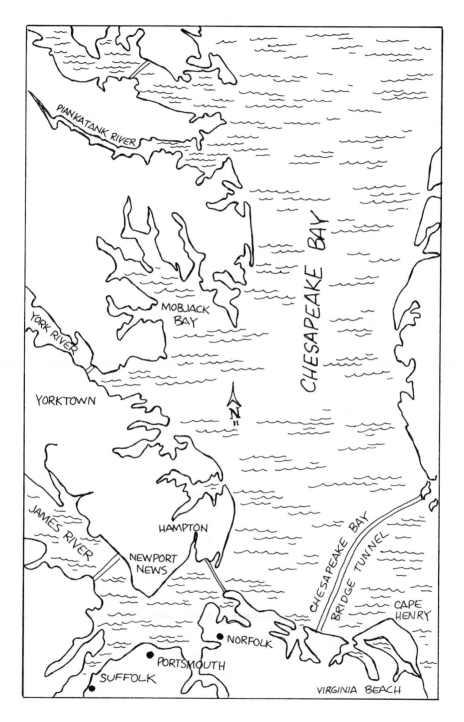

NORFOLK

■ **BACKGROUND**: In 1680, King Charles II, of England, decreed that port cities be created in the colonies. So, in 1682, 50 acres of the Norfolk site were purchased for a mere 10,000 pounds of tobacco from a farmer named Nicholas Wise. The name, Norfolk, was provided by Colonel Thoroughgood, one of the earliest settlers, for his native county in England. In the early 1700's, the post traded with the West Indies. During the Civil War, Norfolk was the chief naval station of the Confederacy. Today Norfolk is a marvelous blend of nautical history. The daily waterfront parade of boats, gentle surf and wide beaches fascinate natives and delight visitors.

Attractions

■ **VISITOR INFORMATION**

Norfolk Visitor's Bureau
236 East Plume Street
Norfolk, Virginia 23510
804-441-5266
800-368-3097

Norfolk Visitor Information Center
4th View Street
Norfolk, Virginia 23503
800-368-3097

■ **AIRPORT**

Norfolk International Airport
Airport Road
Norfolk, Virginia 23518
804-857-3351

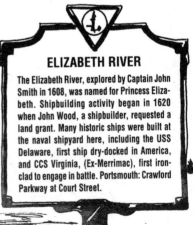

ELIZABETH RIVER

The Elizabeth River, explored by Captain John Smith in 1608, was named for Princess Elizabeth. Shipbuilding activity began in 1620 when John Wood, a shipbuilder, requested a land grant. Many historic ships were built at the naval shipyard here, including the USS Delaware, first ship dry-docked in America, and CCS Virginia, (Ex-Merrimac), first ironclad to engage in battle. Portsmouth: Crawford Parkway at Court Street.

■ BEACHES

Ocean View Beaches
Ocean View Avenue
Norfolk, Virginia 23503
800-368-3097

Beaches provide sun, sand, life guards, picnic shelters, concession stands, and oceans of fun. Free.

Sarah Constant Shrine Beach
East Ocean View Avenue
and Tidewater Drive
Norfolk, Virginia 23503
804-853-6654

This public beach offers lifeguards (on duty from 10 a.m. to 6 p.m.), parking, picnic areas, and restrooms. Free.

■ BOAT CHARTERS: Deep-sea fishing—enjoy a day of fishing or sightseeing, full- or half-day trips. Bring the whole family, and enjoy a day on the water.

Lynnhaven Seafood Marina
3311 Shore Drive
Virginia Beach, Virginia 23451
804-481-4545

Home of the Big "D," the "Nancy Anne" and an entire fleet of deep-sea fishing vessels. Full- and half-day trips. Boats leave 8 a.m. and 1 p.m. daily. Fee.

Virginia Beach Fishing Center
200 Winston Salem Avenue
Virginia Beach, Virginia 23451
804-422-5700

Deep sea fishing, sightseeing, head boats, sport fishing. Full- and half-day trips, year round. Fee.

■ BOAT CRUISES

American Rover Tallship Cruises
P.O. Box 3125
333 Waterside Drive
Norfolk, Virginia 23514
804-627-SAIL

The sails are always set aboard the American Rover, a magnificent 135-foot topsail schooner, offering daily tours of Hampton Road's historic, nautical landmarks. The Rover's design was inspired by historic 19th century cargo schooners. Two-hour cruises depart at 3 p.m. daily and at 11 a.m. Wednesday through Sunday. Three-hour cruises depart 6:30 p.m. from mid-April through October. Admission charge.

Carrie B. Harbor Tours
333 Waterside Drive
Norfolk, Virginia 23510
804-393-4735

The "Carrie B." is an exact replica of a 19th century Mississippi riverboat. Features of the tours include an exciting 1 1/2 hour tour of the Norfolk Naval shipyard and inner harbor where you will see the Norfolk Naval Shipyard founded under the British flag in 1776. Open daily from April 15 through Labor Day. Cruises at 12 noon, 2 p.m., and 4 p.m. Admission charge.

Elizabeth River Ferry
333 Waterside Drive
Norfolk, Virginia 23510
804-627-9291

Pedestrian ferry transportation between Norfolk and Portsmouth. Operates year round. The boat departs from the waterside every half-hour on the quarter-hour. Fee.

Spirit of Norfolk
333 Waterside Drive
Norfolk, Virginia 23510
804-627-7771

This harbor cruise captures all the elements of an oceangoing cruise, including live entertainment, dancing, good food and drink. Cruises depart daily at 10 a.m. and 7 p.m. Admission charge.

■ HISTORIC SITES

Adams-Thoroughgood House
1636 Parish Road
Virginia Beach, Virginia 23455
804-460-0007

The oldest brick house in America was built on the banks of the Lynnhaven River in 1636. Visitors here find authentic 17th century furnishings and marvel at the excellence of construction of this colonial home. Open Tuesday through Saturday 10 a.m. to 5 p.m., Sunday 12 noon to 5 p.m. Admission charge.

Cape Henry Lighthouse
Old Fort Story
Shore Drive
Virginia Beach, Virginia 23459
804-460-1688

Near the lighthouse, the first permanent English settlers in North America landed on American soil on April 26, 1607. From here, they went on to make the settlement at Jamestown. The brick light house was built in 1791. Open mid-March through October. Free.

Historic Sites, cont.

The Lynnhaven House
440 South Wishart Road
Virginia Beach, Virginia 23455
804-460-1688

Built in 1725, this wonderfully preserved, late medieval-style house features frequent demonstrations of period crafts of the early 18th century lifestyle. Open April to November, Tuesday through Sunday, from 12 noon to 4 p.m. Admission charge.

Moses Myers House
323 East Freemason Street
Norfolk, Virginia 23510
804-627-2737

Built in 1792 by one of the first millionaires in America, the Moses Myers House remains one of the most elegant town houses in the country. Baytrippers can stroll through halls once walked by such historic figures as President James Monroe, Daniel Webster, and the Marquis de Lafayette. Open Tuesday through Saturday 10 a.m. to 5 p.m. and Sunday 12 noon to 5 p.m. Admission charge.

St. Paul's Church
201 St. Paul's Boulevard
Norfolk, Virginia 23510
804-627-4353

Built in 1739, St. Paul's Church is the one survivor of a British bombardment by Lord Dunmore in 1776. A cannonball remains embedded in a wall. Open Tuesday through Saturday from 10 a.m. to 4 p.m. Sunday worship services. Donation.

Willoughby-Baylor House
601 East Freemason Street
Norfolk, Virginia 23510
804-627-2737

This house was built in 1794 by Captain William Willoughby on property received in the land grant circa 1636. The furnishings are authentic 18th century pieces which give remarkable insight into the life of a post-Revolutionary American family. Also on the premises is an authentic English herb garden. Open from April through December, 10 a.m. to 5 p.m., Tuesday through Saturday. January through March, open 12 noon to 5 p.m. and closed Sunday. Admission charge.

■ HISTORIC TOWNS

City of Virginia Beach
P.O. Box 200
Virginia Beach, Virginia 23458
800-VA-BEACH

This resort features family attractions, outdoor recreational facilities, year-round events, 35 miles of beaches, a newly renovated 4-mile boardwalk/resort area, and a diverse selection of restaurants and shopping opportunities. Another good reason to visit is to explore the Virginia Marine Science Museum.

19

■ MISCELLANEOUS

Association for Research and Enlightenment, Inc.
67th Street and Atlantic Avenue
Virginia Beach, Virginia 23451
804-428-3588

Headquarters for the work of the late psychic, Edgar Cayce. Open daily 10 a.m. to 5 p.m. Free.

Chesapeake Bay Bridge-Tunnel
Department FT6
Cape Charles, Virginia 23310
804-624-3511

The 17-mile long Bay Bridge-Tunnel connects Norfolk with the eastern shore of Virginia, saving 95 miles and 1 1/2 hours of driving time between Norfolk and points north. Three miles out at sea, there is a stop-over with a gift shop, restaurant, and fishing pier. The passageway is listed as one of the man-made wonders of the world. Fee.

d'Art Center
125 College Place
Norfolk, Virginia 23510
804-625-4211

The Center is a working artistic community for the visual arts. More than 40 artisans create, display, and sell their work. Open Tuesday through Saturday from 10 a.m. to 5 p.m. and on Sunday from 12 noon to 5 p.m. Closed Monday. Free.

Waterside Festive Marketplace
333 Waterside Drive
Norfolk, Virginia 23510
804-627-3300

The waterside is an exciting marketplace on the city's revitalized waterfront, with more than 120 shops and dining places. Open daily from 10 a.m. to 9 p.m. Closed Thanksgiving and Christmas.

■ MUSEUMS

The Chrysler Museum
245 West Olney Road
Norfolk, Virginia 23510
804-622-1211

Chrysler Museum is one of the top 20 art museums in the country. Some of the artists represented include Veronese, Tintoretto, Bernini, Gainsborough, Rodin, Manet, Renoir, Degas, Matisse, Picasso, and Warhol. The museum also exhibits an excellent collection of decorative arts including ceramics, silver, and furniture dating from the 12th century. Hours are 10 a.m. to 4 p.m. Tuesday through Saturday, and 1 p.m. to 5 p.m. on Sunday. Closed Monday and major holidays. Admission charge.

Hampton Roads Naval Museum
One Waterside Drive
Norfolk, Virginia 23510
804-444-8971

The museum presents an extensive naval history of the Hampton Roads area and includes detailed ship models, period photographs, archaeological artifacts, and a superior collection of naval prints and artwork. Open daily 9 a.m. to 4 p.m. Closed major holidays. Free.

Museums, cont.

Hermitage Foundation Museum
7637 North Shore Road
Norfolk, Virginia 23505
804-423-2052

Hermitage Foundation Museum is housed in an elegant riverside mansion on 12 acres of beautifully landscaped grounds on the Lafayette River. The collection includes paintings; sculpture in marble, bronze, and woods; ivories; ritual bronzes; jade; and ceramics including Chinese tomb figures from the T'ang Dynasty. Open 10 a.m. to 5 p.m. Monday through Saturday, and 1 p.m. to 5 p.m. Sunday. Admission charge.

Hunter House Victorian Museum
240 West Freemason Street
Norfolk, Virginia 23510
804-623-9814

This Victorian-era home/museum is located on one of Norfolk's original cobblestone streets. Open April through December, Wednesday through Sun day. Admission charge.

Douglas MacArthur Memorial
City Hall Avenue
and Bank Street
Norfolk, Virginia 23510
804-441-2965

The museum and memorial are about the life and times of General Douglas MacArthur. Open Tuesday through Saturday 10 a.m. to 5 p.m., Sunday 12 noon to 5 p.m. Admission charge.

This memorial contains an extensive collection of exhibits and memorabilia tracing the General's controversial life and military career. It is also his final resting place. The Memorial has nine galleries of exhibits ranging from the General's famous corncob pipe to the surrender documents that ended World War II, plus a film on his life. The General's World War II staff car is also housed within the Memorial.

Nauticus Maritime Center
One Waterside Drive
Norfolk, Virginia 23514
804-623-9084

*"I must go down to the sea
again, for the call of the
running tide."*
—*John Masefield*

From observation decks, Baytrippers will see and learn about the nautical panorama. Exhibits include presentations on marine exploration, navigation, shipbuilding as well as commerce, energy. Nauticus also offers a new film, "The Living Sea" in 70mm. Open daily, March through December, closed January and February. Admission charge.

■ PARKS AND GARDENS

Norfolk Botanical Gardens
Azalea Garden Road
Norfolk, Virginia 23518
804-853-6972

GARDEN FEATURES
1. Tropical Pavilion
2. Japanese Garden
3. Deciduous Azalea Garden
4. Holly Garden
5. Camellia Garden
6. English Border Garden
7. Woodmen of the World Wayside
8. Figure Eight Garden
9. Friendship Pond
10. Renaissance Garden
11. Surprise Garden
12. Purity Garden
13. Colonial Garden
14. Rhododendron Garden
15. Martin House Point
16. Edgewater Wayside and Stone Bridge
17. Horticultural Self Study Area
18. Conifer Garden
19. All America Official Display Garden
20. Doughterty Wayside and Bird Sanctuary
21. Fruit Orchard
22. Flowering Arboretum
23. Frederic Heutte Memorial Garden
24. Perennial Garden
25. Enchanted Forest
26. R.W. Cross Nature Trail
27. Wild Flower Garden
28. Bicentennial Rose Garden
29. Desert Garden
30. Annarino Bog Garden

The Norfolk Botanical Gardens, located in a natural setting covering about 175 acres, are comprised of many gardens within a garden. There are over 12 miles of pathways that lead visitors through such gardens as the fragrance garden for the blind, the sunken garden and a Japanese garden as well as perennial, vista, and colonial gardens. Trackless trains and leisurely drifting canal boats offer a memorable trip through miles of sunlit paths and quiet waterways. Open weekdays 8:30 a.m. to 5 p.m. and weekends from 10 a.m. to 5 p.m. Admission charge.

Parks and Gardens, cont.

Seashore State Park
2500 Shore Drive
Virginia Beach, Virginia 23451
804-481-2131
804-481-4836

You'll find bike trails with bike rentals, boat launching, camping, fishing, group camping, some handicapped facilities, hiking trails, cabins, self-guided walking trails, and great views of the Chesapeake Bay and Atlantic Ocean. Open year round. Admission charge.

Town Point Park
120 West Main Street
Norfolk, Virginia 23510
804-627-7809

Adjacent to the Waterside Festive Marketplace on the Elizabeth River is Town Point Park, site of free concerts and festivals sponsored by Festevents. Write for calendar of events.

Virginia Zoological Park
3500 Granby Street
Norfolk, Virginia 23504
804-441-2706

A 55-acre zoological park exhibiting over 320 animals and birds. The park is open daily from 10 a.m. to 5 p.m. Closed only on Christmas and New Year's Day. Admission charge.

■ SEASONAL EVENTS

Harborfest
207 Granby Street
Suite 311
Norfolk, Virginia 23510
804-627-5329

This event draws over a million visitors yearly. You'll find mock sea battles, a sailboat regatta, waterskiing, crab races, sky diving, fireworks, running events, tug-of-war games, music and concerts. A wondrous variety of seafood makes this one of the most fantastic events in the Chesapeake region. Held early June each year. Free.

International Azalea Festival
420 Bank Street
Norfolk, Virginia 23510
804-622-2312

The Azalea Festival is a salute to NATO, whose maritime headquarters is in Norfolk. Festivities include a parade, ball, and military air show. Events are all centered around downtown and Town Point Park. Activities in clude arts, crafts, international dancing, food, and sports. Free.

Norfolk Tides
150 Parks Avenue
Norfolk, Virginia 23510
804-622-2222

Norfolk's professional baseball team, the Norfolk Tides is a member of the Triple-A International League and the top farm team for the New York Mets. The Tides' season begins in May and ends in September. Call for schedule and times. Admission charge.

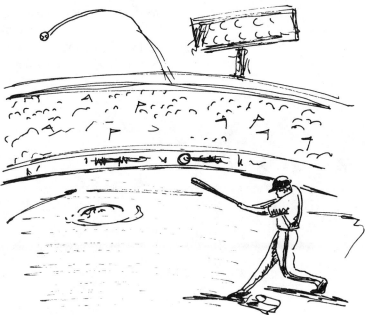

25

■ TOURS

Gray Line Tours
804-363-9644

Let Gray Line's knowledgeable chauffeurs detail Norfolk's historic attractions and modern museums. Tours available year round, Monday through Saturday. Reservations should be made by 5 p.m. the evening before the tour. Admission charge.

Norfolk Navy Base Tour
P.O. Box 2096
9808 Hampton Boulevard
Norfolk, Virginia 23510
804-627-9291
804-444-7955

Tour the world's largest naval base. Home port for more than 126 ships, 51 aircraft squadrons, and 65 shore-based military activities. Operates seasonally. Admission charge.

Norfolk Trolley Tour
P.O. Box 2096
Norfolk, Virginia 23510
804-627-9291

Climb aboard a Norfolk trolley for a 1-hour tour of historic downtown Norfolk, its attractions, and fashionable neighborhoods. Visitors can get off to explore the many attractions and then catch a later trolley. May to September, 11 a.m. to 4 p.m. daily. Fee.

Restaurants

Stretched along the southern shore of the Chesapeake Bay, Norfolk has long been a city famous for its fresh seafood. Many restaurants, some with an excellent waterfront view, offer a sampling of this rewarding harvest. Baytrippers will find dining in Norfolk is a delight.

Alexander's on the Bay
4536 Ocean View Avenue
Virginia Beach, Virginia 23503
804-464-4999

Alexander's on the Bay is located at the foot of Venture Street, near the Chesapeake Bay Bridge-Tunnel. The dining room has a gracious yet relaxed atmosphere. The cuisine is superb yet unpretentious. The tables, glassware, and silverware are spotless and fresh flowers adorn the table. House specialties of our liking include broiled seafood combination platter, soft shell crabs, oysters Rockefeller, clams on the half shell, and shrimp with asparagus bisque. Open daily for dinner. Credit cards: AE, C, MC, and V.

Capt. Johns
4616 Virginia Beach Blvd.
Virginia Beach, Virginia 23464
804-499-7755

The finest seafood buffet — in Virginia Beach. Specials include Fresh Alaskan Snow Crab Legs, Steamed Shrimp, Clams, Mussels and Seafood Dishes, Vegetables, Salads and Desserts. All you care to eat. Open daily for lunch and dinner. Credit cards: AE, D, MC, and V.

SEAFOOD RESTAURANT

Restaurants, cont.

Duck-Inn
3324 Shore Drive
Virginia Beach, Virginia 23451
804-481-0201

It is appropriate that Duck-Inn sits overlooking the mouth of the Chesapeake Bay. Since the lower Bay and the salt marshes of Virginia's shore provide most of our fare, this is the source of the largest seafood industry in the United States. "Our weather station in the lobby is used by watermen, sailors, and sport fishermen to check water and weather conditions before setting up for work or play." Baytrippers won't want to miss a broiled seafood platter dinner with this wonderful view. Open daily for breakfast, lunch, and dinner. Credit cards: AE, D, MC, and V.

Fellini's
123 West 21st Street
Norfolk, Virginia 23517
804-625-3000

Fellini's features 16 gourmet pizzas, Greek and Caesar salads, fresh pasta entrees, and sandwiches, in a casual, European setting. Open daily for lunch and dinner. Credit cards: MC and V.

Fishermen's Wharf
71 Bayville Avenue
Norfolk, Virginia 23510
804-480-3113

Freemason Abbey
209 West Freemason Street
Norfolk, Virginia 23510
804-622-3966

Harbor Grill
333 Waterside Drive
Norfolk, Virginia 23510
804-627-8800

The Fishermen's Wharf is located on the confluence where the Atlantic Ocean flows with the mighty Chesapeake Bay. This restaurant is noted for its world-famous seafood buffet. An extensive list of seafood entrees includes steamed shrimp, shrimp creole, broiled scallops, fried flounder, oysters, boiled fish, seafood au gratin, imperial crab, and baked whole fish. BBQ'd ribs, steamed crabs, clam chowder, fresh breads, and desserts are also offered. Open for lunch and dinner daily. Credit cards: AE, CB, DC, MC, and V.

The Freemason Abbey building was built, and originally dedicated as a church in 1873. Today it's a popular downtown restaurant that features fresh lobster, pasta, fish and choice prime rib. Open Tuesday through Sunday for lunch and dinner. Credit cards: AE, DC, MC, and V.

Relax in a casual atmosphere that has one of the best views of the Norfolk harbor. You can watch your chef prepare your steak or seafood on one of the brass and copper grills while enjoying the sights of the water. Outdoor dining year round. Open for lunch and dinner. Credit cards: AE, DC, D, MC, and V.

Restaurants, cont.

Henry's
3319 Shore Drive
Virginia Beach, Virginia 23451
804-481-7300

Henry's is located at Lynnhaven Inlet. It has featured the finest, freshest seafood since 1938, all with great water views. Special ties include oysters on the half shell, giant crab cakes, and an excellent seafood platter. Most seafood on the menu can be fried or broiled, and don't worry—the waiters won't forget the hush puppies. Open daily for lunch and dinner during summer months and dinner only during winter months. Credit cards: AE, MC, and V.

Il Porto
333 Waterside Drive
Norfolk, Virginia 23510
804-627-4400

Elegantly casual, its reputation precedes itself. Il Porto is on the water, located in the lower level of Harborplace. Open for lunch and dinner. Credit cards: AE, C, DC, MC, and V.

O'Sullivan's Wharf
4300 Colley Avenue
Norfolk, Virginia 23508
804-423-3746
804-423-3753

Dine on an open air deck located on the LaFayette River. Pick your own lobster at this waterfront favorite of locals. Fresh seafood (cooked to order), black angus beef (cut and cooked to order), raw bar, sandwiches, burgers, and lite fare. Open daily for lunch and dinner. Credit cards: AE, DC, MC, and V.

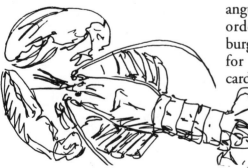

Phillips Waterside
333 Waterside Drive
Norfolk, Virginia 23510
804-627-6600

The place to go for seafood, fabulous steaks, good times, daily specials and a children's menu. Phillips is located in the Harborplace complex and overlooks the bustling Elizabeth River. Phillips is the place to begin your Chesapeake Bay tradition of fine food—a Victorian theme is established by its tiffany-style lamps, stained-glass windows, and sewing machine tables. Open for lunch and dinner. Credit cards: DC, MC, and V.

The Ships Cabin
4110 East Ocean View Avenue
Virginia Beach, Virginia 23503
804-480-2526

The menu says it best: "One of the leading business publications in the country, *Sales and Marketing Management Magazine*, lists the Ships Cabin among the top 100 restaurants in North America." The interior does, indeed, resemble a ship's cabin with dark wood paneled walls, ceiling fans, brass lamps, and exposed timber, but the bayside dining room is the perfect showplace for some of the best seafood in the world. Open daily for lunch and dinner. Credit cards: AE, C, DC, MC, and V.

Accommodations

Norfolk has more than 5,000 hotel and motel rooms to suit every budget. Choose from beachfront properties overlooking the Chesapeake Bay, to downtown hotels in the heart of Norfolk's historic district.

■ BED AND BREAKFASTS

Page House
323 Fairfax Avenue
Norfolk, Virginia 23507
804-625-5033

■ CAMPING

Holiday Trav-L-Park
1075 General Booth Boulevard
Virginia Beach, Virginia 23451
804-425-0249
800-548-0223

Seashore State Park
2500 Shore Drive
Virginia Beach, Virginia 23451
804-481-2131
804-481-4836

Indian Cove Campground
Box 1053, Sandbridge Road
Virginia Beach, Virginia 23456
804-426-2601
804-426-6294

Virginia Beach KOA
1240 General Booth Highway
Virginia Beach, Virginia 23451
804-428-1444

■ HOTEL, MOTELS, AND INNS

Best Western Center Inn
235 North Military Highway
Norfolk, Virginia 23502
804-461-6600
800-237-5517

Comfort Inn
8051 Hampton Boulevard
Hampton, Virginia 23505
804-451-0000

Comfort Inn Town Point
930 Virginia Beach Boulevard
at Tidewater Drive
Norfolk, Virginia 23504
804-623-5700

Days Inn Marina
1631 Bayville Street
Norfolk, Virginia 23503
804-583-4521

Days Inn Norfolk-
5701 Chamber Street
Norfolk, Virginia 23502
804-461-0100

Econo Lodge Airport
3343 North Military Highway
Norfolk, Virginia 23518
804-855-3116
800-424-4777

Hotels, Motels, and Inns cont.

Econo Lodge Azalea Gardens
1850 East Little Creek Road
Norfolk, Virginia 23518
804-588-8888
800-424-4777

Econo Lodge East Ocean View
East Ocean View Avenue
Norfolk, Virginia 23503
804-480-1111
800-424-4777

**Econo Lodge West
Ocean View Beach**
9601 4th View Street
Norfolk, Virginia 23503
800-424-4777

Hampton Inn
1450 Military Highway
Norfolk, Virginia 23502
804-466-7474

**Hampton Inn/
Norfolk Naval Base**
8501 Hampton Boulevard
Norfolk, Virginia 23505
804-489-1000

Hilton/Airport
500 North Military Highway
Norfolk, Virginia 23502
804-466-8000 800-HILTONS

Ho Jo Inn
515 North Military Highway
Norfolk, Virginia 23502
804-461-1800
800-654-2000

Holiday Inn/Waterside
700 Monticello Avenue
Norfolk, Virginia 23510
804-627-5555

Holiday Sands Motel and Tower
1330 East Ocean View Avenue
Norfolk, Virginia 23503
804-583-2621
800-525-5156

Madison Hotel
Granby and Freemason Streets
Norfolk, Virginia 23510
804-622-6682
800-522-0976

Marriott Hotel/Waterside
235 East Main Street
Norfolk, Virginia 23510
804-627-4200
800-228-9290

Old Dominion Inn
4111 Hampton Boulevard
Norfolk, Virginia 23508
804-440-5100

Omni International Hotel
777 Waterside Drive
Norfolk, Virginia 23510
804-622-6664

Quality Inn Lake Wright
6280 North Hampton Boulevard
Norfolk, Virginia 23502
804-461-0251   800-228-5157

Quality Inn/Ocean View
719 East Ocean View Avenue
Norfolk, Virginia 23503
804-583-5211 800-523-0190

Overnight Inn
853 North Military Highway
Norfolk, Virginia 23502
804-461-2380

Ramada Inn/Newtown
6360 Newtown Road
Norfolk, Virginia 23502
804-461-1081

Scottish Inn
1001 North Military Highway
Norfolk, Virginia 23502
804-461-4391

Sheraton Inn
870 Military Highway
Norfolk, Virginia 23502
804-461-9192 800-933-9600

Super 8 Motel
7940 Shore Drive
Norfolk, Virginia 23518
804-588-7888 800-800-8000

PORTSMOUTH

■ **BACKGROUND:** The city of Portsmouth was founded in 1659 by Captain William Carver. In 1716, a grant in the amount of 1,120 acres was made to Colonel William Crawford, who laid out the city's streets. Portsmouth was established as a town in 1752. The name has a double meaning in that it is quite descriptive of the city's location and it was derived from the name of an English naval city. Today Portsmouth still maintains the charm of a picturesque, old English village.

Attractions

■ **VISITOR INFORMATION**

Portsmouth Visitor Center
801 Crawford Street
Portsmouth, Virginia 23704
804-393-5111

■ **BOAT CRUISES**

Carrie B. Harbor Tours
Bay Street
Portsmouth, Virginia 23704
804-393-4735

Expertly narrated tours of the naval shipyard and harbor. Daily April through October. Fee.

Elizabeth River Ferry
Bay Street
Portsmouth, Virginia 23704
804-627-9291

Pedestrian ferry transportation between Portsmouth and Norfolk. Open year round; departs every half hour. Fee.

■ HISTORIC SITES

Hill House
221 North Street
Portsmouth, Virginia 23704
804-393-0241

The Hill House is a four-story English basement dwelling which contains the original furnishings collected by generations of the Hill family. Built in the early 1800's, the house remains in its original condition. Open Tuesday through Saturday 10 a.m. to 5 p.m. and Sunday from 1 p.m. to 5 p.m. Admission charge.

■ MISCELLANEOUS

Pokey Smokey Steam Railroad
City Park Avenue
Portsmouth, Virginia 23704
804-393-5162

The 36-gauge miniature, coal-powered, steam locomotive train runs seasonally. Admission charge.

Portside Marketplace
Crawford Parkway
Portsmouth, Virginia 23704
804-393-5111

Portside is Portsmouth's waterfront compliment to Norfolk's Waterside. Features include the Old Harbor Market, where a dozen open-air shops offer everything from green plants to souvenirs to fresh seafood. Open mid-April to mid-October.

Virginia Sports Hall of Fame
420 High Street
Portsmouth, Virginia 23705
804-393-8031

One hundred exhibits of all types of sports, equipment, and memorabilia from inductees. Tuesday through Saturday 10 a.m. to 5 p.m. and Sunday 1 p.m. to 5 p.m. Free.

■ MUSEUMS

Automobile Museum of Hampton Roads
3535 Airline Boulevard
Portsmouth, Virginia 23701
804-465-0533

More than 50 cars take center stage in the museum's main gallery. Each is a perfectly-preserved or restored automobile with every detail exquisitely presented. Open daily from 10 a.m. to 6 p.m. Admission charge.

Portsmouth Children's Museum
400 High Street
Portsmouth, Virginia 23705
804-393-8393

The only one of its kind in the region, it offers an array of children's hands-on displays that challenge the imagination. Open Tuesday through Saturday from 10 a.m. to 5 p.m., Sunday 1 p.m. to 5 p.m. Admission charge.

Portsmouth 1846 Courthouse Museum
400 High Street
Portsmouth, Virginia 23705
804-393-8543

Dramatic exhibit space provided for travelling and special exhibits that is encompassed by a fine arts gallery. Open Tuesday through Saturday from 10 a.m. to 5 p.m. and Sunday 1 p.m. to 5 p.m. Admission charge.

The Portsmouth Lightship Museum
Londonslip at Water Street
Portsmouth, Virginia 23705
804-393-8741

Historically-equipped vessel exhibiting the important functions of lightships in maritime history as units of the U.S. Coast Guard. Open Tuesday through Saturday from 10 a.m. to 5 p.m. and Sunday from 1 p.m. to 5 p.m. Admission charge.

Portsmouth Naval Shipyard Museum
2 High Street
Portsmouth, Virginia 23705
804-393-8591

History of the Norfolk Naval Shipyard and the Portsmouth area. Ship models, flags, maps, uniforms, and memorabilia of the Armed Forces and local area on display. Open Tuesday through Saturday from 10 a.m. to 5 p.m. and Sunday 1 p.m. to 5 p.m. Admission charge.

Restaurants

The assortment of restaurants in Old Town Portsmouth is enough to whet any appetite whether you're in the mood for fine dining or casual fare. You'll find the right combination of ambience and cuisine sure to please you.

Amory's Wharf
10 Crawford Parkway
Portsmouth, Virginia 23704
804-399-0991

Amory's is located at the Tidewater Yacht Club and offers great views of the Portsmouth waterfront. It is famous for its roasted oysters, crab cakes, and other fresh seafood dishes. There also is a fine array of steak and pasta specialties. Open daily for lunch and dinner. Credit cards: AE, MC, and V.

Baron's Pub
500 High Street
Portsmouth, Virginia 23705
804-399-4840

Delicious food and drinks are provided in a casual English pub atmosphere. House specialties include fried clam strips, fresh perch with hush puppies, steaks, and seafood platters. Open Monday through Friday for lunch and dinner, Saturday for dinner, and closed Sunday. Credit cards: AE, MC, and V.

China Garden
303 High Street
Portsmouth, Virginia 23705
804-399-8888

An enjoyable eating experience with authentic Mandarin and Szechuan cuisine. Features a great and colorful buffet. Open daily for lunch and dinner. Credit cards: AE, MC, and V.

Circle Seafood Restaurant
3010 High Street
Portsmouth, Virginia 23705
804-397-8196

Recognized as one of the best Tidewater restaurants for over 40 years. Open daily for breakfast, lunch, and dinner. Credit cards: MC and V.

Mario's Italian Restaurant
611 Airline Boulevard
Portsmouth, Virginia 23705
804-399-8970

Mario's is a charming, antique-filled restaurant featuring authentic Italian cuisine. House specialties here include chicken parmesan, chicken and dumplings, stuffed peppers, hamburger steak, and linguini with red or white sauce. Open Monday through Friday for lunch and dinner and Saturday and Sunday for dinner only. Credit cards: AE, MC, and V.

41

Restaurants, cont.

The Max
425 Water Street
Portsmouth, Virginia 23705
804-397-1866

The Max is located across the Elizabeth River from Waterside. It sits next to the Pedestrian Ferry Dock. Come by ferry or car and feast on fresh seafood specialties such as our favorite, fresh tuna prepared daily any way you like it—poached, broiled, baked, fried, blackened. Open daily for lunch and dinner. Enjoy Sunday buffet any time from 11 a.m. to 3 p.m. Credit cards: AE, MC, and V.

Scale o'De Whale
3515 Shipwright Street
Portsmouth, Virginia 23703
804-483-2772

Sunsets, seagulls, seafood—Scale o'De Whale is built out on a pier at the water's edge. My favorites here include the crab soup, clam chowder, and oysters Rockefeller. Open daily—Monday through Friday for lunch and dinner, and Saturday and Sunday for dinner only. Credit cards: AE, DC, MC, and V.

＊ Appetizers ＊
Oysters Rockefeller
Roasted oysters topped with a blend of garlic butter, fresh spinach, and bacon
Oysters Hollandaise
Roasted oysters topped with crabmeat and hollandaise sause.

Accommodations

■ HOTELS, MOTELS, AND INNS

Econo Lodge
Downtown Portsmouth
1031 London Boulevard
Portsmouth, Virginia 23704
804-399-4414

Holiday Inn
8 Crawford Parkway
Portsmouth, Virginia 23704
804-393-2573
800-HOLIDAY

London Boulevard Inn
Broad Street and London
Boulevard
Portsmouth, Virginia 23704
804-399-6341

Midtown Motor Lodge
700 Frederick Boulevard
Portsmouth, Virginia 23707
804-399-3066

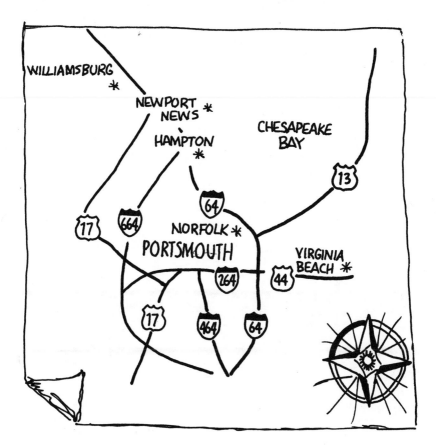

SUFFOLK

■ **BACKGROUND:** The history of Suffolk dates back to 1609 when the Nansemond Indians drove out Captain John Smith who was interested in the oyster beds in the Nansemond River. About 1619, Edward Waters, a plantation owner, became Suffolk's first white settler. The town was chartered in 1742 and named for Suffolk County, England. With its picturesque mix of historic and cultural sites, Suffolk now combines beauty and charm to create its own exciting character, in an area that is truly unique.

Attractions

■ **VISITOR INFORMATION**

Suffolk Chamber of Commerce
1001 West Washington Street
Suffolk, Virginia 23434
804-539-2111

■ **CRABBING/FISHING**

Bennett Creek Park
Shoulder Hill Road
Suffolk, Virginia 23435
804-484-3984

Fishing and crabbing pier, 1 1/4 mile nature trail, bridges over marsh area.

■ MUSEUMS

Riddick's Folly
510 North Main Street
Suffolk, Virginia 23434
804-934-1390

Greek revival town house museum offering art and history exhibits, workshops. Open Tuesday through Friday from 10 a.m. to 5 p.m. and Sunday 1 p.m. to 5 p.m. Free.

Suffolk Museum
118 Bosley Avenue
Suffolk, Virginia 23434
804-925-6311

The museum offers changing exhibits on a regular basis. Exhibits of local art work and artifacts depicting some of Suffolk's early history are displayed as well as travelling exhibits from the Virginia Museum of Fine Arts in Richmond. Open Tuesday through Saturday 10 a.m. to 5 p.m., and Sunday 1 p.m. to 5 p.m. Closed major holidays. Free.

■ PARKS AND GARDENS

Great Dismal Swamp
White Marsh Road
P.O. Box 349
Suffolk, Virginia 23434
804-986-3705

A variety of trails—hiking, biking, boardwalk, and self-guided—are available. Open daily sunrise to sunset in season. Free.

Lone Star Lakes
Bob House Parkway
Chuckatuck, Virginia 23435
804-255-4308

Lone Star Lakes is an 11,000-acre wilderness park featuring 12 lakes and 2 creeks. The park offers fishing, picnic areas, and walking trails. Open 6 a.m. to 8 p.m. during summer months, and hours vary during the winter. Admission charge.

Restaurants

Creekside Restaurant
3305 Ferry Road
Suffolk, Virginia 23435
804-484-8700

I timed my visit with the soft shelled crab season and ordered the house offering. This is where good service and good food begin. The soft shelled crabs were cooked to perfection (golden brown and juicy) and came with sliced tomatoes, homemade french fries, cole slaw, and hush puppies. The results were incredibly delicious. I can't wait to return. Open for dinner Tuesday through Saturday and on Sun day for lunch and dinner. Credit cards: AE, MC, and V.

Front Street House Restaurant
434 North Main Street
Suffolk, Virginia 23434
804-539-5393

Front Street House Restaurant, located on Main Street, offers regional specialties such as scalloped oysters with Peanut City Ham, succulent prime rib, and pan-fried pecan-encrusted rainbow trout. Sounds good, doesn't it? Open Monday through Friday for lunch and dinner and weekends for dinner only. Credit cards: D, MC, and V.

Accommodations

■ HOTELS, MOTELS, AND INNS

Comfort Inn
1503 Holland Road
Suffolk, Virginia 23434
804-539-3600

Holiday Inn
2864 Pruden Boulevard
Suffolk, Virginia 23434
804-934-2311

Econo Lodge
1017 North Main Street
Suffolk, Virginia 23434
804-539-3451

Super 8 Motel
633 North Main Street
Suffolk, Virginia 23434
804-925-0992

JAMES RIVER

Smithfield to Hampton

Follow the water....

- Smithfield
- Surry
- Hopewell
- Petersburg
- Richmond
- Williamsburg
- Newport News
- Hampton

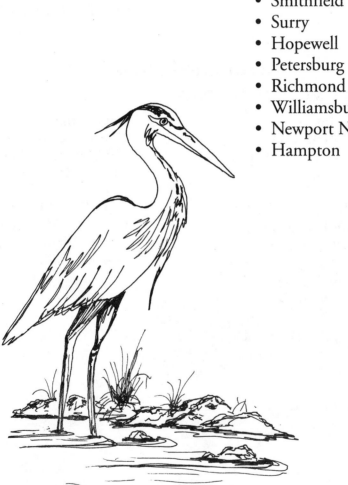

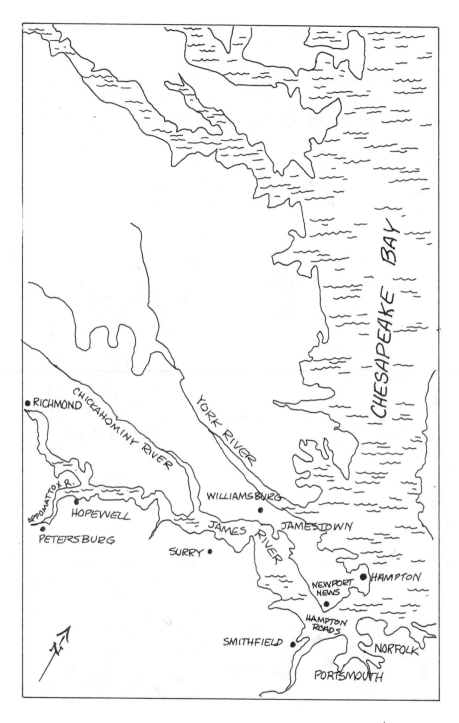

SMITHFIELD

■ **BACKGROUND:** Smithfield was settled in 1752, primarily by British merchants and ship captains. This river port town thrived for more than 20 years as a British colony before the signing of the Declaration of Independence. The town of Smithfield was laid out on a portion of land owned by Arthur Smith IV, an original land grant from the King of England. Smithfield saw battles of both the Revolutionary and Civil Wars. Today Smithfield is home of the world-renowned Smithfield Hams; the town refers to itself as the "ham capital of the world."

Attractions

■ **VISITOR INFORMATION**

Isle of Wight Tourism Bureau
130 Main Street
Smithfield, Virginia 23431
804-357-5182
800-365-9339

Smithfield Chamber of Commerce
132 Main Street
Smithfield, Virginia 23430
804-357-3502

■ **HISTORIC SITES**

The Old Courthouse of 1751
130 Main Street
Smithfield, Virginia 23430
804-357-5182

The Old Courthouse was built in 1750 and used as a county courthouse until 1800. It was a private three-story dwelling during most of the intervening years. It now serves as a visitors center. Open Monday to Friday, 9 a.m. to 5 p.m.

St. Luke's Church
14477 Benns Church Boulevard
Smithfield, Virginia 23430
804-357-3367

Oldest surviving English church in the United States, circa 1632. St. Luke's is affectionately known as "Old Brick" and is the only original Gothic church of English foundation in America. Open daily except major holidays and January.

■ MUSEUMS

Isle of Wight County Museum
103 Main Street
Smithfield, Virginia 23430
804-357-7459

A completely refurbished museum which houses the history of the world-famous Smithfield hams, Indian artifacts, Civil War relics, and fossils from the James River. Open Tuesday through Thursday, 10 a.m. to 4 p.m.; Friday, 10 a.m. to 2 p.m.; Saturday, 10 a.m. to 4 p.m.; Sunday, 1 p.m. to 5 p.m. Free.

■ PARKS AND GARDENS

Ft. Boykin Historical Park
13036 Nike Park Road
Carrollton, Virginia 23314
804-357-7459
804-357-2291

Ft. Boykin has been a part of American history since 1623, and from that time, has been involved in every military campaign fought on American soil. Overlooking the James River, it offers a beautiful respite for visitors. Open daily in season. Free.

Ragged Island Wildlife Park
Route 17
Smithfield, Virginia 23430
804-367-1000

The Ragged Island Wildlife Management Area consists of 1,537 acres of brackish water marsh and small pine islands. Two parking lots have been constructed and the long boardwalk and trail gives birdwatchers, hikers, and photographers access to the marsh. Open daily, sunup to sundown. Free.

Restaurants

C. W. Cowling's
1278 Smithfield Plaza
Smithfield, Virginia 23430
804-357-0044

Specialties include grilled items, pasta, seafood, ribs, steaks, chicken, full selections of sandwiches and salads, and more. Open daily for lunch and dinner. Credit cards: D, MC, and V.

Smithfield Station
415 South Church Street
Smithfield, Virginia 23430
804-357-7700

Savor seafood and specialty dishes featuring world-famous Smithfield ham in the Station's spacious restaurant. You may want to dine outdoors on the back deck with a breathtaking view of the Pagan River. Open daily for breakfast, lunch, and dinner. Credit cards: AE, C, MC, and V.

Accommodations

■ **BED AND BREAKFASTS**

Isle of Wight Inn
1607 South Church Street
Smithfield, Virginia 23430
804-357-3176

■ **HOTELS, MOTELS, AND INNS**

Econo Lodge
Route 258
Smithfield, Virginia 23430
804-357-9057

Smithfield Station
415 South Church Street
Smithfield, Virginia 23430
804-357-7700

SURRY

■ **BACKGROUND:** The earliest names for this Surry County seat were the Crossroads and, later, McIntosh's Crossroads. In 1796, Robert McIntosh, a tavern keeper, donated the land for the county courthouse. Surry is named for its county, formed in 1652, and named after Surry County, England.

Attractions

■ **VISITOR INFORMATION**

Surry County Chamber of Commerce
P.O. Box 353
Surry, Virginia 23883
804-294-3907

■ **BOAT CRUISES**

Jamestown-Scotland Ferry
Route 31
Scotland, Virginia 23890
804-291-3354

The largest vehicle-carrying ferry system in Virginia. The ferry offers a scenic view and trips to various points of interest on both sides of the river. Four boats operate daily from 5 a.m. until 12:30 a.m. They leave at intervals of 30 minutes to one hour. Fee.

NOTICE STOP MOTORS AND SET BRAKES. STARTING ENGINES WHILE FERRY IS MOVING AND BLOWING HORNS IS PROHIBITED

■ HISTORIC SITES

Bacon's Castle
Route 617
Surry, Virginia 23883
804-357-5976

Built in 1665, Bacon's Castle is one the oldest brick dwellings in English America. Its triple diamond stacked chimneys, curvilinear gables, and cruciform design are unique architectural features which give the structure its air of great antiquity and dignity. Open Tuesday through Saturday, 10 a.m. to 4 p.m., and Sunday from 12 noon to 4 p.m., March through September. Admission charge.

Smith's Fort Plantation
Route 31
Surry, Virginia 23883
804-294-3872

Smith's Fort Plantation, an 18th century farmhouse, is a glowing reminder of the prosperity enjoyed by the Surry colonists during the first half of the 18th century. Built on land given by Indian Chief Powhattan to John Rolfe upon his marriage to Pocahontas. Captain John Smith built a fort here on the high banks overlooking Gray's Creek, directly across the James River from Jamestown. Open Tuesday through Saturday, 10 a.m. to 5 p.m., and Sunday, 1 p.m. to 5 p.m. Admission charge.

■ MUSEUMS

Farm and Forestry Museum
Route 634
Surry, Virginia 23883
804-294-3625

The Farm and Forestry Museum is located at Chippokes State Park. The museum features antique farm equipment and logging equipment, along with information on how farmers and loggers worked their trade during the 1850's. Open Memorial Day to Labor Day, Wednesday through Sunday, and holidays, 10 a.m. to 4 p.m. Admission charge.

■ PARKS AND GARDENS

Bacon's Castle Gardens
Route 617
Surry, Virginia 23883
804-357-5976

The Bacon's Castle site is also distinguished by archaeological discovery and restoration..."the largest, earliest, best-preserved, most sophisticated garden that has come to light in North America." Open Tuesday through Saturday from 10 a.m. to 4 p.m. and Sunday from 12 noon to 4 p.m., March through September. Admission charge.

Brandon Gardens
23105 Brandon Road
Spring Grove, Virginia 23881
804-866-8486

Renowned gardens are open daily while visitors see the exterior of the paladian-style mansion believed to be designed by Thomas Jefferson. Open daily except Christmas Day. Admission charge.

Chippokes State Park
Route 634
Surry, Virginia 23883
804-294-3625

Chippokes State Park includes on its grounds the original manor house, a model farm, a visitors' center, and biking and hiking trails, as well as two creeks for fishing and canoeing. Spectacular gardens and an antique farm museum. Open Memorial Day to Labor Day, sunup to sundown. Admission charge.

■ SEASONAL EVENTS

Pork, Peanut, and Pine Festival
Route 634
Surry, Virginia 23883
804-294-3625

Artists and artisans abound at the this annual festival. Exhibits of the pork, peanut, and pine industry, but Baytrippers will want to come just for the food. Pit-cooked barbecue, corn bread, ham biscuits, pig's feet, peanut butter sandwiches, peanut brittle, peanut cookies, peanut pie, peanut soup, and other good foods. A two-day event, Saturday and Sunday, in mid-July. Free admission; parking fee.

■ TOURS

Edward's Smokehouse
Highway 10 and 31
Surry, Virginia 23883
800-222-4267

Visit the smokehouse where you can see first hand how Virginia hams are smoked and cured. Smokehouse tours, March 1 through September 30, Monday through Friday, 9:30 a.m. to 11:30 a.m. and 1:30 p.m. to 4:30 p.m. Tours are every hour on the half-hour. Free.

Restaurants

Surry House Restaurant
Highway 31 East and
Highway 10
Surry, Virginia 23883
804-294-3389

Stop at the Surry House Restaurant for a delicious lunch of traditional Southern cuisine featuring peanut soup, crab cakes, apple fritters, Edward's ham, peanut raisin pie, and other regional Virginia favorites. Open daily for breakfast, lunch, and dinner. Credit cards: AE.

Virginia Diner
Route 460
Wakefield, Virginia 23888
800-899-3106

Specialties include combination platters with chicken and country ham that includes two vegetables, Virginia fried chicken, Virginia ham biscuits, old fashioned potato salad, creamy cole slaw, and peanut tarts. Open daily for breakfast, lunch, and dinner. Credit cards: MC and V.

Accommodations

■ **HOTELS, MOTELS, AND INNS**

Seward House Inn
Route 10
Surry, Virginia 23883
804-294-3810

Wakefield Inn
Route 460
Wakefield, Virginia 23888
804-899-3841

HOPEWELL

■ **BACKGROUND:** Hopewell was first founded under the name of "Bermuda Cittie." Later it was called Old City Point in 1613 by Sir Thomas Dale as the second English settlement in America. In 1622, Indian raids wiped out the population of the town. In 1735, Frances Eppes patented a large tract of land. A portion of the Eppes' Estate was called Hopewell for "Merchants Hope," the ship that brought Eppes to America.

Attractions

■ **VISITOR INFORMATION**

Hopewell Visitor Center
201 D Randolph Square
Route 10
Hopewell, Virginia 23860
804-541-2206

■ **BOAT CRUISES**

Adventure Cruises
901 Riverside
Hopewell, Virginia 23860
804-541-2616
800-405-9990

Adventure Cruises offers a sail through Virginia's plantation country aboard the "Pocahontas II." Baytrippers will visit America's oldest and most famous plantations, as well as major Civil War sites from aboard the ship. You will enjoy cruising around the panoramic shores while learning about the historic Appomattox and James Rivers. Feast on summertime delicacies catered by Captain's Cove Restaurant. Cruises are seasonal and reservations are required. Admission charge.

■ HISTORIC SITES

Flowerdew Hundred
1617 Flowerdew Hundred Road
Hopewell, Virginia 23860
804-541-8897

Flowerdew Hundred, one of the earliest English settlements in the New World and a repository of wealth and archaeological artifacts, dating from 9000 B.C. to the Civil War period, as well as the site of an 18th century style windmill. Open daily except Monday, April 1 through November 30, from 10 a.m. to 5 p.m. daily. Admission charge.

Merchants Hope Church
Route 10
Hopewell, Virginia 23860
804-458-8657
804-732-2680

Site of the oldest Protestant church still standing in America. The 1657 church is praised for its exterior colonial brick work. Open by appointment.

Old Town
201 D. Randolph Square
Hopewell, Virginia 23860
804-541-2206

The Old Town of City Point is a National Historic District. The best way for Baytrippers to enjoy and savor the flavor is to take a walking tour-stop by the Visitor's Center and pick up a map listing 25 of the town's oldest structures.

City Point National Historic District. The city of Hopewell is an outgrowth of old City Point, founded in 1613. Dozens of pre-Civil War houses that survived their war use as commissaries, munitions storage and lodgings for the Federal army during the siege of Petersburg can be viewed in self-guided tours. A brochure with a map detailing the town is available. City Point is at the confluence of the James and the Appomattox rivers. City Point National Cemetery, where several thousand Confederate and Union soldiers are buried, is nearby.

Historic Sites, cont.

Weston Manor
Route 10
Hopewell, Virginia 23860
804-458-4829
804-458-5336

This Georgian frame house on the banks of the Appomattox River belonged to the Eppes' family. Both the house and the institution qualify for consideration of a visit. During the Civil War, the house served as headquarters for General Sheridan, and you can still see the names of Union soldiers scratched into the window pane. Open April 1 through October, Monday through Friday, 10 a.m. to 5 p.m. and Sunday, 1 p.m. to 5 p.m. Admission charge.

■ PARKS AND GARDENS

Presquile National Wildlife Refuge
P.O. Box 189
Prince George, Virginia 23875
804-733-8042

Presquile National Wildlife Refuge is located on a man-made island in the historic James River. Originally, the island's 1,029 acres were approximately four-fifths encircled by water as the river formed a long, ox-bow bend. In 1934, a navigation channel was cut across the base of the peninsula, making Presquile a true island. The refuge has a 3/4-mile nature trail and bird life is abundant. Transportation can be arranged to and from the refuge on a government-operated ferry. Call Monday, Wednesday, or Friday. Free.

Restaurants

Captain's Cove
910 North 21st Street
Hopewell, Virginia 23860
804-452-1368

Captain's Cove is located in the Hopewell Marina. It features daily specials including tantalizing crab legs and spicy steamed shrimp. Fresh Virginia ham is also featured. Open daily for lunch and dinner. Credit cards: AE, C, D, and DC.

Dockside Restaurant
700 Jordan Point Road
·Hopewell, Virginia 23860
804-541-2600

House specialties include fresh tuna, swordfish, and Chesapeake chicken, my favorite. Here a filet of fresh chicken breast is filled with a delightful seafood stuffing. Open daily for lunch and dinner. Credit cards: AE, MC, and V.

Honey Bee's Pancake House
5001 Oaklawn
Hopewell, Virginia 23860
804-541-1800

Although pancakes are the house specialty, there is good news for T-bone and country ham steak lovers. Open for breakfast, lunch, and dinner.

Navigator's Den
701 Randolph Road
Hopewell, Virginia 23860
804-458-9100

Featuring world-famous, all you can eat, seafood buffet with over 45 items served. Beautiful location overlooking the confluence of the Appomattox and James Rivers. Open daily for lunch and dinner. Credit cards: MC and V.

Accommodations

■ HOTELS, MOTELS, AND INNS

Comfort Inn East
5380 Oaklawn Boulevard-
Route 36
Hopewell, Virginia 23860
804-452-0022

Days Inn Hopewell
4911 Oaklawn Boulevard-
Route 36
Hopewell, Virginia 23860
804-458-1500

Evergreen Motel
711 West Randolph Road-
Route 10
Hopewell, Virginia 23860
804-458-8511

Innkeeper
3952 Courthouse Road
Hopewell, Virginia 23860
804-458-2600

FLOWERDEW HUNDRED

PETERSBURG

■ **BACKGROUND:** Petersburg began in the mid-1600's as Fort Henry, a frontier fort and trading post on the Appomattox River. In September of 1732, Colonel William Byrd II changed the name to Petersburg to honor Peter Jones, owner of the trading post. A village was laid out in 1748, and by 1785, four settlements united into Petersburg. The oldest part of town and the commercial heart of the city were located along the banks of the Appomattox River and are known today as "Old Towne."

Attractions

■ **VISITOR INFORMATION**

Petersburg Visitor Center
925 Cockade Alley
Petersburg, Virginia 23803
804-733-2400
800-368-3595

■ **HISTORIC SITES**

Appomattox Iron Works
20-28 Old Street
Petersburg, Virginia 23803
804-733-7300
800-232-IRON

A nearly complete, 19th century iron works, restored on the spot and put into working order. Housed in a complex of brick buildings, the iron works offers exhibits and live demonstrations from American industry's early days. Open daily from 10 a.m. to 5 p.m. Admission charge.

Centre Hill Mansion
Adams and Tabb Streets
Petersburg, Virginia 23804
804-733-2400

Magnificent 1823 Federal Style mansion has been host to three U.S. Presidents. Features high-style wood and plaster work, period furnishings, and a brick tunnel to the Appomattox River. A winter tour seeks out its ghosts. Open daily, 10:30 a.m. to 3:30 p.m. Admission charge.

Farmers Bank
1900 Bollingbrook Street
Petersburg, Virginia 23804
804-733-2400

Built in 1817, an early safe and a currency printing press are on display. Open daily, 10 a.m. to 5 p.m. Admission charge.

Old Blandford Church
319 South Crater Road
Petersburg, Virginia 23804
804-733-2400

A church built in 1735, it is now a Confederate shrine, housing 15 original Tiffany windows. Open year round with tours every 30 minutes from 10 a.m. to 4 p.m. Admission charge.

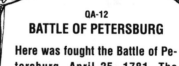

QA-12
BATTLE OF PETERSBURG

Here was fought the Battle of Petersburg, April 25, 1781. The Southside militia, 1,000 strong and commanded by Baron Steuben and General Muhlenberg, made a brave resistance to 2,500 British regulars under Phillips and Arnold. Petersburg: Crater Road at Cameron Street.

Historic Sites, cont.

Petersburg National Battlefield
Highway 36 East
Petersburg, Virginia 23804
804-732-3531

Visitors' center offers a map presentation and short film. Baytrippers, take the driving tour; it's four miles one way. Commemorates the Civil War siege of Petersburg, 1864-1865. Open daily, 8 a.m. to dusk. Admission charge.

Trapezium House
Market and High Streets
Petersburg, Virginia 23804
804-733-2400

Charles O'Hara built his house in 1817 without parallel walls because, as legend has it, such a house could not harbor evil spirits, or was it simply that the lot was of odd angles? Open April through October, 9 a.m. to 4 p.m. Admission charge.

■ MUSEUMS

Quartermaster Museum
Route 36
Fort Lee, Virginia 23801
804-834-1854

Founded in 1775, this fascinating museum has many unique items on display, including uniforms used by General Dwight Eisenhower, General Patton's jeep, and the original artist's model for the Tomb of the Unknown Soldier. Open Monday through Friday, 8 a.m. to 5 p.m., and Saturday, Sunday, and holidays, 11 a.m. to 5 p.m. Free.

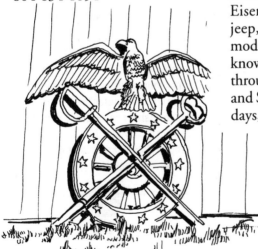

Siege Museum
15 West Bank Street
Petersburg, Virginia 23804
804-733-2400

Exhibits and a film document Petersburg's history during the Civil War's longest siege. Open Monday through Saturday from 9 a.m. to 5 p.m. and Sunday from 12:30 p.m. to 5 p.m. Admission charge.

Slo-Pitch Softball Museum
3935 Crater Road
Petersburg, Virginia 23804
804-732-4099

A 30-minute video details the history of slo-pitch softball. After the tape, you can go through the museum filled with cases of softball jerseys, shoes, and memorabilia. Open Monday through Friday, 9 a.m. to 4 p.m.; Saturday, 11 a.m. to 4 p.m.; and Sunday, 1 p.m. to 4 p.m. Admission charge.

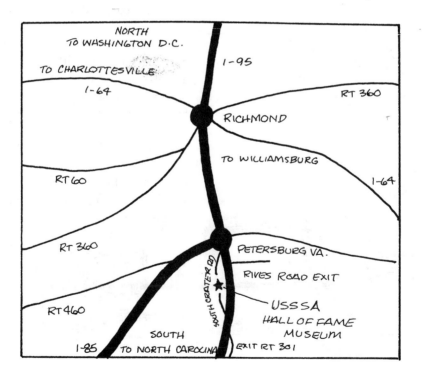

■ SEASONAL EVENTS

Poplar Lawn Art Festival
Sycamore Street
Petersburg, Virginia 23804
800-368-3595

This popular yearly event is held at the City Park and features some of the best artisans in plantation country. It corresponds with Garden Week of Virginia and is held the third weekend of April. Free.

Restaurants

Alexander's Fine Food
101 West Bank Street
Petersburg, Virginia 23803
804-733-7134

Alexander's is located across from the D.M.V. Italian, Greek, and American foods are featured including award-winning salads. Open for breakfast, lunch, and dinner, Monday through Saturday. Closed Sunday.

Annabelle's
2733 Park Avenue
Petersburg, Virginia 23803
804-732-0997

This location housed in an old dairy barn is filled with antiques and is a legend throughout the South. Annabelle's is a chain of family-run restaurants. Their specialties are steaks and prime rib, but they also present interesting preparations of local seafoods. Open daily for lunch and dinner. Credit cards: AE, D, DC, MC, and V.

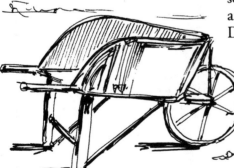

Accommodations

■ BED AND BREAKFASTS

High Street Inn
405 High Street
Petersburg, Virginia 23803
804-733-0505

Mayfield Inn
3348 West Washington Street
Petersburg, Virginia 23805
804-733-0866
804-861-6775

■ CAMPING

Petersburg KOA
2809 Courtland Avenue
Petersburg, Virginia 23805
804-732-8345

■ HOTELS, MOTELS, AND INNS

Comfort Inn West
12002 South Crater Road
Petersburg, Virginia 23805
804-732-2000

Howard Johnson Hotel
530 East Washington Street
Petersburg, Virginia 23803
804-732-5950

Days Inn
12208 South Crater Road
Petersburg, Virginia 23805
804-733-4400

Quality Inn-Steven Kent
12205 South Crater Road
Petersburg, Virginia 23805
804-733-0600

Flagship Inn
815 South Crater Road
Petersburg, Virginia 23803
804-861-3470

RICHMOND

■ **BACKGROUND:** Captain John Smith bought a tract of land from Chief Powhattan in 1609 and founded the settlement of "None Such." By the mid-1600's, Richmond had a population of about 500 people. The city was named in 1733 by Colonel William Byrd II. The name was given because Colonel Byrd thought this new town resembled Richmond-on-Thames, England. Richmond was the county seat of Henrico County in 1752 and became the state capital in 1779. The Civil War began in 1861; Richmond fell to the Union in 1865. Today Richmond blends the new with the old and remembers its past without losing sight of the future.

Attractions

■ **VISITOR INFORMATION**

The Richmond Visitors Bureau
550 East Marshall Street
Richmond, Virginia 23219
800-365-7272
804-782-2777

■ **AIRPORTS**

Richmond International Airport
Airport Drive
Richmond, Virginia 23231
804-226-3056

■ BOAT CRUISES

Annabel Lee
4400 East Main Street
Richmond, Virginia 23231
804-222-5700
800-752-7093

The Annabel Lee's riverboat excursion is reminiscent of that time in America when river travel was common, and travelers expected uncommon atmosphere. Lunch, brunch, dinner, and party plantation cruises are offered on the historic James River aboard the Annabel Lee. Reservations are necessary. Open April through December. Call for departure time. Fee.

Richmond Raft Company
4400 East Main Street
Richmond, Virginia 23231
804-222-RAFT

Prepare to get wet. Ride a rubber raft for 10 1/2 miles down the James River. An experienced guide will get you through some tricky white water. Departs on Monday through Friday at 10 a.m. and on Saturday at 9 a.m. and 3 p.m., Sunday, 10 a.m. Fee.

■ FISHING

Bass Unlimited Guide Services
2813 Shiloh Church Road
Midlothian, Virginia 23112
804-744-2732

Fishing on the James River, the Chickahominey River, or the Appomattox River. Trips may be custom-tailored for individual groups or company outings. All boats are fully rigged. Taxidermy, video services, and instruction also available. Open year round. Fee.

■ HISTORIC SITES

Agecroft Hall
4305 Sulgrave Road
Richmond, Virginia 23221
804-353-4241

This unique Tudor manor house was moved here from England and painstakingly reconstructed on the banks of the James River. Magnificent, authentic gardens. House and grounds are open year round-Tuesday through Friday, 10 a.m. to 4 p.m.; Saturday and Sunday, 2 p.m. to 5 p.m. Admission charge.

The Fan Historic District
804-782-2777

Historic district named for the layout of its streets which fan out toward the western part of town. This city-within-a-city reflects in its architecture the wealth which occurred to Richmond as a commercial center in the last part of the 19th century. The Fan is bordered by Monument Avenue to the North and Main Street to the South, Laurel Street to the East, and Boulevard to the West.

Jefferson Hotel
101 West Franklin Street
Richmond, Virginia 23220
804-788-8000
800-325-3535

This working hotel, originally built in 1895, was damaged severely by fire in 1901. Edward Valentine's statue of Thomas Jefferson stands in the upper lobby and windows are of Tiffany glass. Baytrippers are invited in for walking tours.

The Jefferson Hotel

St. John's Church
2401 East Broad Street
Richmond, Virginia 23223
804-648-5015

The St. John's Church is where Patrick Henry made his famous "Give me liberty or give me death" speech. Guided tours, Monday through Saturday, 10 a.m. to 3 p.m. Re-enactment Sundays at 2 p.m. Summer services, 8:30 a.m. to 11 a.m. Donations.

Shockoe Slip
East Cary and 12th Streets
Richmond, Virginia 23219
804-782-2777

Historic district in the downtown area of Richmond which was once the hub of commercial activity. Today it's busy with shops and restaurants. It's nice, it's quaint, it's the cobblestone warehouse district of old Richmond with many structures dating back a century or more.

State Capitol
9th and Capitol Square
Richmond, Virginia 23219
804-786-4344

Designed by Thomas Jefferson in 1785, Richmond was the capital of the Confederacy during the Civil War. This neoclassical building is the meeting of the oldest legislative body in America. The huge white building sits atop a hill facing the James River. Open April through November, daily, 9 a.m. to 5 p.m.; December to March, Monday through Saturday, 9 a.m. to 5 p.m., Sunday, 1 p.m. to 5 p.m. Free.

Historic Sites, cont.

Virginia House
4301 Sulgrave Road
Richmond, Virginia 23226
804-353-4251

Virginia House is a 16th century English manor house moved to Richmond in 1925 from England. Furnished with antiques from all over the world. Home of the late Ambassador Alexander and Mrs. Virginia Weddell. Tours by appointment, requires two days' advance notice. Open, 9 a.m. to 3 p.m. daily. Admission charge.

Maggie Walker Historic Site
110 1/2 East Leigh Street
Richmond, Virginia 23219
804-780-1380
804-226-1981

Visit the restored home of Maggie Walker, a Black woman who arose from poverty to become a financially successful banker. Park rangers conduct house tours Wednesday through Sunday from 9 a.m. to 5 p.m. Free.

Wilton House
South Wilton Road
Richmond, Virginia 23226
804-282-5936

Wilton House is a Georgian brick, James River plantation built by William Randolph III in 1753. General Lafayette made it his headquarters during the American Revolution. The building was moved 10 miles up the James River to its present site in 1933. Open Tuesday through Saturday, 10 a.m. to 4:30 p.m., and Sunday from 1:30 p.m. to 4:30 p.m. Admission charge.

■ MISCELLANEOUS

Farmer's Market
17th Street between
East Main and East Franklin
Streets
Richmond, Virginia 23219

Farmers roll into Richmond in their trucks early in the morning and set up their stands in this rustic marketplace, built on the site of an Indian Trading Village. Baytrippers won't want to miss it; it's been here for over 300 years, but the vegetables and fruits are fresh as fresh can be. Open daily all year.

Kanawha Canal Locks
12th and Byrd Streets
Richmond, Virginia 23219
804-782-2777

These locks are what's left of the country's first canal system which brought western Virginia products to Richmond in the late 18th century until the 19th century. Today there is a picnic area and audio-visual display explaining how the locks worked. Open daily. Free.

Monument Avenue
Downtown
Richmond, Virginia 23219
800-365-7272

America's most beautiful boulevard, named for its many statues including those of Robert E. Lee, Stonewall Jackson, and Jefferson Davis. This historic avenue is lined with handsomely restored old homes.

Richmond International Raceway
600 East Laburnum Avenue
Richmond, Virginia 23227
804-345-7223

This 3/4 mile, state-of-the-art track features four weekends of major league NASCAR auto racing each year. Call for seasonal schedule. Admission charge.

Miscellaneous, cont.

Skydeck-Richmond City Hall
900 East Broad Street
Richmond, Virginia 23219
804-780-5757

The City Hall Skydeck rises 18 stories above the modern and historic Richmond skyline. Open Monday through Thursday, 8 a.m. to 8 p.m., and Friday through Sunday, 8 a.m. to 5 p.m. Free.

■ MUSEUMS

Federal Reserve Money Museum
701 East Byrd Street
Richmond, Virginia 23219
804-697-8108

The Money Museum houses an exhibit on the history of money in the United States, a currency printing press, and more than 500 items depicting the history of currency. Open Monday through Friday, 9:30 a.m. to 3:30 p.m. Free.

The Museum of the Confederacy
1202 East Clay Street
Richmond, Virginia 23219
804-649-1861

Uniforms and Swords...

Civil War buffs can have a field day in Richmond, particularly at the Museum of the Confederacy, an ultramodern facility which houses the largest collection of Confederate memorabilia in the world. The displays include the uniform and the sword which General Robert E. Lee was wearing the day he surrendered at Appomattox.

This museum is the center for the study of the Confederacy and Civil War. Displays feature the largest comprehensive collection of Civil War-related material. The museum's principal exhibition interprets the South's role in the Civil War. The museum includes the White House of the Confederacy which was President Jefferson Davis' war time residence when he lived in Richmond. Open Monday through Saturday, 10 a.m. to 5 p.m., and Sunday, 2 p.m. to 5 p.m. Admission charge.

Edgar Allan Poe Museum
1914 East Main Street
Richmond, Virginia 23223
804-648-5523

The Poe Museum is located in a stone house built in 1737 and houses Poe memorabilia, exhibit rooms, a model of Richmond in Poe's time, and also features an enchanted garden. Open Tuesday through Saturday from 10 a.m. to 4 p.m., and on Sunday and Monday it's open from 11 a.m. to 3:30 p.m. Closed Christmas Day. Admission charge.

Richmond Children's Museum
740 North Sixth Street
Richmond, Virginia 23219
804-788-4949

Celebrate childhood-children explore their own creativity through painting, listening to opera, playing musical instruments, or creating sculpture. The emphasis is on the importance of participating in the artistic process. For children ages 2 to 12. Open Tuesday through Friday, 10 a.m. to 4 p.m., and Sunday, 1 p.m. to 5 p.m. Admission charge.

Science Museum of Virginia
2500 West Broad Street
Richmond, Virginia 23220
804-367-1013

Take an old train station, convert it into a museum devoted to the wonders of science, and what do you have? The Science Museum of Virginia. Exhibits range from astronomical telescopes to a 325-gallon salt water aquarium. One of the features is a marine "touch tank" in which visitors may handle such creatures as tulip snails and starfish.

The Science Museum is housed in the former Broad Street Train Station which itself is a beautiful arched structure and features hands-on exhibits on aerospace, astronomy, crystals, electricity, illusions, and more. It will delight Baytrippers of all ages. Open daily, 9:30 a.m. to 5 p.m.; hours vary in winter. Admission charge.

Museums, cont.

Valentine Museum
1015 East Clay Street
Richmond, Virginia 23219
804-649-0711
804-225-8730

Baytrippers after sunset, head to the Valentine Riverside Courtyard and you will see the Spectacular Sound and Light Show, Valentine Riverside's signature event.

This historic museum compliments the history and lifestyle of Richmond's past. The museum contains many artifacts and replicas of early American inhabitants and an exemplary collection of Virginian, Victorian exhibits-historic homes and gardens. Open Tuesday through Saturday from 10 a.m. to 5 p.m. and Sunday from 12 noon to 5 p.m., closed Monday. Admission charge.

Virginia Aviation Museum
5701 Huntsman Road
Sandston, Virginia 23150
804-371-0371
804-222-8690

The Aviation Museum houses a collection of antique aircraft circa 1914 to the 1930's. It's located at the Richmond International Airport on Route 60 east of the city. It's a division of the Science Museum of Virginia. Newest exhibits show early flights and display various craft. Open Tuesday through Saturday from 10 a.m. to 4 p.m. Admission charge.

Virginia Museum of Fine Arts
2800 Grove Avenue
Richmond, Virginia 23221
804-367-0844

The museum features outstanding collections of art Nouveau, art Deco, Indian, contemporary, and impressive art, and the largest public collection of Fabrege eggs outside of Russia. Open Tuesday through Saturday from 11 a.m. to 5 p.m. and on Thursday until 10 p.m.; Sunday hours are 1 p.m. to 5 p.m. Admission charge.

■ PARKS AND GARDENS

James River Park
700 Blanton Street
Richmond, Virginia 23221
804-226-1981

Take a nature walk in the James River Park, one of only two wilderness parks in the U.S. located in an urban setting. The park features several miles of hiking paths and foot bridges connecting the small river islands in the park. You can ride a hand-operated ferry that connects three small islands. Open dawn to dusk. Free.

Paramount's Kings Dominion
Highway 64
Doswell, Virginia 23047
804-876-5000

The world-famous Paramount's Kings Dominion entertainment complex offers over 100 rides and attractions, hosts numerous live concerts, and big name entertainment throughout the season. One of the most popular rides is the Rebel Yell Roller Coaster that was featured in the movie "Roller Coaster." Open daily, March through October; call for hours. Admission charge.

Parks and Gardens, cont.

Lewis Ginter Botanic Gardens
7000 Lakeside Avenue
Richmond, Virginia 23228
804-262-9887

Restored Victorian gardens. Outstanding collection of daffodils, daylillies, rhododendrons, azaleas, annuals, and perennials. Open daily, 9:30 a.m. to 4:30 p.m. Admission charge.

Maymont Park
1700 Hampton Street
Richmond, Virginia 23220
804-358-7166

Maymont is a 100-acre Victorian estate featuring a restored house, gardens, wildlife, a children's farm, and carriage and tram rides. Grounds open daily, 10 a.m. to 5 p.m. Free.

Richmond National Battlefield Park
3215 East Broad Street
Richmond, Virginia 23223
804-226-1981

Highlights McClellan's 1862 peninsula campaign and Grant's 1864 attack at Cold Harbor. This battlefield park was once the site of the Confederate Army's defense of the city of Richmond during the Civil War. The park headquarters offers exhibits and audio-visual programs and maps the 97-mile tour through Hanover, Henrico, and Chesterfield County sites. Open daily from 9 a.m. to 5 p.m. Admission charge.

■ SEASONAL EVENTS

Chesapeake Bay Days
2500 West Broad Street
Richmond, Virginia 23220
804-367-6792

Bay Days gives visitors an opportunity to meet the people who work the Bay and whose organizations preserve and protect the Chesapeake. Last year 10,000 visitors enjoyed Bay Days. Join in this year and celebrate the Chesapeake Bay. This two-day event is held in early March. Open 9:30 a.m. to 5 p.m. Admission charge.

Richmond's Children's Festival
1435 West Main Street
Richmond, Virginia 23220
804-355-7200

Held annually at Byrd Park, it is one of the country's largest such events. This collection of dancers, workshops, and performances provides an introduction to the arts every kid will love. Free.

Virginia State Fair
P. O. Box 26805
Henrico Turnpike and Laburnam Avenue
Richmond, Virginia 23261
804-228-3200

Every year Virginia's State Fair fills its 350-acre fairgrounds with thousands of animals and scores of rural skill contests. Hundreds of performances are held on eight stages. Annually, 600,000 persons attend the fair. Plenty of free parking. Held mid-September. Admission charge.

■ SIGHTSEEING TOURS

Events, Etc.
11503 Allecingie Parkway
Richmond, Virginia 23235
804-794-2138

See historic Richmond and Virginia, with a personal touch. Small and large groups welcome as are individual tours. Special event planning available. Fee.

Historic Richmond Tours
2407 East Grace Street
Richmond, Virginia 23223
804-780-0107

Historic Richmond Tours offer guided van tours daily with pickup at major hotels. Walking tours, April through October. Civil War Battlefields, second, third, and fourth Sunday. Call for your schedule. Fee.

Richmond Discoveries
8620 Varina Road
Richmond, Virginia 23231
804-795-5781

Individuals may join for Sunday afternoon walking tours, March through October. In April and October, Baytrippers can take the Civil War walking tour. Provides step-on guide service, souvenirs, historical entertainment, and more. Unique historical bus and walking tours; seasonal themed walking tours. Fee.

Restaurants

Blue Point Seafood Restaurant
550 East Grace Street
Richmond, Virginia 23219
804-783-8138

Delicacies of the sea are featured, including sauteed crab Norfolk in sherry and butter; and if you have a fish dinner in mind, you'll find it at Blue Point Seafood. Ten different varieties are listed and all are fresh. Open daily for lunch and dinner. Credit cards: AE, D, DC, MC, and V.

Captain George's Seafood Restaurant
4700 West Broad Street
Richmond, Virginia 23230
804-359-0222

Home of the original world-famous, all-you-can-eat, seafood buffet with over 70 items on the table. Offerings include crab legs, steamed shrimp, crab imperial, and more than 15 desserts. Open daily, dinner-Sunday, lunch and dinner. Credit cards: AE, MC, and V.

Extra Billy's Ribs and Barbecue
5205 West Broad Street
Richmond, Virginia 23294
804-282-3949

Richmond is famous for its barbecue and at Extra Billy's, it's extra good. House specialties include ribs, pork, beef brisket, roasted chicken, and deluxe salad bar. Open Monday through Friday, lunch and dinner; Saturday, dinner only; closed Sunday. Credit cards: AE, D, DC, MC, and V.

Lemarie Restaurant
The Jefferson Hotel
Franklin and Adams Streets
Richmond, Virginia 23220
804-788-8000

Our restaurant is named for Etienne Lemaire, who served as maitre d'hôtel to Thomas Jefferson from 1794 through the end of his presidency. Jefferson was known for his appreciation of fine wines, and Lemaire is widely credited for introducing to America the fine art of cooking with wines.

Jefferson was also known for his fondness of meals prepared with light sauces, garden-fresh herbs and creative uses for the region's abundant variety of ingredients. Through research and trial, it is that spirit which inspires this menu.

If you only have time to eat one meal while you're visiting in Richmond, do it at the Jefferson Hotel. Lemarie Restaurant features innovative Virginia cuisine in gilded era elegance. Original 1890's decor has been faithfully restored. Also on the premises is T.J.'s Grill and Bar. While it's less formal, it's great for laid back dining. The kitchen serves American fare. Open daily, breakfast, lunch, and dinner. Credit cards: AE, DC, MC, and V.

Restaurants, cont.

Sam Miller's Warehouse
1210 East Cary Street
Richmond, Virginia 23219
804-644-5465

Sam Miller's is located in the Shockoe Slip District and is one of my favorite restaurants. The management's job is to make you feel as comfortable and contented as possible, The kitchen vies with the serving staff for top honors. Specialties include live Maine lobster, Chesapeake Bay seafood, and prime rib. Open for lunch and dinner, Monday through Saturday; Sunday brunch, 10 a.m. to 2 p.m. Credit cards: AE, DC, MC, and V.

Mr. Patrick Henry's Inn
2300 East Broad Street
Richmond, Virginia 23219
804-644-1322

Experience European and Southern cuisine in a pre-Civil War Inn. The menu features innovative dishes using fresh herbs. Open Monday through Saturday for lunch and dinner. Credit cards: AE, D, DC, MC, and V.

O'Toole's Restaurant
4800 Forrest Hill Avenue
Richmond, Virginia 23225
804-233-1781

At O'Toole's the daily specials include traditional meals of seafood, steak, and sandwiches. You don't last for over 25 years without being special. Open daily for lunch and dinner. Credit cards: AE, MC, and V.

Pierce's Bar-B-Que Inc.
10825 Hull Street Road
Richmond, Virginia 23113
804-674-4049

If you love bar-b-que, you'll love Pierce's, a Virginia institution since 1971. Some say Pierce's pit style is the best in the South. We'll let you be the judge. Open daily for lunch and dinner. Credit cards: MC and V.

Ruth's Chris Steakhouse
11500 Huguenot Road
Midlothian, Virginia 23113
804-378-0600

Restaurant News Magazine selects this place as one of the best, you will too. Ruth Chris serves up serious portions cooked to order and served on sizzling hot plates with a side order of bearnaise if you so desire. Open daily for dinner only. Credit cards: AE, DC, DIS, MC and Visa.

The Tobacco Company Restaurant
12th and East Cary Streets
Richmond, Virginia 23219
804-782-9431

This upscale restaurant is located in historic Shockoe Slip and was once a tobacco warehouse. Outstanding new American menu featuring fresh seafood, choice beef, and daily chef specials. Open daily for lunch and dinner. Credit cards: AE, DC, MC, and V.

87

Accommodations

■ BED AND BREAKFASTS

Be My Guest Bed and Breakfast
2926 Kensington Avenue
Richmond, Virginia 23221
804-358-9901

Benson House Bed and Breakfast
2036 Monument Avenue
Richmond, Virginia 23220
804-648-7500

William Catlin House
2304 East Broad Street
Richmond, Virginia 23223
804-780-3746

Emmanuel Hutzler House
2036 Monument Avenue
Richmond, Virginia 23220
804-353-6900

West-Bobcock House
1107 Grove Avenue
Richmond, Virginia 23220
804-358-6174

■ CAMPING

Americamps
396 Air Park Road
Ashland, Virginia 23005
804-798-5298

Pocahontas State Park
10300 Beach Road
Chesterfield, Virginia 23832
804-796-4255

■ HOTELS, MOTELS, AND INNS

Berkeley Hotel
12th and Cary Streets
Richmond, Virginia 23219
804-780-1300

Best Western Governor's Inn
9848 Midlothian Turnpike
Richmond, Virginia 23235
804-323-0007

Best Western Hanover House
I-95 Atlee Exit 86
Ashland, Virginia 23005
804-550-2805

Best Western King's Quarters
I-95 and Route 30
Doswell, Virginia 23047
800-528-1234

Commonwealth Hotel
9th and Bank Streets
Richmond, Virginia 23219
804-343-7300
800-343-7302

**Courtyard by Marriott
Richmond West**
6400 West Broad Street
Richmond, Virginia 23230
804-282-1881
800-321-2211

Cricket Inn
7300 West Broad Street
Richmond, Virginia 23294
804-672-8621

Days Inn
1600 Robin Hood Road
Richmond, Virginia 23220
804-353-1287
800-325-2525

Days Inn Downtown
612 East Marshall Street
Richmond, Virginia 23219
804-649-2378

Days Inn West Broad
2100 Dickens Road
Richmond, Virginia 23230
804-282-3300
800-325-2525

Econo Lodge Airport
5408 Williamsburg Road
Sandston, Virginia 23150
804-222-1020

Econo Lodge North
5221 Brook Road
Richmond, Virginia 23227
804-266-7603
800-637-3297

Econo Lodge West
6523 Midlothian Turnpike
Richmond, Virginia 23225
804-270-8241
800-446-6900

Hojo Inn
801 East Parham Road
Richmond, Virginia 23227
804-266-8753

Hojo's
101 South Carter Road
Ashland, Virginia 23005
804-798-9291

Holiday Inn Airport
5203 Williamsburg Road
Sandston, Virginia 23150
804-222-6450

Holiday Inn Central
3207 North Boulevard
Richmond, Virginia 23230
804-359-9441

Holiday Inn Crossroads
2000 Stapes Mill Road
Richmond, Virginia 23230
804-359-6061

Hotels, Motels, and Inns cont.

Holiday Inn Downtown
301 West Franklin Street
Richmond, Virginia 23220
804-644-9871
800-HOLIDAY

**Holiday Inn Executive
Conference Center**
1021 Koger Center Boulevard
Richmond, Virginia 23235
804-379-3800
800-HOLIDAY

Holiday Inn Fanny's
6531 West Broad Street
Richmond, Virginia 23230
804-285-9951
800-HOLIDAY

Holiday Inn Midtown
3200 West Broad Street
Richmond, Virginia 23230
804-359-4061
800-HOLIDAY

Holiday Inn Richmond-Chester
2401 West Hundred Road
Chester, Virginia 23831
804-748-6321
800-HOLIDAY

**Holiday Inn Southeast
(Bells Road)**
4303 Commerce Road
Richmond, Virginia 23234
804-275-7891

**Howard Johnson Diamond
Stadium**
1501 Robin Hood Road
Richmond, Virginia 23222
804-353-0116
800-IGO-HOJO

Hyatt Richmond
6624 West Broad Street
Richmond, Virginia 23230
804-285-1234
800-233-1234

Jefferson Hotel
101 West Franklin Street
Richmond, Virginia 23220
804-788-8000
800-325-3535

Knights Inn Airport
5252 Airport Square Lane
Sandston, Virginia 23150
804-226-4519

LaQuinta Motor Inn
6910 Midlothian Turnpike
Richmond, Virginia 23225
804-745-7100
800-531-5900

Marriott Residence Inn
2121 Dickens Road
Richmond, Virginia 23230
804-285-8200
800-331-3131

Omni Richmond
100 South 12th Street
Richmond, Virginia 23219
804-344-7000

Quality Inn North
2002 Brook Road
Glen Allen, Virginia 23060
804-266-2444
800-221-2222

Radisson Hotel Richmond
555 East Canal Street
Richmond, Virginia 23219
804-788-0900
800-333-3333

Ramada Inn North
5701 Chamberlayne Road
Richmond, Virginia 23227
804-266-7616
800-776-4667

Ramada Inn South
2126 Willis Road
Richmond, Virginia 23237
804-271-1281
800-228-2828

Red Roof Inn
4350 Commerce Road
Richmond, Virginia 23234
804-271-7240
800-THE-ROOF

Richmond Marriott Hotel
500 East Broad Street
Richmond, Virginia 23219
804-643-3400

The Roof Chippenham
100 Greshamwood Place
Richmond, Virginia 23225
804-745-0600

Sheraton Airport Inn
4700 South Laburnam Avenue
Richmond, Virginia 23231
804-226-4300
800-628-7601

Sheraton Park South
9901 Midlothian Turnpike
Richmond, Virginia 23235
804-323-1144

Shoney's Inn Richmond
7007 West Broad Street
Richmond, Virginia 23294
804-672-7007
800-222-2222

Super 8 Motel
5615 Chamberlayne Road
Richmond, Virginia 23227
804-262-8880
800-800-8000

Super 8 Motel
7200 West Broad Street
Richmond, Virginia 23294
804-672-8128
800-843-1991

WILLIAMSBURG

■ **BACKGROUND:** Williamsburg began as a colonial town named Middle Township. It was an outpost of Jamestown. It became Virginia's capital in 1699 and was named to honor King William III. It remained the state center for government until 1780 when Governor Thomas Jefferson moved the state's capital to Richmond. Today the town of Williamsburg is an 18th century community restored to the time when it was the cultural center of the largest colony in the new world. A 173-acre outdoor living museum. There are more than 500 buildings in the historic area, among them 88 original, restored 18th century structures.

Attractions

■ **VISITOR INFORMATION**

Colonial Williamsburg Foundation
Box 1776
Williamsburg, Virginia 23187
800-HISTORY

Williamsburg Visitor's Bureau
201 Penniman Road
Williamsburg, Virginia 23187
804-253-0192

■ **AIRPORTS**

Newport News/Williamsburg International Airport
Bland Boulevard
Newport News, Virginia 23602
804-877-0221

Williamsburg-Jamestown Airport
100 Marclay Road
Williamsburg, Virginia 23185
804-229-9256

■ HISTORIC SITES

Berkeley Plantation
Route 5
Charles City, Virginia 23030
804-829-6018

THIS IS A REPLICA OF
"THE GOOD SHIP MARGARET"
COMMISSIONED IN BRISTOL
ENGLAND IN 1618
ON THE 5TH OF DECEMBER,
1619 38 SETTLERS LANDED
HERE AND GAVE THANKS
FOR THE SAFE JOURNEY.

40 TONS
35 FEET LONG
38 PASSENGERS
A CREW OF 8

Berkeley has no peer among the James River Plantations as a center of historic interest and as a beautifully restored example of the mansions that graced Virginia's "Golden Age." Site of the first official Thanksgiving in 1619, birthplace of Benjamin Harrison, Signer of the Declaration of Independence, and William Henry Harrison, 9th U.S. President. Ancestral home of 23rd President Benjamin Harrison. Headquarters for General McClellan, and "Taps" composed here in 1862. Plantation mansion built in 1726. Today, in its traditional condition with exceptionally fine antiques authentic to the period. Terraced boxwood gardens. Open daily, 8 a.m. to 5 p.m. Admission charge.

Historic Sites, cont.

Carter's Grove
Route 60
Williamsburg, Virginia 23187
804-220-7645

Today, this magnificent river estate is open to the public and provides an absorbing glimpse of the past. A leisurely walk through this fine home and its grounds will help you visualize a way of life that is a cherished part of our heritage.

Carter's Grove is approached by a seven-mile scenic drive through woods, meadows, and marshes. Begin your visit at the reception center, a 14-minute slide presentation will prepare you for the 400 years of history you will encounter while at Carter's Grove. The plantation grounds have been the site of ongoing archaeological excavations, revealing the remains of a 17th century settlement. Many objects have been found and are on display in the Winthrop Rockefeller Archaeological Museum. Also on the grounds are the partially reconstructed remains of Wolstenholme Towne. Open daily, 9 a.m. to 5 p.m, mid-March through November, and during the Christmas season. Admission charge.

Edgewood Plantation
Route 5
Charles City, Virginia 23030
804-829-2962

Gothic revival 1849 home filled with antiques, old charm, and Civil War history. Open daily, 10 a.m. to 5 p.m. Closed Monday. Admission charge.

Christmas is a special and popular time at Edgewood. Make arrangements early to share the season's spirit in special tours from December 1 through January 1. Both day and evening candlelight tours are offered.

The "trimmings" at Edgewood will delight you: a Victorian hostess, an old-fashioned sleigh, eight to twelve decorated trees, hot mulled cider and hundreds of antique and country decorations.

Evelynton Plantation
Route 5
Charles City, Virginia 23030
804-829-5075
800-473-5075

Evelynton was originally part of Westover, home since 1847 to Ruffin family, whose patriot, Edmund Ruffin, fired the first shot of the Civil War. Evelynton was the site of fierce Civil War skirmishes in 1862 when General George McClellan waged his destructive peninsula campaign. The house, lush grounds, and gardens are open daily, 9 a.m. to 5 p.m. Admission charge.

Jamestown Settlement
Route 31 and Colonial Parkway
Williamsburg, Virginia 23187
804-229-1607

Living history museum depicts life in America's first permanent English colony. Features replicas of the three ships in which the first settlers arrived. The ships are Godspeed, Discovery, and Susan Constant. Other features include an Indian village, exhibition galleries, and film telling the history of Jamestown and the Powhattan Indians. Open daily, 9 a.m. to 5 p.m. Closed Christmas and New Year's Day. Admission charge.

Sherwood Forest
Route 5
Charles City, Virginia 23030
804-829-5377

Sherwood Forest Plantation was the home of President John Tyler and was built circa 1730. It is considered the longest frame house in America. It measures 300 feet along its front facade. It is furnished with an extensive collection of 18th and 19th century family heirlooms. Open daily except Christmas from 9 a.m. to 5 p.m. Admission charge.

Historic Sites, cont.

Shirley Plantation
Route 5
Charles City, Virginia 23030
804-829-5121
800-232-1613

The ninth and tenth generations of the Hill-Carter family welcome you to visit their home, where their ancestors entertained George Washington, Thomas Jefferson, and prominent Americans. The original crested silver, furniture, and portraits still remain. The famous "Hanging" stairway, with no visible means of support, and the Queen Anne Forecourt are the only ones of their kind in America. Shirley Plantation was the home of Anne Hill Carter, mother of Robert E. Lee. Open daily, 9 a.m. to 4:30 p.m. Admission charge.

■ MISCELLANEOUS

Historic Air Tours, Inc.
100 Marclay Road
Williamsburg, Virginia 23187
804-253-8185

Here's a great way to enhance the appreciation of historic sites through the added dimension of the aerial view. Historic air tours will tailor a narrative air flight that will help you discover the splendor of 15 James River plantations. Flights originate at Williamsburg-Jamestown Airport. Call for same day or advance reservations. Fee

Water Country, U.S.A.
176 Water Country Parkway
Williamsburg, Virginia 23185
804-229-9300
800-343-SWIM

Forty-acre family water park. Over 25 water rides, slides, pools, and shows-offering something for all ages from exciting rapid rides to lazy river tube rides. Open, May through mid-September. Hours will vary during peak season. Admission charge.

Williamsburg Pottery Factory
Route 60
Lightfoot, Virginia 23090
804-564-3326

Virginia's premier tourist attraction. Wild, wonderful shopping bargains from around the world. Exhibits on pottery making. Open daily. Hours will vary during peak season.

Williamsburg Winery
2638 Lake Powell Road
Williamsburg, Virginia 23185
804-229-0999

The Williamsburg Winery is located three miles from Colonial Williamsburg. Tours and tastings are available for Baytrippers Tuesday through Sunday from 10 a.m. to 5 p.m. Closed Monday. Admission charge.

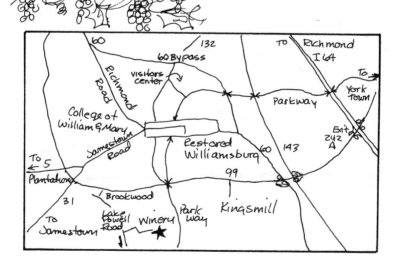

■ MUSEUMS

Abby Aldrich Rockefeller Folk Art Center
307 South England Street
Williamsburg, Virginia 23185
804-229-1000

The Abby Aldrich Rockefeller Folk Art Center is the oldest institution in this country devoted exclusively to collecting, exhibiting, and researching American folk art. The core of the collection is composed of 424 objects given to Colonial Williamsburg in 1939 by Mrs. John D. Rockefeller, Jr., whose husband made possible the restoration of 18th century Williamsburg. Open daily, 10 a.m. to 6 p.m. Admission charge.

■ PARKS AND GARDENS

Anheuser-Busch Gardens
Route 60
Williamsburg, Virginia 23185
804-253-3350

The old country European themed, 360-acres family entertainment park featuring re-creations of England, France, Italy, and Germany hamlets to visit. Exciting rides, shows, and unique attractions. Open daily at 10 a.m.; closing hours will vary in peak season. Admission charge.

Jamestown Island
Colonial Parkway
Williamsburg, Virginia 23185
804-229-1733

The Colonial National Historic Park features preserved remains of 1607 settlement, museum, film, pottery, and glass-blowing demonstrations. Self-guided tours. A five-mile nature drive that rings the island is posted with historically informative signs and paintings. Open daily, June to Labor Day, 9 a.m. to 6:30 p.m.; September to May, 9 a.m. to 5 p.m. Admission charge.

Westover Garden
Route 5
Charles City, Virginia 23030
804-829-2882

This fine plantation features an outstanding Georgian boxwood garden. Only the gardens and grounds are open to Baytrippers. Open daily, 9 a.m. to 6 p.m. Admission charge.

Restaurants

Backfin Seafood Restaurant
1193 Jamestown Road
Williamsburg, Virginia 23188
804-220-2249

Quite simply, they serve great seafood here, such as stuffed shrimp, crab imperial and sauteed soft shell crabs. Entrees include hush puppies, fresh vegetable, and your choice of potato. Open Monday through Saturday, lunch and dinner; Sunday, dinner only. Credit cards: MC and V.

Captain George's Seafood Restaurant
5363 Richmond Road
Williamsburg, Virginia 23188
804-565-2323

Home of the original world-famous seafood buffet, it's a sight to see and pure joy to eat. On the regular menu are featured seafood shish kabob and prime cut steaks. Open daily Monday through Saturday, dinner only; Sunday, lunch and dinner. Credit cards: AE, MC, and V.

Chowning's Tavern
Duke of Gloucester Street
Williamsburg, Virginia 23185
804-229-2141

Chowning's is a true Virginia-style ale house. Try the mouthwatering beefsteak ribs and hearty brunswick stew. Wash it down with a pint of brew. Open daily for lunch and dinner. Closed Wednesday and Thursday during winter. Credit cards: AE, MC, and V.

Coach House Tavern
12604 Harrison Landing Road
Charles City, Virginia 23030
804-829-6003

The Coach House Tavern is located at historic Berkeley Plantation and features such favorites as colonial onion soup or Chesapeake oyster stew, accompanied by shrimp with dill, served with fresh fruit, green salad, and fresh baked bread. The results are mighty good. Open for lunch and dinner. Credit cards: AE, MC, and V.

Cracker Barrel Old Country Store
200 Bypass Road
Williamsburg, Virginia 23185
804-220-3384

The Cracker Barrel chain of restaurants is famous throughout the south, not for fancy fixin's so much but for authentic country fare-from BBQ ribs to country steak to a delicious soup and sandwich. Open daily for breakfast, lunch, and dinner. Credit cards: AE, D, MC, and V.

Indian Fields Tavern
9220 John Tyler Memorial Highway
Charles City, Virginia 23030
804-829-5004

Indian Fields Tavern is housed in a beautifully restored farmhouse. The special of the house that I fell in love with was the "crab cake Harrison." Here two lump crab cakes were served on grilled Sally Lunn bread with Smithfield ham and topped with hollandaise sauce. I could go on, but I'll leave the rest for you to discover. Will I see you there? Open daily for lunch and dinner, except during January and February. Closed Monday. Credit cards: AE, D, MC, and V.

Restaurants, cont.

Kingsmill
100 Golf Club Road
Williamsburg, Virginia 23185
804-253-3900

Here at Kingsmill you may select from several dining options to suit your mood or needs. Whatever you try, you will have a beautiful view of the James River. Kingsmill offers a menu of special selections each evening and offers only the freshest of local seafood. Open daily, breakfast, lunch and dinner. Credit cards: AE, D, DC, MC, and V.

Shields Tavern
Duke of Gloucester Street
Williamsburg, Virginia 23185
804-229-2141

The food and decor of Shields Tavern represents life as it was in the late 1740's. The rustic, even austere, interior perfectly sets the mood to enjoy authentically prepared chicken and beef over an open fire. Strolling balladeers in period costumes will play you a song and make your heart light. Open daily, lunch and dinner. Credit cards: AE, MC, and V.

The Trillis
Duke of Gloucester Street
Williamsburg, Virginia 23185
804-229-8610

The Trillis is located in Merchants Square. This nationally-acclaimed restaurant offers a seasonal menu served via contemporary atmosphere. There are several rooms to choose from. Fresh Chesapeake seafood and Smithfield ham are several of the featured items that you don't want to miss. Open daily for lunch and dinner. Credit cards: AE, MC, and V.

Accommodations

■ BED AND BREAKFASTS

Applewood Colonial
605 Richmond Road
Williamsburg, Virginia 23185
804-229-0205
800-899-2753

Colonial Capital
501 Richmond Road
Williamsburg, Virginia 23185
804-229-0233
800-776-0570

Fox Grape
701 Monumental Avenue
Williamsburg, Virginia 23185
804-229-6914
800-292-3699

Governor's Trace
303 Capital Landing Road
Williamsburg, Virginia 23185
804-229-7552

The Homestay
517 Richmond Road
Williamsburg, Virginia 23185
804-229-7468

Legacy of Williamsburg Tavern
930 Jamestown Road
Williamsburg, Virginia 23185
804-220-0524
800-962-4722

Liberty Rose
1022 Jamestown Road
Williamsburg, Virginia 23185
804-253-1260
800-545-1825

War Hill Farm
4560 Long Hill Road
Williamsburg, Virginia 23188
804-565-0248

Williamsburg Sampler
922 Jamestown Road
Williamsburg, Virginia 23185
804-253-0398
800-722-1169

103

Camping, cont.

■ CAMPING

Anvil Campground
5243 Mooretown Road
Williamsburg, Virginia 23188
804-565-2300
800-633-4442

Brass Lantern Campground
1782 Jamestown Road
Williamsburg, Virginia 23185
804-229-4320
804-229-9089

Fair Oaks Holiday Travel
901 Lightfoot Road
Williamsburg, Virginia 23090
804-565-2101

First Settlers Campground
Route 31 South and Jamestown
Road
Williamsburg, Virginia 23187
804-229-4900

Jamestown Beach Campsites
2117 Jamestown Road
Williamsburg, Virginia 23187
804-229-7609
804-229-3300

Williamsburg Campsites, Inc.
6967 Richmond Road
Williamsburg, Virginia 23090
804-564-3101

Williamsburg KOA Campground
5210 Lightfoot Road
Williamsburg, Virginia 23188
804-565-2907
800-635-2717

■ HOTELS, MOTELS, AND INNS

Best Western Colonial Capitol Inn
111 Penniman Road
Williamsburg, Virginia 23185
804-253-1222
800-446-9228

Best Western Patrick Henry Inn
York and Page Streets
Route 60 East
Williamsburg, Virginia 23185
804-229-9540

Captain John Smith Motor Lodge
2225 Richmond Road
Williamsburg, Virginia 23185
804-220-0710
800-933-6788

Colonel Waller Motel
917 Capitol Landing Road
Williamsburg, Virginia 23185
804-253-0999

Colonial Motel
1452 Richmond Road
Williamsburg, Virginia 23185
804-229-3621
800-232-1452

Comfort Inn Historic Area
120 Bypass Road
Williamsburg, Virginia 23185
800-544-7774

**Courtyard by Marriott
Williamsburg**
510 McLaws Circle
Williamsburg, Virginia 23187
800-321-2211

Days Inn Historic Area
331 Bypass Road
Williamsburg, Virginia 23185
804-221-0637
800-759-1166

Days Inn West
5437 Richmond Road
Williamsburg, Virginia 23187
804-565-2700
800-635-5366

Econo Lodge Midtown
1420 Richmond Road
Williamsburg, Virginia 23185
800-582-3729

**Friendship Inn at Busch
Gardens**
7247 Pocahontas Trail
Williamsburg, Virginia 23185
804-220-2000
800-763-3344

Holiday Inn Downtown
814 Capitol Landing Road
Williamsburg, Virginia 23185
804-229-0200

Holiday Inn Patriot
3032 Richmond Road
Williamsburg, Virginia 23185
804-565-2600

Kingsmill Resort
1010 Kingsmill Road
Williamsburg, Virginia 23185
804-253-1703
800-832-5665

Quality Inn Downtown
300 Bypass Road
Williamsburg, Virginia 23185
804-229-6270

Quality Suites Williamsburg
152 Kings Gate Parkway
Williamsburg, Virginia 23185
804-229-6800
800-333-0924

Ramada Inn Historic Area
351 York Street
Williamsburg, Virginia 23185
800-962-4743

NEWPORT NEWS

■ **BACKGROUND:** It is believed that Newport News was named for Captain Christopher Newport, Commander of the ships that brought the "news" and supplies to the earliest settlers in Jamestown. In 1619, the name Newport News Point was recorded for the first time in English record. Today Newport News is Virginia's fourth largest city and home of the world's largest shipbuilder.

■ **VISITOR INFORMATION**

Newport News Tourism Office
50 Shoe Lane
Newport News, Virginia 23606
804-594-7475
800-333-RSVP

■ **AIRPORTS**

Newport News/Williamsburg International Airport
Bland Boulevard
Newport News, Virginia 23602
804-877-0221

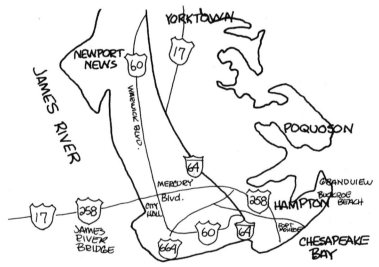

Attractions

■ BOAT CRUISES

Wharton's Wharf Harbor Cruises
530 12th Street
Newport News, Virginia 23607
804-245-1533

This cruise gives you a view of the world's largest commercial shipyard-Newport News shipbuilding, as well as trips to Norfolk's waterside and moonlight dining and dance cruises. Cruise Schedule: From April 1 to April 30, one trip daily, departs 1 p.m. From May 1 to June 12, one trip daily, leaves 12:30 p.m. From June 13 to Sept. 6, three trips daily at 10 a.m., 12:30 p.m., and 3 p.m. From Sept. 7 to Oct. 31, one trip daily, leaving at 12 noon. Fee.

■ HISTORIC SITES

Victory Arch
Downtown
Newport News, Virginia 23606

Hampton Roads was the WWII port of embarkation, returning men of our armed forces marched through this victory arch during their homecoming. A permanent stone arch serves today as a continuing memorial.

■ MUSEUMS

Mariners Museum
Museum Drive
Newport News, Virginia 23606
804-595-0368

"If you think all the sea's treasures lie beneath the waves, you've only scratched the surface." The Mariners Museum traces 3,000 years of maritime history with figureheads, miniature ships, and nautical artifacts. Open: Monday through Saturday, 9 a.m. to 5 p.m.; Sunday, 12 noon to 5 p.m. Closed Christmas Day. Admission charge.

U. S. Army Transportation Museum
Building 300, Besson Hall
Fort Eustis, Virginia 23604
804-878-1182

If you're a history buff, you're gonna love this place. Explore the world of motion from mighty steam locomotives of days past to the world's only captive "flying saucer." See the world's first helicopter to land at the South Pole-a vertical take-off and landing aircraft and the Army's largest helicopter, The Flying Crane. Open daily, 9 a.m. to 4:30 p.m. Closed major holidays. Free.

Virginia Living Museum
524 J. Clyde Morris Boulevard
Newport News, Virginia 23601
804-595-1900

The Virginia Living Museum is a spectacular combination of the best and most enjoyable elements of a narrative wildlife park, science museum, aquarium, botanical preserve, and planetarium. Open daily Memorial Day to Labor Day, Monday through Saturday, 9 a.m. to 6 p.m., and Sunday, 10 a.m. to 6 p.m. Winter Hours: Labor Day to Memorial Day, Monday through Saturday, 9 a.m. to 5 p.m., and Sunday, 1 p.m. to 5 p.m. Closed major holidays. Admission charge.

War Memorial Museum of Virginia
9285 Warwick Boulevard
Newport News, Virginia 23607
804-247-8523

The fascinating saga of military history unfolds in the galleries of the War Memorial Museum of Virginia with over 50,000 artifacts on display which document America's wars from 1775 to the present. Open daily Monday through Saturday, 9 a.m. to 5 p.m., and Sunday, 1 p.m. to 5 p.m. Closed major holidays. Admission charge.

■ PARKS AND GARDENS

Huntington Park
9200 Warwick Boulevard
Newport News, Virginia 23607
804-886-7912

Located at the foot of the James River Bridge, this park offers a public beach with lifeguards. Open, sunrise to sunset. Free.

Newport News Park
13564 Jefferson Avenue
Newport News, Virginia 23606
804-886-7912
804-888-3333

This large 8,000-acre municipal park offers a wide variety of family fun such as paddle boating, canoeing, archery, fishing, sheltered picnic areas, nature trails, wildlife and bird study programs, and a Nature and Historical Interpretive Center. Open daily, sunrise to sunset. Free.

Restaurants

Bill's Seafood House
10900 Warwick Blvd.
Newport News, Virginia 23602
804-595-4320

Bill's Seafood House takes great pride in good food, at reasonable prices and quick service. Bill's Seafood was established in July of 1980. Since that time the restaurant has captured the hearts of both travelers and a fiercely loyal local clientele. My visit recalls a perfectly prepared flounder, shrimp combo. It arrived quickly, and it was served with flair. The combo was heaping with the delicate fish and was served with french fries and coleslaw. And don't worry, your waitress won't forget the hushpuppies. Open for lunch and dinner. Closed Sunday.

Herman's Harbor House
663 Deep Creek Road
Newport News, Virginia 23606
804-595-3474

Herman's Harbor House is the place to go for local seafood dishes. Specialties include imperial crab, crab cakes, prime rib, seafood buffet. Open Sunday through Friday, lunch and dinner; Saturday, dinner only. Credit cards: AE, D, M, and V.

Japan Samural
12233 Jefferson Avenue
Newport News, Virginia 23602
804-249-4400

Located in the Jefferson Green Shopping Center, the Japan Samural features authentic Japanese delicacies prepared at your table right before your eyes. Open daily for dinner. Credit cards: AE, D, MC, and V.

Accommodations

■ CAMPING

Newport News Park Campsites
13564 Jefferson Avenue
Newport News, Virginia 23603
804-886-2844

■ HOTELS, MOTELS, AND INNS

Comfort Inn
12330 Jefferson Avenue
Newport News, Virginia 23602
804-249-0200
800-228-5150

Knights Inn
797 J. Clyde Morris Boulevard
Newport News, Virginia 23601
804-595-6336

Days Inn Warwick
14747 Warwick Boulevard
Newport News, Virginia 23602
804-874-0201
800-325-2525

Omni Newport News Hotel
1000 Omni Boulevard
Newport News, Virginia 23606
804-873-6664
800-THE-OMNI

Governor's Inn
741 Thimble Shoals Road
Newport News, Virginia 23606
804-873-1701

Ramada Inn
950 J. Clyde Morris Boulevard
Newport News, Virginia 23601
804-599-4460

Holiday Inn Newport News
6128 Jefferson Avenue
Newport News, Virginia 23605
804-826-4500
800-465-4329

Super 8
945 J. Clyde Morris Boulevard
Newport News, Virginia 23601
804-595-8888

King James Best Western
6045 Jefferson Avenue
Newport News, Virginia 23605
804-245-2801
800-528-1234

Thr-Rift Inn
6129 Jefferson Avenue
Newport News, Virginia 23605
804-838-6852

IF YOU WANT TO SEE SOME OF THE BEST CRAFTSMANSHIP ON EARTH, LOOK TO THE SEA.

Since the beginning of time, the sea has captured the imagination of men. The many inspired to explore her waters could not have done so were it not for the extraordinary craftsmanship of the few who chose to build the vessels in which they sailed.

It is to these craftsmen—and to others who captured the lure and lore of the sea and her vessels in paintings, ceramics and miniature replicas—that The Mariners' Museum is dedicated.

Enter the Great Hall and a gilded eagle with a wing span of 18 1/2 feet—once the figurehead of a U.S. Navy frigate—soars above you. Hand-carved trailboards, rudder heads, and paddleboxes line the walls. Model ships crafted from metal, ivory and wood draw you through galleries where great moments in naval history come alive in photographs, costumes, tools, weapons, and other marine memorabilia.

HAMPTON

The Indians called it Kecoughtan, translated it means "Inhabitants of the great town." The city was established by the court system in 1610. In 1619 it was one of the original boroughs in the Virginia Legislature. It became an industrial port way back in 1705 and sits at the mouth of the confluence where the Chesapeake Bay meets the Atlantic Ocean. Today the river is the center for the seafood industry, shelters pleasure craft, and serves the cruise ship industry.

■ VISITOR INFORMATION

Hampton Department of Conventions and Tourism
2 Eaton Street
Hampton, Virginia 23667
804-722-1222
800-487-8778

Hampton Visitor Center
710 Settlers Landing Road
Hampton, Virginia 23669
804-727-1102
800-800-2202

■ AIRPORTS

Norfolk Airport Authority
Norfolk International Airport
Norfolk, Virginia 23518
804-857-3351

Attractions

■ BEACHES

Buckroe Beach
Pembroke Avenue
Hampton, Virginia 23669
804-727-6347

Buckroe Beach has lots of clean sand and a gentle, calming surf. Open Memorial Day to Labor Day with lifeguards. Free.

■ BOAT CRUISES

Miss Hampton II
710 Settlers Landing Road
Hampton, Virginia 23669
804-727-1102

See the harbor of Hampton on a two-decked, 65-foot tour boat. It takes you from the Hampton Visitors' Center Dock out onto the Chesapeake Bay. Cruise past the world's largest naval base and see the mightiest ships in the U.S. Navy. Your tour boat docks for a visit of Fort Royal, an artificial island recently opened to civilians. The Fort was active during the Civil War with its guns rocking the skies during the famous battle between the Monitor and the Merrimac. Open Memorial Day through Labor Day, cruises depart 10 a.m. and 2 p.m. Fee.

■ HISTORIC SITES

Hampton Carousel
610 Settlers Landing Road
Hampton, Virginia 23669
804-727-6479

Take a spin on the Hampton Carousel and experience an American tradition. Built in 1920 the Carousel has been completely restored to its original beauty and is now housed in its own pavilion on the downtown waterfront. Open April through seasonal hours, 12 noon to 8 p.m. Admission charge.

St. John's Church
100 West Queens Way
Hampton, Virginia 23669
804-722-2567

Established in 1610, it is the oldest, continuous English-speaking parish in the United States. Since 1728 the church has been on its present site. The baptism of Indian Princess Pocahontas is depicted in one of the exquisite stained-glass windows. Open Monday through Friday, 9 a.m. to 3:30 p.m.; Saturday, 9 a.m. to 12 noon. Closed Sunday. Free.

■ HISTORIC TOWNS

Town of Poquoson

Poquoson, which derives its name from the Indian (Po-ko-son) word meaning low, flatland, was settled in 1628. It soon became an important shipping point for tobacco, and today Poquoson is a town of scenic beauty and home port for many fishing boats.

■ MISCELLANEOUS

FISHING PIER

Grandview Fishing Pier
Beach Road
Hampton, Virginia 23666
804-851-2811

Grandview Fishing Pier juts out into the Chesapeake Bay and caters to the fisherman in search of the Bay's bounty. Open 24 hours a day, Memorial Day until Labor Day. Fee.

Hampton Coliseum
1000 Coliseum DRive
Hampton, Virginia 23668
804-838-4203

Sporting events, trade shows, conventions, and concerts are showcased here. The grounds include a 14-acre lake set in a landscaped park.

■ MUSEUMS

The Casemate Museum
Box 341, Mercury Boulevard
Fort Monroe, Virginia 23651
804-727-3391

The Casemate Museum opened on 1 June 1951 to display the cell in which Jefferson Davis had been imprisoned after the Civil War. Since then, the museum has expanded to depict the history of Fort Monroe and the Coast Artillery Corps. Exhibits include weapons, uniforms, models, and drawings by Frederick Remington and R. F. Zogbaum. The museum also serves as the Army's Coast Artillery Museum.

The Casemate Museum is housed within the thick walls of Fort Monroe and relates to the battles of Hampton Road during the Civil War. The battle of the Monitor and Merrimac is told here. Fort Monroe, sometimes called the "Gibraltar of Chesapeake Bay," is the largest stone fort ever built in the country and the only moat-encircled fort still used today by the Army. Open daily, 10:30 a.m. to 5 p.m. Closed: Thanksgiving, Christmas and New Year's Day. Free.

The Hampton Institute Museum
Marshall Street, Hampton University
Hampton, Virginia 23668
804-727-5308

This museum on the campus of Hampton University features traditional art from African and American Indian cultures and works by noted black artists. Open September through May; Monday to Friday, 8 a.m. to 5 p.m.; Saturday and Sunday, 12 noon to 4 p.m. Free.

The Virginia Air and Space Center
600 Settlers Landing Road
Hampton, Virginia 23669
800-296-0800

The Air and Space Center is a fitting addition to Hampton's downtown sky line. This seaport city was the training site for NASA's original seven astronauts. Exhibited inside the Center are some of NASA's most dramatic artifacts including moon rocks and space capsules. Open daily, 10 a.m. to 5 p.m. Admission charge.

■ PARKS AND GARDENS

Air Power Park
413 West Mercury Boulevard
Hampton, Virginia 23666
804-727-1163

Outdoor exhibit of missiles, rockets, and military aircraft. Open 9 a.m. to 5 p.m., Wednesday through Sunday. Closed Thanksgiving, Christmas, New Year's Day. Free.

Bluebird Gap Farm
60 Pine Chapel Road
Hampton, Virginia 23669
804-727-6347

This 60-acre farm/park/zoo, operated by the City of Hampton, is home to hundreds of farm animals and animals that a farmer might encounter in the area surrounding the farm. Playground, picnic, hiking, and recreational facilities are available. Closed Monday, Tuesday, and all major holidays. Open 9 a.m. to 5 p.m., Wednesday through Sunday. Free.

Grandview Nature Preserve
Beach Road
Hampton, Virginia 23669
804-727-6347

Sometimes one finds surprising natural attractions in most unexpected places, such as Grandview Nature Preserve. This is a fine place to visit the Chesapeake Bay to watch a wild mallard duck raising her young during the summer. Miles of beach, sand dunes, and exciting views. Open daily, dawn to dusk. Free.

■ SEASONAL EVENTS

The Hampton Bay Days Festival
Downtown Area
Hampton, Virginia 23669
804-727-1102

Old Hampton comes alive with top entertainment, sports, arts, and crafts. Come learn about the Chesapeake Bay and the environment through more than 35 exhibits ranging from world-renowned organizations such as the Cousteau Society to local watermen. Early September. Free.

Hampton Jazz Festival
Marshall Street, Box 7309
Hampton, Virginia 23666
804-838-5650

This annual, three-day event is held at the Hampton Coliseum and brings together top name jazz entertainers from around the world. Held mid-June. Admission charge.

Restaurants

The Chamberlain Hotel Restaurant
Old Point Comfort
Hampton, Virginia 23651
804-722-3636

From your restaurant table, you can look out through the large windows and see all types of boats from a trawler to a tanker. On Friday night the seafood buffet is as bountiful a gift from the sea as you will ever see. House specialties: crab bisque, clam chowder, crab Norfolk, stuffed flounder, crab cakes, coconut shrimp, and a scrumptious seafood combination platter. Open: Monday through Saturday, dinner only; Sunday, brunch and dinner. Credit cards: AE, DC, MC, and V.

Restaurants, cont.

Fisherman's Wharf
14 Ivy Home Road
Hampton, Virginia 23669
804-723-3113

Fisherman's Wharf features one of the largest and the best seafood buffets you will find anywhere: steamed shrimp, jumbo snow crab legs, shrimp creole, broiled scallops, fried flounder, select oysters, gulf fried shrimp, broiled fish, seafood au gratin, imperial crab supreme, baked whole fish, deviled crab, steamed blue crabs, clam chowder, fresh salads, vegetables, and desserts-all this and a view of the Hampton Roads area. Open, dinner only, Monday through Saturday; Sunday, open lunch and dinner. Credit Cards: AE, D, DC, MC, and V.

Sam's Seafood Restaurant
23 Water Street
Phoebus, Virginia 23663
804-723-3709

Entrees include seafood fried, broiled, in a sauce, or sauteed. I especially enjoyed the broiled flounder. Other specials include steak served the way you like it. Open daily for lunch and dinner. Credit Cards: AE, MC, and V.

> *Blackbeard the Pirate, whose head was severed and displayed on a pole at the mouth of the Hampton River. Since that time the point of land has been known as Blackbeard's Point.*

Strawberry Banks Restaurant
Strawberry Banks Lane
Hampton, Virginia 23663
804-723-6061

According to legend, Strawberry Banks witnessed our Founding Fathers' arrival. Captain John Smith was greeted by friendly Kecoughtan Indians from these banks as he and his English settlers sailed toward Jamestown in 1607. The Captain noticed the abundance of wild berries on the shore and called this spot "'Strawberry Bankes.'" Open: Monday through Saturday, breakfast, lunch, and dinner; Sunday, brunch and dinner. Credit cards: AE, DC, and MC.

Accommodations

■ CAMPING

Gosnold Hope Park
901 Little Back River Road
Hampton, Virginia 23669
804-727-6347

■ HOTELS, MOTELS, AND INNS

The Chamberlain Hotel
Fort Monroe
Hampton, Virginia 23651
804-723-6511

Days Inn
1918 Coliseum Drive
Hampton, Virginia 23666
804-826-4810

Econo Lodge
2708 West Mercury Boulevard
Hampton, Virginia 23666
804-826-8970

Holiday Inn Coliseum
1815 West Mercury Boulevard
Hampton, Virginia 23666
804-838-0200

Sheraton Inn Coliseum
1215 West Mercury Boulevard
Hampton, Virginia 23666
804-838-5011

Strawberry Banks
30 Strawberry Banks Lane
Hampton, Virginia 23663
804-723-6061

121

THE YORK RIVER AND THE RAPPAHANNOCK RIVER

Yorktown to Kilmarnock

Follow the water....

- Yorktown
- West Point
- Gloucester
- Deltaville
- Urbanna
- Tappahannock
- Fredericksburg
- Warsaw
- Lancaster
- Irvington
- Kilmarnock

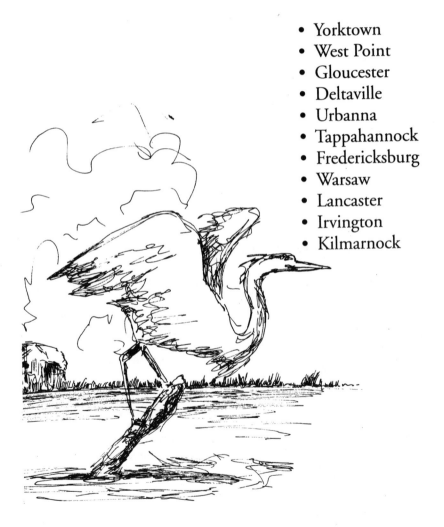

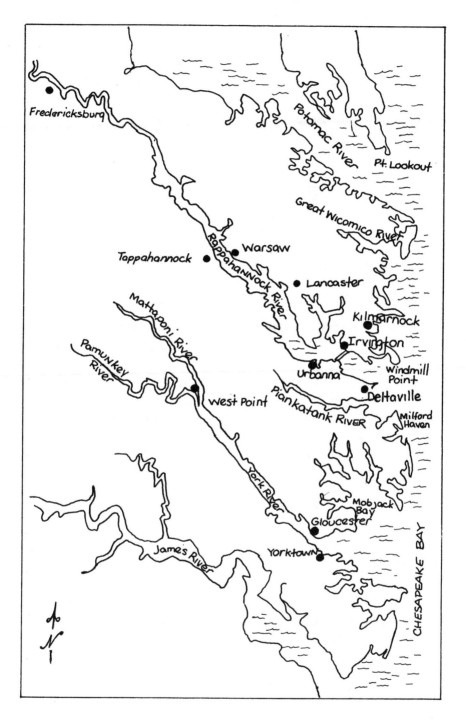

YORKTOWN

■ **BACKGROUND:** In 1630, a French engineer secured a grant for the land on which Yorktown was built. The Virginia Assembly established a port here in 1680. Nothing about the town seemed strategic enough during the Revolutionary War to suggest that it would be the site of the battle which would end the conflict. However, the Battle of Yorktown played a role when George Washington overcame the British here as the Brits' escape to the sea was blockaded at the mouth of the Chesapeake Bay. Today visitors to Yorktown can enjoy many historic sites and reflect on events that shaped the beginning of a great nation.

Attractions

■ **VISITOR INFORMATION**

Colonial National Historic Park
Box 532
Yorktown, Virginia 23690
804-890-3300

York River Cruise Ship "Miss Yorktown"
Evening river cruises & fishing parties. Docks at Watermen's Museum. Special charters available. Call Erin Kay Charters: daytime (804) 879-8276 or evening (804) 642-5096.

York County Information Office
224 Ballard Street
Yorktown, Virginia 23690
804-890-3300

Yorktown Victory Center
Box 1776
Yorktown, Virginia 23690
804-887-1776

■ **BEACHES**

Yorktown Beach
Water Street, Box 210
Yorktown, Virginia 23690
804-898-0090

This two-acre, public Yorktown Beach is open year round and is staffed with lifeguards from Memorial Day through Labor Day. Open from 10 a.m. to 5 p.m. for swimming, fishing, and boating. Free.

■ HISTORIC SITES

Moore House
106 Hamilton House Road/
Route 238
Yorktown, Virginia 23690
804-898-3400

The terms of surrender for the British Army were negotiated here in 1781. The house is now restored and refurbished. Living history programs are presented by costumed actors in period dress on weekends in the spring and fall and daily during the summer. Admission charge.

Nelson House
508 Main Street
Yorktown, Virginia 23690
804-898-3400

This early 18th century mansion is an impressive example of Georgian architecture. It was the home of Thomas Nelson, Jr., a signer of the Declaration of Independence. The brickwork still bears the scars of the siege of 1781. Open daily except in the winter months. Hours vary; call for schedule. Admission charge.

■ MISCELLANEOUS

Colonial Parkway

Yorktown and Jamestown, together with Williamsburg, form Virginia's "Historic Triangle," a region which had a major role in the creation of the United States.

The Colonial Parkway is a 23-mile drive that links Jamestown, Williamsburg, and Yorktown. Along the way interpretive markers and overlooks allow Baytrippers to enjoy both the history and the natural beauty of the area. There are spectacular views of both the James and York Rivers.

On-The-Hill Cultural Arts Center
121 Alexander Hamilton Boulevard
Yorktown, Virginia 23690
804-898-3076

The Art Center features changing exhibitions of fine arts and crafts by regional artists. Open 10 a.m. to 5 p.m., Tuesday through Saturday, and 12 noon to 5 p.m. on Sunday. Free.

Yorktown Victory Center
Old Road 238, Box 1976
Yorktown, Virginia 23690
804-253-4838

The Victory Center, operated by the Commonwealth of Virginia, presents the story of the Revolutionary War through audio-visual exhibits, a film, and an outdoor Continental Army camp. Open from 9 a.m. to 5 p.m. daily. Closed Christmas and New Year's Day. Admission charge.

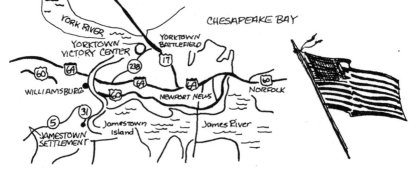

■ MUSEUMS

Watermen's Museum
309 Water Street
Yorktown, Virginia 23690
804-887-2641

The first Virginia watermen were native American Indians who taught the colonists to fish and set nets. From Revolutionary times to the present, learn about "Wooden Boats and Iron Men."

The museum tells the story of Virginia's watermen who for centuries have worked and harvested the rivers and the tributaries of the Chesapeake Bay year round. Open 10 a.m. to 4 p.m., Tuesday through Friday, and Saturday, 1 p.m. to 4 p.m. Admission charge.

■ PARKS AND GARDENS

Yorktown Battlefield Visitor Center
Colonial Parkway
P.O. Box 210
Yorktown, Virginia 23690
804-898-3400

Operated by the National Park Service, the Visitor Center has a museum and a film that recreates the excitement of the Revolutionary War. The battlefield is the scene of the last major battle of the war in 1781. Hours of operation are 8:30 a.m. to 5 p.m. (extended hours spring, summer, and fall). Free.

Restaurants

Nick's Seafood Pavilion
Water Street
Yorktown, Virginia 23690
804-887-5269

Beauty and luxury envelop you at Nick's Seafood Pavilion, and the special dishes will no doubt add to your sense of well being. Featured are such selections as Seafood Shishkabob or the Crab Meat ala Pavilion. A Baked Alaska will make a wonderful end to the meal if you still have room. Open daily for lunch and dinner. Credit Cards: AE, CB, DC, M, and V.

Yorktown Pub
540 Water Street
Yorktown, Virginia 23690
804-898-8793

The Yorktown Pub is a popular beach front restaurant, and the atmosphere is definitely casual. There's a good selection to choose from on the menu with steamed clams, oysters, and shrimp getting top raves. Open daily for lunch and dinner.

Accommodations

■ HOTELS, MOTELS, AND INNS

Duke of York Motor Hotel
508 Water Street
Yorktown, Virginia 23690
804-898-3232

Thomas Nelson Motel
7833 George Washington Highway
Yorktown, Virginia 23692
804-898-5436

Yorktown Motor Lodge
8829 George Washington Highway
Yorktown, Virginia 23692
804-898-5451
800-950-4003

WEST POINT

■ **BACKGROUND:** The town of West Point on the York River was named during the 17th century after the four West Brothers: Thomas, Nathaniel, Francis, and John. Three of them became governors of Virginia. Today local attractions include boat cruises, nearby Indian reservations, hiking, and an annual Crab Carnival.

Attractions

■ **VISITOR INFORMATION**

West Point Area Chamber of Commerce
10th and Main Streets
West Point, Virginia 23181
804-843-4620

■ **BOAT CRUISES**

Tidewater River Adventures
Box 157
Walkerton, Virginia 23177
804-769-1602

Chances are there is a trip that's "just right" for you. Special boat tours focus on river ecology, river history, land-use issues, or flora and fauna, among other subjects. Call for their schedule. Open daily. Fee.

■ HISTORIC SITES

Mattaponi Indian Reservation
Highway 625
West Point, Virginia 23181
804-769-2229
804-769-2194

In 1658, this Indian Reservation was established just north of the Pamunkey River. The Mattaponi Indian Museum built here in 1954 exhibits tribal artifacts including the tomahawk used by Opecahanough in the battles of 1622 and 1644. Open 10 a.m. to 6 p.m. daily. Admission charge.

Pamunkey Indian Reservation
Highway 673
King William, Virginia 23086
804-843-4792

Of particular interest here is the Pamunkey Indian Museum which shows their way of life throughout history from the ice age to the present. Powhatan and Pocahontas once lived among the Pamunkey people. The Museum is open from 10 a.m. to 4 p.m., Monday through Saturday, and on Sunday from 1 p.m. to 5 p.m. Admission charge.

■ PARKS AND GARDENS

New Kent Nature Trail
Route 33
West Point, Virginia 23181
804-843-5402
804-843-5290

A considerable variety of wild-life has been seen on or near the New Kent Nature Trail. Be on the lookout for wild turkey, deer, opossums, snakes, skunks, and birds of many kinds. Various flowers and plants are identified on markers along the path. Open daily, sunup to sundown. Free.

York River State Park
5526 River View Road
Croaker, Virginia 23188
804-566-3036
804-786-1712

The York River State Park is known for its rare and delicate estuarine environment, where fresh and salt water meet to create a habitat rich in marine and plant life. The park area was the site of a 17th and 18th century Public Tobacco Warehouse. Remnants of wooden "corduroy" roads dating from this period can be seen along Taskinas Creek at low tide. Open daily, 8 a.m. to dusk. Admission charge.

ATAMASCO LILY

■ SEASONAL EVENTS

Crab Carnival
Box 1035
West Point, Virginia 23181
804-843-4620

This three-day annual event highlights the crab and features activities that the entire family can enjoy. If the weather permits, you can take a hot air balloon ride or how about a tug boat tour? Need more? Okay, there's food, fabulous food, arts and crafts, parades, and fireworks. Held in early October. Free.

Restaurants

Anna's Italian Restaurant
3040 King William Avenue
West Point, Virginia 23181
804-843-4035

Anna's concentrates on a wide variety of Italian cuisine from delicious subs and pizzas to a number of signature dishes like flounder filet. Their most frequently touted entrees are the chef's many preparations of fork-tender veal. Open daily for lunch and dinner.

Restaurants, cont.

Harbor House Restaurant
7th Street
West Point, Virginia 23181
804-843-2015

The Taylor Family presents casual waterfront dining overlooking the Mattaponi River. The owners here come from a long line of seafood lovers (Taylor's Restaurant, Deltaville, Virginia). If you love seafood, too, you'll love the Harbor House. Open daily for lunch and dinner. Credit cards: MC and V.

Tony and George's
2880 King William Avenue
West Point, Virginia 23181
804-843-4448

There are two ways of dining at Tony and George's. You can take advantage of the fresh seafood dishes such as stuffed flounder and trout, or you can dig into a menu that features appetizing Italian pasta. Two soups are always on the menu—beef vegetable and clam chowder—and both should be tried. Open daily for lunch and dinner. Credit cards: MC and V.

The Chesapeake Bay has one of the highest concentrations of bald eagles in the conterminous forty-eight states. The Bay is home for twenty percent of the breeding birds on the eastern coast of the United States. In addition to the year-round breeding population, there are visitors from Canada in the winter and Florida in the summer.

The Chesapeake bald eagles feed along the Bay waters and marshes on a variety of fish, waterfowl, mammals and some turtles and snakes. Their diet consists mainly of catfish, mallard, carp, muskrat and stinkpot turtles.

Accommodations

■ HOTELS, MOTELS, AND INNS

Washington Burgess Inn
Routes 30 and 33
West Point, Virginia 23181
804-843-2100

GLOUCESTER

■ **BACKGROUND:** Gloucester County was named for the third son of Charles I—Henry, Duke of Gloucester. The county figured prominently in the history of the colony and the Commonwealth of Virginia. When English settlers arrived at Jamestown in 1607, the Indian stronghold of Chief Powhatan was located on the north side of the York River in Gloucester. It was here that Powhatan built his home, Werowocomoco. According to legend, his daughter, the Princess Pocahontas, saved the gallant Captain John Smith from a tragic death at the hands of the Indians, and she thus entered the pages of Virginia's history. Today the town survives "as a classic example of an early Virginia county seat." The walled courtyard and cluster of government buildings are one of the most picturesque groupings of its type. A visit here is a step back in time.

Attractions

■ **VISITOR INFORMATION**

Gloucester Chamber of Commerce
Box 296
Gloucester, Virginia 23061
804-693-2425

Matthews County Chamber of Commerce
Box 1126
Matthews, Virginia 23109
804-725-9029

■ **BEACHES**

Gloucester Point Beach
Route 1206
Gloucester Point, Virginia
23061
804-693-2355

This five-acre park is located on the York River. Facilities include a fishing pier, picnic areas, horseshoe court, volleyball court, and plenty of room for sunbathing and swimming. Open daily, sunup to sundown. Free.

■ HISTORIC SITES

Gloucester Courthouse Square
Historic District
Main Street, Box 1176
Gloucester, Virginia 23061
804-693-1236

Gloucester's historic district includes a debtors prison, the old county courthouse dating from 1776, and fine examples of handsome 18th and 19th century homes. Debtors prison is open Wednesday and Friday, 10 a.m. to 2 p.m. Free.

■ MUSEUMS

Gwynn's Island Museum
Route 633 and Rose Lane
Gwynn's Island, Virginia 23064
804-725-7949

This Museum is dedicated to preserving the island's history. Its extensive collection includes memorabilia relating to island watermen, old schools, homes, stores, and much more. Open Saturday and Sunday, 1 p.m. to 4 p.m. Free.

Virginia Institute of Marine Science
U.S. Route 17
Gloucester Point, Virginia 23061
804-642-2111

The Marine Science Museum offers a variety of displays highlighting the marine world including several aquariums, a large collection of shells, and a salt marsh. Open daily. Hours are 8 a.m. to 4:30 p.m., Monday through Friday, and 10 a.m. to 4:30 p.m., Saturday and Sunday. Free.

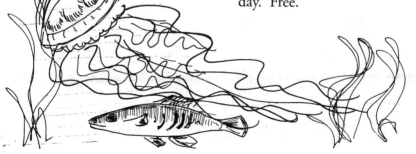

■ PARKS AND GARDENS

Tindall's Point Park
Route 1208
Gloucester, Virginia 23061
804-693-2355

This four-acre Park has historical significance relating to both the American Revolution and Civil War. The Park has a picnic area and is surrounded by earthworks that were used to protect the soldiers in battle. Open daily, 8 a.m. to dusk. Free.

■ SEASONAL EVENTS

Annual Daffodil Show
P. O. Box 296
Gloucester, Virginia 23061
804-693-2425

Sponsored by the Gloucester Chamber of Commerce, this annual weekend festival and show celebrates daffodil harvest time. Dates vary slightly depending upon the blooming season which usually extends from early March to mid-April. Free.

Restaurants

Courthouse Restaurant
Main Street
Gloucester, Virginia 23061
804-693-6801

Anytime you get within 30 miles of Gloucester and it's time to eat, head for the Courthouse Restaurant. Specials are all home cooked and very, very good. Open daily for breakfast, lunch, and dinner.

Golden Anchor Restaurant
Old Ferry Road
Gwynn's Island, Virginia 23064
804-725-2152

House specialties: baked stuffed shrimp, captain's seafood platter, crab cakes, stuffed flounder, imperial crab, fried shrimp. Open April through October for breakfast, lunch, and dinner. Credit Cards: MC and V.

Restaurants, cont.

Shores and Ruack Seafood
Melford Haven Road
Gwynn's Island, Virginia 23064
804-725-4696

Eat fresh crabs at a picnic table while looking out at the water. It's one way to truly experience the Chesapeake Bay at its finest. The steamed crabs are great and the island puts you at ease. Open for lunch and dinner.

Seabreeze Restaurant
Route 223 at the Bridge
Gwynn's Island, Virginia 23064
804-725-4000

You'll know they serve seafood when you see the distinctive Bay Country style decor. Expect fresh homemade crab cakes and spicy steamed shrimp. Open daily for lunch and dinner.

Sandpiper Reef
Godfrey Bay Road
Hallieford, Virginia 23068
804-725-3331

The Sandpiper Reef Restaurant at Misti Cove offers fine dining on the Piankatank River. If you would like to sample a little bit of Heaven, try the "Heavenly Flounder." It's topped with Swiss and parmesan cheese and broiled to perfection. Open Thursday through Saturday for dinner only; Sunday open for brunch only (12 noon to 3 p.m.). Credit cards: AE, MC, and V.

Accommodations

■ BED AND BREAKFASTS

Ravenswood Inn
Box 715, Poplar Grove Lane
Matthews, Virginia 23109
804-725-7272

The Willows
Route 614, Featherbed Lane
Gloucester, Virginia 23061
804-693-4066

Riverfront B&B
Route 14 East
Box 310
Matthews, Virginia 23109
804-725-9975

■ CAMPING

New Point Campground
Route 602
New Point, Virginia 23125
804-725-5120

■ HOTELS, MOTELS, AND INNS

The Islander
Gwynn's Island
Grimstead, Virginia 23064
804-725-2151

Tidewater Motel
Route 17
Gloucester Point, Virginia 23072
804-642-2155

BALLOON RIDES
ALONG THE
CHESAPEAKE
BAY
(804)694-5800

DELTAVILLE

■ **BACKGROUND:** This town (originally called Unionville) was named after the Union of Two Churches. When the post office was established, the name changed to Deltaville because the community sits on a delta on the Chesapeake Bay. It was near here that a grave was dug for Captain John Smith when he almost died following an encounter with a sting ray. Today Deltaville is known as "the capital of wooden boat building" because there are more than a half dozen boat yards turning out vessels that the watermen use for working on the Bay.

Attractions

■ **VISITOR INFORMATION**

Middlesex County Chamber of Commerce
Cross Street
Urbanna, Virginia 23175
804-758-5540

■ **BOAT CHARTERS**

C&L Charters
Chesapeake Cove Marina
Deltaville, Virginia 23043
804-758-4535

C&L Charters offer Chesapeake Bay fishing where the Rappahannock River joins the Bay. Call Captain Cliff Heiser for your schedule. Fee.

Restaurants

The Galley
Route 33
Deltaville, Virginia 23043
804-776-6040

The Galley offers a comfortable and informal atmosphere. Featured is a selection of seafood and traditional specials. Open Monday for lunch; Tuesday through Sunday for breakfast, lunch, and dinner. Credit cards: MC and V.

Red Sky Restaurant
Route 1102
Deltaville, Virginia 23043
804-776-6913

Imaginative continental cuisine in a friendly, casual atmosphere. Red Sky specializes in regional seafood as well as Southwestern dishes. Open Wednesday through Saturday for dinner only.

Taylor's Restaurant
Route 33
Deltaville, Virginia 23043
804-776-9611

The specialties to try here are the seafood creations, especially the catch of the day and the soft shell crabs (in season). And if you want a real taste sensation, try the excellent Seafood Buffet. Open daily for breakfast, lunch, and dinner. The Buffet is offered on Friday, Saturday, and Sunday.

Accommodations

■ CAMPING

The Cross Rip Ltd.
Route 33, Box 362
Deltaville, Virginia 23043
804-776-9324

■ HOTELS, MOTELS, AND INNS

Dockside Inn
Route 33
Deltaville, Virginia 23043
804-776-9224

URBANNA

■ **BACKGROUND:** Urbanna is one of the four remaining towns of the 20 sites designated by an Act of the Assembly in 1680 as ports through which all tobacco, then the currency of the colony, would be shipped. All imports, goods, slaves, or servants also passed through these ports. The town was laid out in 1681 in the pattern preserved today. It received the name Urbanna, City of Anne, in 1704 to honor Queen Anne, who was the reigning monarch. The town celebrates its major claim to fame the first weekend in November each year when thousands visit the Annual Urbanna Oyster Festival.

Attractions

■ **VISITOR INFORMATION**

Middlesex/Saluda Chamber of Commerce
Cross Street
Urbanna, Virginia 23175
804-758-5540

■ **BOAT CRUISES**

Rivah Cruises
210 Oyster Road
Urbanna, Virginia 23175
804-758-4349

The Rappahannock River provides miles of tranquil picturesque shorelines abundant with nature unique to Virginia's Tidewater area. Baytrippers can cruise the river aboard the *Bethpager*, a traditional Chesapeake Bay deadrise vessel. Seasonal operations. Call for schedule. Fee.

144

■ HISTORIC SITES

Historic District
Downtown
Urbanna, Virginia 23175
804-758-5540

The center portion of Urbanna has been designated as a historic district and is listed on the Virginia Landmarks Register and the National Register of Historic Places.

■ SEASONAL EVENTS

Urbanna Oyster Festival
Downtown Area
Urbanna, Virginia 23175
804-758-5540

This event marks the beginning of another oyster harvest, and a highlight of the two-day celebration is the Virginia Oyster Shucking Championship. The winner will represent the State in the National Oyster Shucking Championship. Also featured are numerous street booths offering arts, crafts, and oysters...either fried, frittered, stewed, roasted, or raw. First weekend in November. Free.

Restaurants

Awful Arthur's
213 Virginia Street
Urbanna, Virginia 23175
804-758-0758

Don't judge this restaurant by its name; in fact, it could be called Wonderful. At lunch you could choose a Reuben sandwich or a Philly cheese steak sub. For dinner it's Prime Rib or fried oysters or fresh rockfish grilled to perfection. Open daily for lunch and dinner. Credit cards: AE, MC, and V.

Urbanna Inn
250 Virginia Street
Urbanna, Virginia 23175
804-758-4852

Relax and enjoy your meal in the casual colonial dining room. Delicacies of the Bay are offered including crab cakes. They are the house specialty and are usually our first choice.

Virginia Street Cafe
Virginia Street
Urbanna, Virginia 23175
804-758-3798

This cozy cafe located in the historic district is worth a stop. It specializes in local seafood. I recommend the clam chowder. The steak is also great. Open daily for breakfast, lunch, and dinner.

Accommodations

■ **BED & BREAKFASTS**

Atherston Hall B&B
217 Virginia Street
Urbanna, Virginia 23175
804-758-2809

Duck Farm Inn B&B
Route 227
Urbanna, Virginia 23175
804-758-5685

Bradwick's White Swan B&B
350 Virginia Street
Urbanna, Virginia 23175
804-758-3367

■ **CAMPING**

Bethpage Camp-Resort
Route 602
Urbanna, Virginia 23175
804-758-4349

■ **HOTELS, MOTELS, AND INNS**

Urbanna Inn
250 Virginia Street
Urbanna, Virginia 23175
804-758-4852

TAPPAHANNOCK

■ **BACKGROUND:** Captain John Smith landed here in 1608 but was driven back to his ship by local Indians. A warehouse and trading post were established in the early 1600's by Jacob Hobbs, and for many years this area was known as Hobb's Hold. The 1682 port at this location was called New Plymouth. Tappahannock, the name itself is a variation of Rappahannock, is derived from the Algonquian word meaning "on the rise and fall of water" or "on the running water." As you drive through Tappahannock today, the past is very much present. Its buildings, ranging from prerevolutionary to modern, are located on the banks of the Rappahannock River in a lovely setting of stately old trees.

Attractions

■ **VISITOR INFORMATION**

Tappahannock-Essex County Chamber of Commerce
Box 481
Tappahannock, Virginia 22560
804-443-5241

■ **BOAT CRUISES**

Rappahannock River Cruises
Route 1, Box 1332
Reedville, Virginia 22539
804-453-2628

Take a trip up the Rappahannock River to the Ingleside Plantation Winery and Saunders Wharf at Wheatland. During May through October, the Captain Thomas departs at 10 a.m. from Tappahannock at the Hoskins Creek Bridge every day except Monday and returns at 5 p.m. Admission charge.

Restaurants

Lowery's Seafood Restaurant
528 Church Lane S.
Tappahannock, Virginia 22560
804-443-4314

Lowery's Seafood Restaurant has been specializing in crab cakes, oysters, shrimp, fish, beef, and all American chicken for over 50 years. It's hard for many Bay-trippers to remember when this restaurant wasn't here serving prodigious portions of authentic Bay Country food in an old country rural atmosphere. Open daily for breakfast, lunch, and dinner.

Accommodations

■ **BED AND BREAKFASTS**

Linden House
Route 17 South
Champlain, Virginia 22438
800-622-1202

■ **HOTELS, MOTELS, AND INNS**

Super 8 Motel
Route 360 and 17
Tappahannock, Virginia 22560
804-443-3888

Tappahannock Motel
360 Church Lane
Tappahannock, Virginia 22560
804-443-3366

FREDERICKSBURG

■ **BACKGROUND:** Fredericksburg was officially founded and given its name in 1727. The city was named for Frederic, Prince of Wales and father of George the III. Frederic(k) is the anglicization of Friedrich. Fredericksburg and the surrounding countryside were the sites of four major battles during the Civil War; in fact, 17,000 died and more than 80,000 were wounded in these conflicts. Fredericksburg was George Washington's boyhood stomping grounds and is also home to Mary Washington College, which is named in honor of George Washington's mother. The passing of time changes all places, but George Washington would still know much of the Fredericksburg that stands today.

Attractions

■ **VISITOR INFORMATION**

Fredericksburg Department of Tourism
706 Caroline Street
Fredericksburg, Virginia 22401
703-373-1776
800-678-4748

Here you can enjoy a special orientation film on Fredericksburg, receive your tour directions, hotel or restaurant information, and free parking passes.

Then you're ready to visit one of the oldest cities in America—a city with more than 350 original buildings built before 1870.

Spotsylvania County Visitor's Center
4704 Southpoint Parkway
Fredericksburg, Virginia 22407
703-891-8687

■ **HISTORIC SITES**

Chatham
120 Chatham Lane
Falmouth, Virginia 22405
703-373-4461

Walk in Washington's footsteps. Stand where brave men fell.

This home served as a Union headquarters during the battle of Fredericksburg, and Clara Barton and Walt Whitman joined in the treatment of hundreds of wounded soldiers. Chatham contains exhibits about its colorful history. Open daily, 9 a.m. to 5 p.m. Free.

Ferry Farm (Washington's Boyhood Home)
240 Kings Highway
Falmouth, Virginia 22405
703-372-4485

According to legend, it was here on the eastern bank of the Rappahannock River that George Washington, father of our country, chopped down the cherry tree. The site was recently acquired by Stafford County for restoration, and it's now open. Call for schedule. Free.

Kenmore
1201 Washington Avenue
Fredericksburg, Virginia 22401
703-373-3381

Kenmore is one of the most elegant colonial mansions in America. It was the home of Fielding Lewis and his wife, Betty, the only sister of George Washington. The mansion contains three of the most elaborately decorated rooms of the period. On March 1 through November 30, open daily, 9 a.m. to 5 p.m. On December 1 through February 28, open daily, 10 a.m. to 4 p.m. Closed major holidays. Admission charge.

Historic Sites, cont.

Hartwood Winery
345 Hartwood Road
Hartwood, Virginia 22471
703-752-4893

Virginia is becoming well-known for its regional wine production. This Virginia farm winery offers free tours and tastings as well as a gift shop and a selection of Hartwood fine wines. Open summer days, 11 a.m. to 5 p.m.; weekends and by appointment the remainder of the year. Free.

Hugh Mercer Apothecary Shop
1020 Caroline Street
Fredericksburg, Virginia 22401
703-373-3362

As a doctor, Mercer practiced medicine and operated this shop from 1771 to 1776.

As one of Fredericksburg's five Revolutionary War generals, he gave his life at the Battle of Princeton rather than surrender to the British.

Here you can see such oddities as silver plated pills, an apothecary jar decorated from the inside, an original prescription in Mercer's handwriting, and the sitting room Mercer's friend, George Washington, used as an office during his visits to Fredericksburg.

This 18th century building restored as the Mercer Apothecary Shop presents a living history interpretation of colonial medical practices. On March 1 through November 30, open daily, 9 a.m. to 5 p.m. On December 1 through February 28, open daily, 10 a.m. to 4 p.m. Closed major holidays. Admission charge.

Rising Sun Tavern
1304 Caroline Street
Fredericksburg, Virginia 22401
703-371-1494

The Rising Sun Tavern was built by Charles Washington in 1760 as his home. The building was later operated as a tavern in the bustling port city of Fredericksburg. Visitors at the Rising Sun today may feel as though they had just stepped off the stagecoach. On March 1 through November 30, open daily, 9 a.m. to 5 p.m. On December 1 through February 28, open daily, 10 a.m. to 4 p.m. Closed major holidays. Admission charge.

Mary Washington House
1200 Charles Street
Fredericksburg, Virginia 22401
703-373-1569

George Washington bought this home for his mother in 1772, and she lived here during the last 17 years of her life as a neighbor to her daughter Betty who lived at Kenmore. Among the period furnishings are some of Mary's personal possessions, including her best dressing glass which she willed to her son George. On March 1 through November 30, open daily, 9 a.m. to 5 p.m. On December 1 through February 28, open daily, 10 a.m. to 4 p.m. Closed major holidays. Admission charge.

■ MISCELLANEOUS

Belmont
224 Washington Street
Falmouth, Virginia 22405
703-899-4860

This 18th century estate was owned by the internationally renowned American artist, Gari Melchers. The home is handsomely furnished. A stone studio features the works of Melchers. On April 1 through September 30, open Monday through Saturday, 10 a.m. to 5 p.m., and Sunday, 1 p.m. to 5 p.m. On October 1 through March 31, open Monday through Saturday, 10 a.m. to 4 p.m., and Sunday, 1 p.m. to 4 p.m. Closed major holidays. Admission charge.

■ MUSEUMS

Fredericksburg Area Museum and Cultural Center
905 Princess Anne Street
Fredericksburg, Virginia 22401
703-371-3037

This museum contains six permanent exhibit galleries which help tell the story of the area's rich and varied past-from prehistoric to 20th century days. On March 1 through November 30, open Monday through Saturday, 9 a.m. to 5 p.m. and Sunday, 1 p.m. to 5 p.m. On December 1 to February 28, open Monday through Saturday, 9 a.m. to 4 p.m. and Sunday, 1 p.m. to 4 p.m. Admission charge.

Kirkland Museum
912 Lafayette Boulevard
Fredericksburg, Virginia 22401
703-899-5565

This museum presents through documents and artifacts a history of the United States with a special emphasis on Fredericksburg and the Civil War. Open daily, 10 a.m. to 5 p.m. Closed major holidays. Admission charge.

Masonic Lodge No. 4 A.F. and A.M.
803 Princess Anne Street
Fredericksburg, Virginia 22401
703-373-5885

Young George Washington became a Mason in this lodge. The lodge museum today contains memorabilia and relics relating to his membership, including an original Gilbert Stuart portrait of Washington. Open daily, 9 a.m. to 4 p.m.; Sunday, 1 p.m. to 4 p.m. Closed major holidays. Admission charge.

The James Monroe Museum
908 Charles Street
Fredericksburg, Virginia 22401
703-899-4559

James Monroe practiced law in this building from 1786 to 1789. Today the museum houses the beautiful possessions of the fifth President, which he purchased in Paris in 1794 and later used in the White House. On March 1 through November 30, open daily, 9 a.m. to 5 p.m. On December 1 through February 28, open daily, 10 a.m. to 4 p.m. Closed major holidays. Admission charge.

National Bank Museum
900 Princess Anne Street
Fredericksburg, Virginia 22401
703-899-3243

Nearly two centuries of American banking history are housed in this museum in one of the oldest buildings in America serving continuously as a bank. Objects on display reflect the history of the City's more prosperous times. Open Monday through Friday, 9 a.m. to 1 p.m. Closed weekends and Federal holidays. Free.

■ PARKS AND GARDENS

Fredericksburg/Spotsylvania National Military Park
1013 Lafayette Boulevard
Fredericksburg, Virginia 22401
703-373-6122

Retrace some of the history of the Civil War at four battlefields: Fredericksburg, The Wilderness, Spotsylvania Courthouse, and Chancellorsville. Open daily until dusk. Free.

■ SEASONAL EVENTS

Fredericksburg Art Festival
William and Prince Edward
Streets
Fredericksburg, Virginia 22401
703-373-1776
800-654-4118

A fine arts and crafts festival
with the juried works of professionals and amateur artists from
up and down the east coast.
Nationally known judges, cash
prizes, and awards. Held in early
June as a two-day event, Saturday and Sunday, from 10 a.m.
to 6 p.m. Free.

**Great Rappahannock River
Whitewater Canoe Race**
Caroline Street
Fredericksburg, Virginia 22401
703-373-1776
800-654-4118

A 4.5-mile race including
flatwater, whitewater, and por-
tage. Spectators line the banks
to watch this thrilling race.
Held early June. Free.

Restaurants

Battlefield Restaurant
1018 Lafayette Blvd.
Fredericksburg, Virginia 22401
703-373-9661

The Battlefield Restaurant is located adjacent to the Battlefield
Park Visitor Center and is my
recommendation for the best
food at reasonable prices in all
of Fredericksburg. You can't go
wrong with all-American favorites like "Liver and Onions",
"Grilled Pork Chops" and a "T-
Bone Steak" served with hot
rolls and your choice of two
veggies. Open daily for breakfast, lunch and dinner.

George Street Grill
106 George Street
Fredericksburg, Virginia 22401
703-371-9500

Italian food of a traditional nature is featured here. Every dish is cooked to order. For the Garlic Shrimp Fettucini, the tender large shrimp are sauteed with mushrooms, peppers, pancetta bacon, garlic, and herbs, and then finished with a light seafood sauce. Need more? Open daily for lunch and dinner. Credit cards: AE, C, MC, and V.

La Petite Auberge
311 William Street
Fredericksburg, Virginia 22401
703-371-2727

La Petite Auberge is located in the downtown historic district and it's been chef-owned and operated since 1981. The menus vary on a daily basis. A sampling of the dinner menu consists of Blackened Redfish With Bananas and Spring Onions or how about Poached Norwegian Salmon with Fresh Hollandaise Sauce? Open daily for lunch and dinner. Credit cards: AE, MC, and V.

Smythe's Cottage
303 Fauquier Street
Fredericksburg, Virginia 22401
703-373-1645

Southern cooking in a quaint, early 19th century cottage. Open daily, except Tuesday, for lunch and dinner. Credit cards: D, MC, and V.

Restaurants, cont.

Spirits
816 Caroline Street
Fredericksburg, Virginia 22401
703-371-9595

Offerings include Antipasto, Caesar Salad, pasta salad, Greek Salad, as well as pastas of many descriptions, along with Chicken Parmesan, spaghetti, baked lasagna, manicotti, a sufficient wine list, and a delightful selection of sandwiches. Open daily for lunch and dinner. Credit cards: AE, D, MC, and V.

Virginia Deli
101 William Street
Fredericksburg, Virginia 22401
703-371-2233

The restaurant is small and quaint but features a large selection of tasty sandwiches. Try the Virginian-baked Virginia ham and Swiss topped with cole slaw served on an onion roll with Russian dressing, or the Thomas Jefferson-breast of turkey with bacon strips, Swiss cheese, lettuce, and mayonnaise on an onion roll. Open daily for lunch and dinner.

Accommodations

■ BED AND BREAKFASTS

Renaissance Manor
2247 Courthouse Road
Stafford, Virginia 22554
703-720-3785

The Spooner House
1300 Caroline Street
Fredericksburg, Virginia 22401
703-371-1267

Selby House B&B
226 Princess Anne Street
Fredericksburg, Virginia 22401
703-373-7037

■ CAMPING

Aquia Pines Campground
3071 Jefferson Davis Highway
Stafford, Virginia 22554
703-659-3447

Fredericksburg/KOA Campgrounds
4100 Guinea Station Road
Fredericksburg, Virginia 22408
703-898-7252

■ HOTELS, MOTELS, AND INNS

Dunning Mill Inn
2305 Jefferson Davis Highway
Fredericksburg, Virginia 22401
703-373-1256

Richard Johnston Inn
711 Caroline Street
Fredericksburg, Virginia 22401
703-899-7606

Econo Lodge
Virginia Route 3 West
Fredericksburg, Virginia 22404
703-786-8374

Motel 6
401 Warrenton Road
Fredericksburg, Virginia 22401
703-371-5443

Fredericksburg Colonial Inn
1707 Princess Anne
Fredericksburg, Virginia 22401
703-371-5666

Ramada Inn
Route 3 West
Fredericksburg, Virginia 22404
703-786-8361

Hampton Inn
2310 William Street
Fredericksburg, Virginia 22401
703-371-0330
800-HAMPTON

Sheraton Inn
2801 Plank Road
Fredericksburg, Virginia 22404
703-786-8321

Holiday Inn
564 Warrenton Road
Fredericksburg, Virginia 22401
703-371-5550

Thunderbird Motel
Route 3 West
Fredericksburg, Virginia 22401
703-786-7404

WE'VE ENJOYED SHARING YOUR COMPANY AND WE HOPE YOU'LL JOIN US AGAIN SOON!!

WARSAW

■ **BACKGROUND:** Warsaw, the county seat since 1730, was originally called Richmond County Courthouse. The village was renamed Warsaw in 1831 in sympathy with the Polish struggle for liberty. Today it's a place where life is informal and warm hospitality is a cherished tradition.

Attractions

■ **VISITOR INFORMATION**

Richmond County Visitor Information
Box 1000
Warsaw, Virginia 22572
804-333-3415

Warsaw-Richmond County Chamber of Commerce
Box 730
Warsaw, Virginia 22572
804-333-3737

■ BEACHES

Naylor's Beach
Route 634
Warsaw, Virginia 22572
804-333-3951

Located along the attractive Rappahannock River, Naylor's Beach is a perfect spot for sunbathing, swimming, fishing, crabbing, and watersports of all types. There are numerous scenic vistas. Open Memorial Day to Labor Day. Admission charge.

■ MUSEUMS

Richmond County Museum
Highway 360 at Route 3
Warsaw, Virginia 22572
804-394-4901

In the old clerk's office (circa 1816) adjacent to the 1748 courthouse in Warsaw, see a display of Richmond County history and enjoy special exhibits and programs. There are self-guided tours of historic sites, and genealogical inquiries are by referral. Open Thursday through Friday, 11 a.m. to 3 p.m.; Saturday, 10 a.m. to 2 p.m.; or by special arrangement. Free.

Restaurants

Main Street Cafe
15 Main Street
Warsaw, Virginia 22572
804-333-0130

Main Street Cafe is a place known for its friendliness and warmth. It is also famous for its pan-sauteed soft shell crabs. My friend Joan Bruce says, "It's the best restaurant in the entire Northern Neck Area." I think you may agree. P.S. If you are a steak lover, you are in for a treat. Open Monday through Wednesday, lunch only; open Thursday, Friday, and Saturday for lunch and dinner. Closed Sunday. Credit cards: MC and V.

Roma Italian Restaurant
500 West Richmond Road
Warsaw, Virginia 22572
804-333-9222

This popular spot has been providing the finest in Italian cuisine since 1976. Offerings include lasagna, spaghetti, subs, veal, steak, and seafood. Open daily for lunch and dinner. Credit cards: MC and V.

San Remo
603A Highway 360
Warsaw, Virginia 22572
804-333-3679
804-333-0130

At San Remo Restaurant, Italian and American cuisine is offered. Choose from steaks, seafood, chicken, pizza, and subs. Open daily for lunch and dinner. Credit cards: MC and V.

Accommodations

■ BED AND BREAKFASTS

Greenwood
Route 1026/Maple Street
Warsaw, Virginia 22572
804-333-4353

■ CAMPING

Naylor's Beach Campground
Route 634
Warsaw, Virginia 22572
804-333-3951

Whelan's Campground
Route 1, Box 334
Farnham, Virginia 22460
804-394-9500

LANCASTER

■ **BACKGROUND:** Lancaster, the seat of Lancaster County, takes its name from the county. Lancaster County was formed in 1651 and named for Lancaster, England. The town's rich history is still evident. Visitors will want to take a leisurely walk along a tree shaded sidewalk. The Town Green is a wonderful location to spread a blanket and enjoy a picnic.

Attractions

■ **VISITOR INFORMATION**

Northern Neck Travel Council
Box 312
Reedville, Virginia 22539
800-453-6167

■ **BOAT CRUISES**

Merry Point Ferry
Route 604/Ottoman Wharf
Lancaster, Virginia 22503

Merry Point Ferry has been in operation since 1668. It offers a delightful crossing of the Western Branch of the Corrotoman River. Open 7 a.m. to 7 p.m. Closed Sunday. Free.

■ MUSEUMS

Mary Ball Washington Museum and Library
Route 3
Lancaster, Virginia 22503
804-462-7280

The museum is located in the historic village of Lancaster on the Courthouse Green. Tour the 18th century clerk's office (1797) and jail (1863). The museum which honors the Lancaster-born mother of George Washington offers a glimpse of life in early Tidewater Virginia. There is an extensive library and a historical and genealogical research center. Open all year, 9 a.m. to 5 p.m., Tuesday through Friday. In April through November open Saturday, 10 a.m. to 4 p.m. Free.

■ PARKS AND GARDENS

Chesapeake Nature Trail
Route 3
Lancaster, Virginia 22503
804-843-5402

Three marked trails of .08 miles, 1.25 miles, and .28 miles along the Western Branch of the Corrotoman River. These well-labeled trails through both upland and wetland habitats identify many native trees and wildflowers. Open dawn to dusk. Free.

Restaurants

Conrad's Upper Deck
Route 624
Mollusk, Virginia 22517
804-462-7400

The upper deck offers no menu but features a fantastic seafood buffet. Open March through November, Friday and Saturday only. Memorial through Labor Day, open Thursday through Saturday for dinner only.

The Oaks Restaurant
Route 3
Lively, Virginia 22507
804-462-7050

The Oaks offers casual family dining in a warm, friendly atmosphere. The seafood specials get the most raves. Open daily for lunch and dinner. Credit cards: MC and V.

Accommodations

■ BED AND BREAKFASTS

Greenvale Manor
Box 70, Route 354
Mollusk, Virginia 22517
804-462-5995

The Inn at Levelfields
Route 3
Lancaster, Virginia 22507
703-435-6887
800-238-5578

IRVINGTON

■ **BACKGROUND:** Irvington is a small town settled by John Carter in 1649. Rich in history, Irvington was home to most of the first families of Virginia. Three governors, two presidents, and Robert E. Lee all came from this area. Today Irvington maintains its share of wealth with several of the finest yachting complexes on the Bay. Many beautiful homes line the shores of Carter Creek.

Attractions

■ **VISITOR INFORMATION**

Irvington Chamber of Commerce
Box 1357
Kilmarnock, Virginia 22482
804-438-6053

■ **BOAT CHARTERS**

Windmill Point Marine Resort
Route 695
White Stone, Virginia 22578
804-435-1166
800-228-5151

Windmill Point Marine Resort offers recreational luxuries, such as a golf course, sparkling pool, tennis courts, deep-water slips for over 150 yachts, and many other amenities. Rental accommodations range from waterfront rooms to beachside villas, and charter boat captains take out fishing parties from this resort. Open year round. Fee.

■ **MISCELLANEOUS**

Wood-A-Drift Art Shop
Tidewater Drive
Irvington, Virginia 22480
804-438-6913

Proprietors Bonita and Graham Bruce invite you to visit their most unusual gift shop. Specialties offered are nautical gifts and art from the Chesapeake Bay region.

■ MUSEUMS

Historic Christ Church
Route 222
Irvington, Virginia 22480
804-438-6855

Historic Christ Church was completed around 1735. It is the only virtually unchanged colonial church in America, retaining its original pews and rare triple-decked pulpit with sounding board. In April through November, open daily, 10 a.m. to 4 p.m., weekdays; 1 p.m. to 4 p.m., Saturday; and 2 p.m. to 5 p.m., Sunday. Free.

■ SEASONAL EVENTS

Rappahannock River Waterfowl Show
Route 695
White Stone, Virginia 22578
804-435-6355

The show features wildfowl art and carving exhibits, as well as carving competitions for decorative and gunning decoys. Held mid-March, 10 a.m. to 4 p.m., Saturday; 10 a.m. to 5 p.m., Sunday. This two-day annual event is held at the Whitestone Firehouse.

Restaurants

Annabel Lee Restaurant
Old Ferry Road
White Stone, Virginia 22578
804-435-2123

Sunset dining overlooking the scenic Rappahannock River. House specialties include Prime Rib, Baby Back Ribs, steamed or broiled seafood seasoned just right, and homemade pizza. All entrees include house salad, fresh baked potato, and your choice of fresh vegetable of the day. Open daily for dinner. Credit cards: MC and V.

Restaurants, cont.

River Cafe
Windmill Point Road
White Stone, Virginia 22578
804-435-0113

Specialties include fresh seafood, hand-cut beef, homemade soups, and desserts. Open for dinner only, Tuesday through Saturday, 5 p.m. to 10 p.m. Credit cards: D, MC, and V.

The Tides Inn
King Carter Drive
Irvington, Virginia 22480
804-438-5000
800-TIDESINN

The Captain's Quarters at the Tides Inn offers fresh-as-fresh-can be-soft shell crabs-pan fried to perfection and oh so good. I can't wait to return. Open daily for breakfast, lunch, and dinner, mid-March to January 1. Credit cards: AE, MC, and V.

The Tides Lodge
One Saint Andrews Lane
Irvington, Virginia 22480
804-438-6000
800-248-4337

The sun has set, but your day isn't over. After cocktails over-looking the marina, enjoy a highly praised dinner in the Royal Stewart Dining Room which is well-known for its in-novative cuisine. Open daily for breakfast, lunch, and dinner. Credit cards: MC and V.

White Stone Wine and Cheese
Route 3, Rappahannock Drive
White Stone, Virginia 22578
804-435-2000

Stop in this gourmet specialty shop for fresh baked French bread and croissants, salads, and sandwiches. Tell Maggie that Whitey sent you! And don't forget the wonderful desserts. Open for lunch and early dinner. Credit cards: MC and V.

Accommodations

■ BED AND BREAKFASTS

The King Carter Inn
Box 425, King Carter Drive
Irvington, Virginia 22480
804-438-6053

■ HOTELS, MOTELS, AND INNS

The Tides Inn
King Carter Drive
Irvington, Virginia 22480
804-438-5000
800-843-3746

Whispering Pines Motel
Route 3
White Stone, Virginia 22578
804-435-1101

The Tides Lodge
One St. Andrews Lane
Irvington, Virginia 22480
804-438-6000
800-248-4337

Windmill Point Resort
Route 695
White Stone, Virginia 22578
804-435-1166
800-228-5151

KILMARNOCK

■ **BACKGROUND:** Local historians trace the earliest mention of Kilmarnock to a deed filed in December 1776 by Robert Gilmour, a silversmith who was a native of Kilmarnock, Scotland. The name can be traced to a town in 4th century Scotland where an Irish missionary named "Marnoc" established his "church" (in Scottish, "kil"). Hence "Kilmarnock" was formed. Today Kilmarnock is the commercial trade center of Virginia's Northern Neck.

Attractions

■ **VISITOR INFORMATION**

Kilmarnock Chamber of Commerce
Box 1357
Kilmarnock, Virginia 22482
804-435-1552

■ **BOAT CRUISES**

Ingram Bay Marina
Route 609
Wicomico Church, Virginia 22579
804-580-7292

Captain Billy Pipkin is your host and guide for scenic Great Wicomico River cruises. Departing from Ingram Bay Marina, Baytrippers can sit back and enjoy the sights or cruise to waterfront dining at Horn Harbor Restaurant. Open daily except Tuesday, 4:30 p.m. to dark. Fee.

■ FISHING CHARTERS

Captain Billy's Charters
Route 609
Wicomico Church, Virginia
22579
804-580-7292

The Northern Neck is considered one of the best fishing areas on the east coast. If you're not from the area and want to try your luck, who better to go fishing with than "Fishing Columnist" Captain Billy Pipkin. Open seasonally. Fee.

Restaurants

The Crab Shack
Route 672
Kilmarnock, Virginia 22482
804-435-2700

The Crab Shack features fresh seafood plates and specialties like the "Royal Beef and Reef" (Filet Mignon topped with Crab Meat) or how about shrimp and scallops (sauteed with green peppers and onions). My favorite is the soft crabs "Fried To Perfection". I ordered a couple to go— just for the ride home. Open May through November for lunch and dinner, closed Monday. Credit cards: DC, DIS, MC, and V.

Harry's Barbecue
Route 3
Kilmarnock, Virginia 22482
804-435-3366

Here you'll discover the hardwood coals, smoke, and slow cooking, and Harry's produces some of Virginia's finest barbecued pork, beef, and chicken. Open Tuesday through Sunday for lunch and dinner. Closed Monday.

POTOMAC RIVER,
VIRGINIA SIDE
Reedville to Arlington

Follow the water....

- Reedville
- Kinsale
- Montross
- Colonial Beach
- Occoquan
- Alexandria
- Arlington

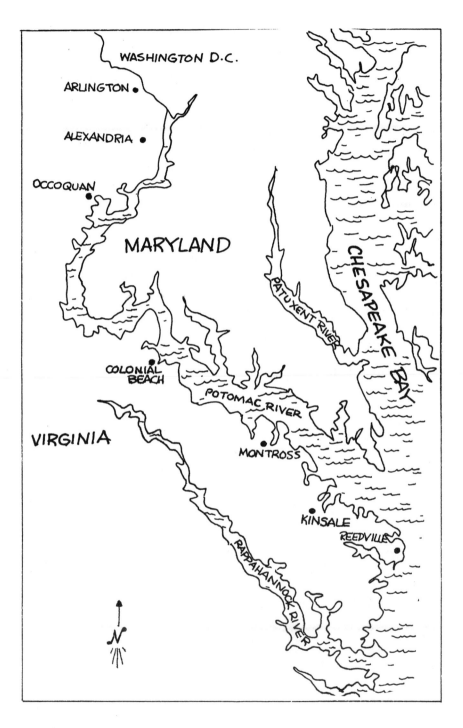

REEDVILLE

■ **BACKGROUND:** The story of Reedville begins with Elijah Reed, a 19th century Sea Captain. In 1873, Captain Reed purchased a 33-acre point of land on Cockrell Creek at the entrance channel of the Great Wicomico River. Earlier names for this spit of land were Windmill Point and then Reed Point. The town prospered around the harvesting of the Menhaden, a fish similar to shad. Main Street became known as "Millionaires' Row." Reedville did not recover from the Great Depression and the over-fishing of the Menhaden. Today the village provides a living image of the past with its magnificent Victorian mansions and seafaring atmosphere.

Attractions

■ **VISITOR INFORMATION**

Northern Neck Travel Counsel
Box 312
Reedville, Virginia 22539
800-453-6167

■ **BOAT CRUISES**

Tangier and Chesapeake Cruises, Inc.
Box 36
Warsaw, Virginia 22572
804-333-4656

Cruise aboard the "Chesapeake Breeze" on a relaxing 1 1/2-hour narrated trip. The ship docks at Tangier Island where you are met by a friendly guide. Walk around this quaint island or take a tour on a mini-bus. The people of Tangier, who speak with a lingering trace of Elizabethan accent, are warm, and they're proud of this island. Tours depart from Reedville at 10 a.m. and return at 3:45 p.m. during May through October 15. Reservations necessary. Fee.

TANGIER ISLAND
CRUISES
BUZZARD'S
POINT
MARINA

Island and Bay Cruises, Inc.
Box 1910, Route 650
Reedville, Virginia 22539
804-453-3430
804-453-3854

Cruise 13 1/2 miles across the storied Chesapeake Bay to Smith Island. See waterways with interlacing creeks, canals, and tiny clusters of islands. Sail from KOA Campground Reedville, Virginia; departs 10 a.m. and returns 4:15 p.m. Fee.

■ FISHING CHARTERS

Captain Billy's Charters
Route 2, Box 270
Heathsville, Virginia 22473
804-580-7292

This fish captain's charters on the Chesapeake Bay are aboard "Liquid Assets," a 40-foot vessel designed for fishing parties and sightseeing. Whether you're a devoted fisherman or you just want to get away from it all, you're sure to have an enjoyable day. Call Captain Billy Pipkin for your schedule. Fee.

■ MUSEUMS

Fisherman's Museum
Box 306, Route 360
Reedville, Virginia 22539
804-453-6529

Built in 1875 as a waterman's home, this house is the oldest in Reedville and is located on a waterfront site in the historic district. You'll find various exhibits including the Menhaden fishing industry of the Reedville area. Other artifacts featured are those of the oystering, crabbing, and pound net industries. Open May 1 to October 31. Hours on Monday through Friday are 3 p.m. to 5 p.m., and on Saturday and Sunday, 1 p.m. to 5 p.m. Admission charge.

Restaurants

The Deli at Cockrells Creek Seafood
Fleeton Road
Reedville, Virginia 22539
804-453-6326

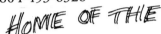

HOME OF THE

QUARTER POUND

CRAB CAKE

No visit I take to Reedville is complete until I stop at the Deli at Cockrells Creek Seafood for salads, deviled crab, Crab Imperial, shrimp salad, seafood salad, wonderful crab cakes, and perfectly prepared soft crabs. Open Monday through Saturday for breakfast and lunch.

Horn Harbor House
Route 810
Burgess, Virginia 22432
804-453-3351

The specialties to try here are the seafood creations, especially the seafood Norfolk-style dishes and the "Steamboat Platter" with lobster tail, crab claws, shrimp, and crab legs. The chowders are homemade and excellent. Open April through November for dinner only.

Accommodations

■ BED AND BREAKFASTS

Cedar Grove Bed and Breakfast
Fleeton Road, Box 2535
Reedville, Virginia 22539
804-453-3915

Janet's Bed and Breakfast
Main Street, Route 360
Reedville, Virginia 22539
804-453-5222

Elizabeth House Bed and Breakfast
Route 360
Reedville, Virginia 22539
804-453-7016

■ CAMPING

Great Wicomico River Campground
Route 810
Burgess, Virginia 22432
804-453-3351

KOA Kampgrounds
Route 650, Box 1910
Reedville, Virginia 22539
804-453-3430

■ HOTELS, MOTELS, AND INNS

Bay Motel
Route 360
Reedville, Virginia 22539
804-453-5171

KINSALE

■ **BACKGROUND:** Named for Kinsale County Cork, Ireland. In Gaelic, Kinsale means "head of the salt water." The town was designated by an act of the Assembly in 1706 and given town status in 1784. Kinsale was twice burned, once during the War of 1812 and a second time during the War Between the States. Though it is little more than an hour's drive from major cities, it has maintained its charming atmosphere.

Attractions

■ **VISITOR INFORMATION**

Westmoreland County Visitor Center
Courthouse Square
Montross, Virginia 22520
804-493-8440

■ **MUSEUMS**

Ball Memorial Library and Museum
Route 360
Heathsville, Virginia 22473
804-580-8581

The museum houses Civil War, medical, and prehistoric artifacts, as well as a vast collection of silver, china, and crystal. Open on Monday, Wednesday and Thursday, and every second and fourth Saturday, 9 a.m. to 4 p.m. Free.

Kinsale Museum
Main Street
Kinsale, Virginia 22488
804-472-3001
804-472-3895

The museum is housed in a recently restored early meat market. Permanent exhibits include wartime aspects of town history and an extensive collection of Indian artifacts. Open Thursday, Friday, and Saturday, 10 a.m. to 5 p.m.; open Sunday, 1 p.m. to 5 p.m. Free.

Restaurants

Driftwood II
Route 612
Coles Point, Virginia 22442
804-472-3892

KEYS TO MAP

1. MUSEUM • C. 19th C • MEAT MKT
2. THE GREAT HOUSE • PRESENT C. 1828
3 BAILEY CEMETERY GRAVE
OF MIDSHIPMAN SIGOURNEY . U.S S.A&P
4 WHARF • SITE OF EARLY TOMATO CANNERY
5. ICE CREAM PARLOR • EARLY 1900's
6. "LITTLE HOUSE" C. MID 19th C
7. PARKS GENL. STORE · C. MID 1800's

This small country restaurant is owned by Ruth and Joe McCoy who cook up some terrific seafood. I personally recommend the soft crab sandwich and the crab cakes. Some of the locals claim it's home to the best steaks in Virginia. Open seasonally for unch and dinner.

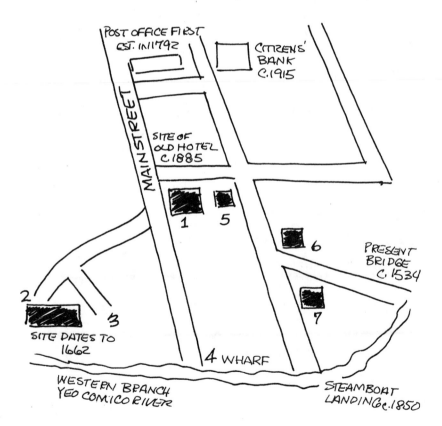

POST OFFICE FIRST EST. IN 1792

CITIZENS' BANK C. 1915

MAIN STREET

SITE OF OLD HOTEL C. 1885

1   5

6   PRESENT BRIDGE C. 1534

2   3

7

SITE DATES TO 1662

4 WHARF

WESTERN BRANCH YEO COMICO RIVER

STEAMBOAT LANDING C. 1850

Restaurants, cont.

The Mooring Restaurant
Route 608
Kinsale, Virginia 22488
804-472-2971

The Mooring Restaurant is tucked in a cove on the outskirts of town at the water's edge. The white-shingled building with its beautiful lawn and climbing roses is at the end of a mile-long gravel drive in a lovely wooded setting. The Mooring offers such entrees as Cajun Crab Dip, Caesar Salad with Fried Oysters, crab cakes, broiled sea scallops, and Gulf Shrimp Tempura. Open seasonally except Tuesday for dinner; Saturday and Sunday, open for lunch and dinner. Credit cards: MC and V.

The Pilot's Wharf
Route 612
Coles Point, Virginia 22442
804-472-4761

The Pilot's Wharf restaurant prides itself on its pleasant staff and traditional favorites. Seafood is the specialty here and it's Great! The Pilot's Platter consists of a medley of flounder, scallops, shrimp, soft shell crabs, and crab cakes served broiled or fried. Open daily for lunch and dinner.

Accommodations

■ BED AND BREAKFASTS

Pondside
Route 203 @ Route 1001
Kinsale, Virginia 22488
804-472-4075

■ CAMPING

Ragged Point Harbor Campground
Route 612
Coles Point, Virginia 22442
804-472-3955

Yeocomico Campground
Route 608
Kinsale, Virginia 22488
804-472-2971

Ragged Point was the last lighthouse built in the Chesapeake Bay area, although the initial request for its erection had been made in 1896; "This shoal makes off from the west bank of the river at a short turning point. It is important that this point be marked by a light at night and a fog signal during thick weather. It is estimated that a light and fog signal station can be established here for $20,000, and it is recommended that an appropriation of this amount be made therefor." The Lighthouse Board in 1901 complained that the cost of labor and materials had risen so much since the request was made that an additional $10,000 would be required for construction. In 1906, Congress appropriated the $30,000 needed for the lighthouse. When it was finally completed, on March 15, 1910, the total cost had risen to $34,223. The delay had cost the Treasury almost $15,000.

The hexagonal screwpile light was built on the Virginia side of the Potomac, off Coles Neck, a few miles across the river from Piney Point. It is ironic that this light, last to be built, was one of the first to be dismantled under the Coast Guard automation program. However, the foundation was retained as support for a 44-foot tower from which a white light still flashes.

MONTROSS

■ **BACKGROUND:** The earliest name for this town was Westmoreland Court House (1676). In 1853 the name was changed to Montross. It is, however, believed that the name Montross was used as early as 1752. It's possible that this town was named for a village on the east coast of Scotland. Montross is the county seat and it has a central location. The town offers many services and activities.

Attractions

■ **VISITOR INFORMATION**

Westmoreland County Visitor Center
Courthouse Square
Montross, Virginia 22520
804-493-8440

■ **HISTORIC SITES**

Stratford Hall Plantation
Route 214
Stratford, Virginia 22558
804-493-8038

Stratford Hall is the ancestral home of the only brothers to sign the Declaration of Independence, Richard Henry Lee and Francis Lightfoot Lee. It was also the birthplace of Robert E. Lee. Built in the 1720's, the restored great house is furnished with period pieces. The 1600-acre plantation includes gardens, a stable, a working gristmill, and cliffs overlooking the Potomac. Open daily except Christmas, 9 a.m. to 4:30 p.m. Admission charge.

■ MUSEUMS

Westmoreland County Museum and Visitor Center
Route 3
Montross, Virginia 22520
804-493-8440

You'll find artifacts of local history, a Charles Wilson Peale portrait of William Pitt, and changing exhibits. Open daily from 10 a.m. to 4 p.m. Free.

■ PARKS AND GARDENS

George Washington Birthplace
Route 204
Washington's Birthplace, Virginia 22443
804-224-1732

The site of our first President's birthplace provides a glimpse of 18th century plantation life. Of interest are the birthplace site, a memorial house of 18th century design, a colonial working farm, the family burial grounds, and a walking trail. Open daily, 9 a.m. to 5 p.m., except Christmas and New Year's Day. Admission charge.

Westmoreland State Park
Route 347
Montross, Virginia 22520
804-493-8821
804-786-1712

Westmoreland State Park on the Potomac River offers camping, hiking, cabins, picnic areas, a public boat ramp, and swimming at the beach or in a new Olympic-size swimming pool. Open year round; pool open in season. Admission charge.

Restaurants

The Inn at Montross
Court House Square
Montross, Virginia 22520
804-493-9097

Dine in a cozy, colonial setting with entrees, wine, and spirits to delight even the most discriminating palate. Open daily for lunch and dinner. Credit cards: AE, D, MC, and V.

Mt. Holly Steamboat Inn
Route 202
Mt. Holly, Virginia 22524
804-472-3336

Originally built as a steamboat hotel to serve the needs of the weary traveller, today it's a bed and breakfast inn. A fixed lunch and dinner is served family style. The tavern dinner comes well recommended. Open for lunch on Thursday and Friday, and for dinner, Thursday through Saturday.

Stratford Hall Dining Room
Route 214
Stratford, Virginia 22558
804-493-9696

There's no better way to get a feel for the Northern Neck of Virginia. Once you're plugged into the menu, there is a lot of food to enjoy beginning with the house appetizer and ending with the Apple Brown Betty. Open daily, March to December 23. Lunch only.

Accommodations

■ BED AND BREAKFASTS

The Inn at Montross
Court House Square
Montross, Virginia 22520
804-493-9097

Pearson's House
Route 3
Montross, Virginia 22520
804-493-9547

Mt. Holly Bed and Breakfast
Route 202
Mount Holly, Virginia 22524
804-472-3336

■ CAMPING

Westmoreland State Park
Route 347
Montross, Virginia 22520
804-493-8821

■ HOTELS, MOTELS, AND INNS

Washington and Lee Motel
Route 3
Montross, Virginia 22520
804-493-8093

COLONIAL BEACH

■ **BACKGROUND:** Colonial Beach is located on the Potomac River on land that was patented about 1650 by Samuel Bonum. Late in the 19th century there was active development on the waterfront property. The town was promoted as the "playground of the Potomac" when great sidewheel steamboats brought thousands for summer fun. Colonial Beach is still a bustling resort in summer with its municipal pier and sandy beach.

Attractions

■ **VISITOR INFORMATION**

Colonial Beach Town Hall
18 Irving Avenue
Colonial Beach, Virginia 22443
804-224-7181

■ **BEACHES**

Colonial Beach
Municipal Pier and Boardwalk
Colonial Beach, Virginia 22443
804-224-7181

Colonial Beach has been a popular summer resort for over a century featuring a safe public bathing beach with a netted area and lifeguards. Open from the end of May to Labor Day. Free.

■ **BOAT CRUISES**

Fisherman's Inc.
Fisherman's Pier
Colonial Beach, Virginia 22443
804-224-0896

You will enjoy your cruise around Monroe Bay and up the Potomac River. It could be the highlight of your visit to the scenic Northern Neck. Cruises depart at 2 p.m. and 7 p.m. on Saturday and Sunday beginning June 30 until Labor Day. Fee.

■ FISHING PIER

Municipal Pier at Boardwalk
Colonial Beach, Virginia 22443
804-224-7181
804-224-7148

The Colonial Beach Municipal Pier extends from the boardwalk out into the Potomac River. Try your hand at bottom fishing. There are limits and size restrictions on all fish caught. Call for information. Fee.

■ MISCELLANEOUS

Colonial Beach Dragway
Route 631
Colonial Beach, Virginia 22443
804-224-7455
703-777-6232

See hundreds of top racers compete at the quickest and fastest racetrack around. Open Friday and Sunday-weather permitting-February to November. Call for your schedule. Admission charge.

Ingleside Plantation Vineyard
Route 638
Oak Grove, Virginia 22443
804-224-8687

The Plantation occupies 2,500 acres of the highest land in the northern neck. Since 1832 it has been the site of a school, a Civil War garrison for Union Troops, a courthouse, and a dairy. Today it produces an award-winning Virginia wine. If you would like a sample, stop in the wine-tasting room. Open year round except major holidays. Hours on Monday through Saturday are 10 a.m. to 5 p.m., and Sunday, 12 noon to 5 p.m. Free.

■ PARKS AND GARDENS

Caledon Natural Area
Route 218/11617 Caledon Road
King George, Virginia 22485
703-663-3861

At Caledon Natural Area, over 120 species of birds have been seen, and it is one of the most significant summering areas for the American Bald Eagle on the east coast. Four hiking trails wind throughout the 2,300 acres of hardwood forest. Open daily from 8 a.m. to sunset. Free.

Westmoreland Berry Farm and Orchard
Route 637
Oak Grove, Virginia 22443
804-224-9171

The Westmoreland Berry Farm is a 1,600-acre property. Over 60 acres of 16 different crops are cared for on a year round basis. You're invited to visit. Stop at the farmer's market. You're able to pick your own or buy some that's already picked. Open daily from 8 a.m. to 6 p.m.; except Sunday, open 10 a.m. to 6 p.m.

■ SEASONAL EVENTS

Potomac River Festival
Boardwalk
Colonial Beach, Virginia 22443
804-224-7181

Any festival that has endured as long as the Colonial Beach River Festival is a good one. The festival draws annually more than 25,000 visitors. Highlights of the three-day Festival are a fishing contest, baby contest, parade, fireworks, dances, and a beauty contest. Held mid-June. Free.

Restaurants

Dockside Restaurant
Monroe Point
Colonial Beach, Virginia 22443
804-224-8726

Specialties include broiled, steamed, and raw seafood. Feast outdoors on an open-air crab deck overlooking the Potomac River. Also on premises is Martin's Tavern, a British-style pub, which I think you'll find enjoyable. Open daily for breakfast, lunch, and dinner. Credit cards: AE, D, MC, and V.

The Happy Clam
Route 205
Colonial Beach, Virginia 22443
804-224-0248

The Happy Clam is located on the former terminus of the Potomac River Car Ferry. You can still see the pilings jutting out into the Potomac from your table at the window in the restaurant. The owners are proud to serve fresh, local products whenever possible. Do try it. I know you're gonna love it. Open daily for lunch and dinner. Credit Cards: MC and V.

Restaurants, cont.

Parker's Crab Shore
1016 Monroe Bay Avenue
Colonial Beach, Virginia 22443
804-224-7090

SINCE 1927

When you arrive at Colonial Beach, the first thing you should do is drive through the tiny streets of town to the Potomac River and then up Monroe Bay Avenue. When you reach Parker's Crab Shore, stop for a visit. The house specialty (and my favorite) is the wonderfully-prepared steamed crabs. Open daily for lunch and dinner.

Wilkerson's Seafood Restaurant
Route 205
Colonial Beach, Virginia 22443
804-224-7117

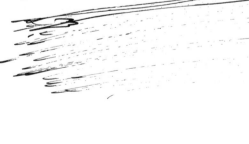

At Wilkerson's, you'll find a great sampling of the local favorites. Specialties include stuffed shrimp, fried shrimp, a broiled fish dinner, an oyster platter, a crab meat Norfolk Platter, a crab cake platter, and a combination platter. Open daily for lunch and dinner. Credit cards: MC and V.

Accommodations

■ BED AND BREAKFASTS

Mt. Stuart
Route 218
King George, Virginia 22485
703-775-9763

Quiet Water Cove B&B
306 Hamilton Street
Colonial Beach, Virginia 22443
804-224-7595

■ CAMPING

The Leedstown Campground
Route 638
Leedstown, Virginia 22443
804-224-7445

Monroe Bay Camping Grounds
551 Lafayette Street
Colonial Beach, Virginia 22443
804-224-7418

■ HOTELS, MOTELS, AND INNS

Comfort Inn
Route 301
Dahlgren, Virginia 22448
703-663-3060
800-221-2222

Nightingale Motel
101 Monroe Bay Avenue
Colonial Beach, Virginia 22443
804-224-7956

Days Inn
30 Colonial Avenue
Colonial Beach, Virginia 22443
804-224-0404

Wakefield Motel
1513 Irving Avenue
Colonial Beach, Virginia 22443
804-224-7311

Doc's Motor Court
11 Irving Avenue
Colonial Beach, Virginia 22443
804-224-7840

OCCOQUAN

■ **BACKGROUND:** Occoquan translated in the Dogue Indian language means "at the end of the water." In 1729 at the falls of the Occoquan River, "King" Carter built a landing from which he could ship copper ore. That town became known as Colchester. Colchester lasted until about 1804 when the name was changed to Occoquan. The charm of this 18th century mill town still exists. There are over 100 shops that line the tiny streets and are open to visitors.

Attractions

■ **VISITOR INFORMATION**

Fairfax Tourist Center
7764 Armistead Road
Lorton, Virginia 22079
800-7-FAIRFAX

Occoquan Tourist Information Center
200 Mill Street
Occoquan, Virginia 22125
703-491-2168

Prince William County Visitors Bureau
4349 Ridgewood Center Drive
Prince William, Virginia 22192
703-792-6680
800-334-9876

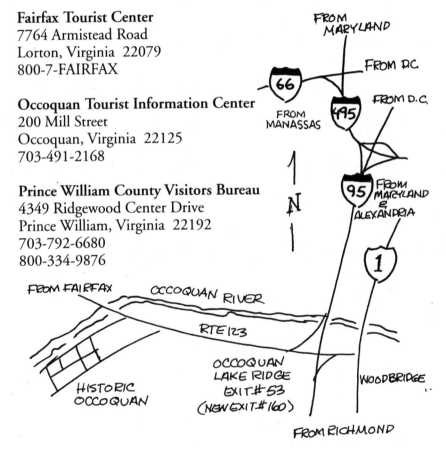

194

■ MUSEUMS

Gunston Hall
10709 Gunston Road
Lorton, Virginia 22079
703-550-9220

George Mason, father of the Bill of Rights, built Gunston Hall in 1755 on land overlooking the Potomac River. The house is an outstanding example of Colonial Virginia architecture and it contains a fine collection of 18th-century furnishings, a number of which belong to the Mason family. Baytrippers may walk through formal gardens, view the deer park, hike the nature trail to the river, and enjoy exhibitions in the visitors' center. Open daily from 9:30 a.m. to 5 p.m. Closed major holidays. Admission charge.

Mill House Museum
Mill Street
Occoquan, Virginia 22125
703-491-7525

Historic artifacts and memorabilia of Occoquan's past are featured here. Open daily from 11 a.m. to 4 p.m. Free.

GUNSTON HALL

195

■ PARKS AND GARDENS

Mason Neck State Park
7301 High Point Road
Mason Neck, Virginia 22079
703-339-7265

Encompassing 1,804 acres, the Park is dedicated to recreation and wildlife management. Of interest to Baytrippers are four hiking trails, a canoe launch, a visitors' center, and marsh and scenic overlook. Open daily from 8 a.m. to dusk. Free.

Pohick Bay Regional Park
Gunston Hall Road
Lorton, Virginia 22079
703-339-6104
703-352-5900

The Algonquin Indians named the area "Pohick" which means "water place." The natural beauty of the Potomac River and parkland are both relaxing and refreshing. Baytrippers can cool down in the giant swimming pool or walk a dense forest trail. Open daily, dawn to dusk. Free.

Restaurants

Occoquan Inn
301 Mill Street
Occoquan, Virginia 22125
703-491-1888

The Occoquan Inn is rated tops when it comes to fresh seafood, but steak and poultry lovers are also in for a treat. High marks go to Chicken Roanoke and Filet Mignon. Open daily for lunch and dinner. Credit cards: AE, DC, MC, and V.

Pilot House
16216 Neabsco Road
Woodbridge, Virginia 22191
703-221-1010

The structure of the Pilot House started as a barge and it has been built to look like a paddle boat. Their menu offers more than 30 seafood and 7 meat entrees. The atmosphere here is very nautical and very nice. Open Tuesday through Sunday for dinner only. Credit cards: AE, D, DC, MC, and V.

Sea Sea and Company Restaurant
201 Mill Street
Occoquan, Virginia 22125
703-494-1365

Noted for its seafood selections. Look for fresh swordfish steak, Shrimp Scampi, and Crab Imperial. If you have room, try the gourmet ice cream. Open daily for lunch and dinner. Credit cards: AE, DC, MC, and V.

Accommodations

■ CAMPING

Pohick Bay Regional Park
Gunston Road
Lorton, Virginia 22079
703-339-6104
703-352-5900

■ HOTELS, MOTELS, AND INNS

Rockledge Inn
410 Mill Street
Occoquan, Virginia 22125
703-690-3377

Historic Occoquan is a place to enjoy yourself. Shopping is a pleasant change in this authentic waterfront mill town. Here you'll find a wonderful selection of specialty shops and restaurants filled with art and antiques, handcrafts and gifts, and the kind of warm Virginia hospitality you'd expect from an unusual community of merchants and artisans. We hope you have a pleasant stay and we welcome your return.

197

ALEXANDRIA

■ **BACKGROUND:** The city of Alexandria was established in 1749 by a group of Scottish merchants. Alexandria was named for John Alexander, who acquired the land in 1669, and it became one of the main colonial trading centers. It was a part of the original District of Columbia but was returned to Virginia in 1847. Today Alexandria is a city filled with celebration, music, and tradition. Baytrippers can bask in the warmth of yesteryear or shine in the sparkling ambiance of today.

Attractions

■ **VISITOR INFORMATION**

**Alexandria Convention and
Visitors Bureau**
221 King Street
Alexandria, Virginia 22314
703-838-4200

William Ramsay House
221 King Street
Alexandria, Virginia 22314
703-838-4200

All tours to Old Town Alexandria should begin here. Built in 1724 by William Ramsay, Alexandria's first Lord Mayor and a fellow patriot of George Washington, this is now a visitors' center. The visitors' center offers parking passes and a 15-minute film to help you discover what Alexandria has to offer. Open daily, 9 a.m. to 5 p.m.

■ **AIRPORT**

Washington National Airport
George Washington Memorial Parkway
Arlington, Virginia 20001
703-661-2700

■ BOAT CRUISES

Dandy Restaurant Cruise
Zero Prince Street
Alexandria, Virginia 22314
703-683-6090

The Dandy Cruise Ship offers dining, dancing, and an unparalleled view of Washington, D.C. and the Alexandria Waterfront. Dinner boarding daily. Call for your cruise schedule. Fee.

Schooner Alexandria Tallship
1000 South Lee Street
Alexandria, Virginia 22314
703-549-7070

With her distinctive Red Sails, the 125-foot long Schooner Alexandria is a classic Scandinavian vessel built in Sweden in 1929 and then remodelled for passengers in the 1970's. When in port, the ship is open for viewing. Open Saturday and Sunday, 12 noon to 5 p.m. Free.

The Admiral Tilp
205 The Strand
Alexandria, Virginia 22314
703-548-9000
703-684-0580

Cruise the Potomac River aboard the Admiral Tilp. Offered is a 40-minute, narrated sightseeing excursion along the waterfront of historic old town. You will find a concession stand for beverages and snacks, or feel free to bring your own lunch. Open daily, May through Labor Day. Cruises leave on the hour from the City Pier Monday through Friday, 11 a.m. to 3 p.m., and from 10 a.m. to 4 p.m., Saturday and Sunday. Fee.

■ GUIDED SIGHTSEEING TOURS

Accent on Alexandria
Box 23343
Alexandria, Virginia 22304
703-751-5756

Take a walk back in time and discover the history of Old Town Alexandria during an hour-long walking tour with an "18th century lady." In addition to Twilight Tours, Accent on Alexandria provides step-on bus tours including historical properties or nearby plantations. Call for schedule. Fee.

■ HISTORIC SITES

Just as history has preserved the names of famous early Americans, the city of Alexandria, Virginia keeps safe the homes and buildings where many of them lived and visited. The old part of the city is fairly compact, making it perfect for walking.

Boyhood Home of Robert E. Lee
607 Oronoco Street
Alexandria, Virginia 22314
703-548-8454

"Light Horse Harry" Lee, Revolutionary War hero and father of the more famous Robert E. Lee, brought his family to this house in 1812. Robert E. Lee lived and studied here in his early formative years. The preserved house is beautifully furnished with rare antiques and Lee memorabilia. Open daily, 10 a.m. to 4 p.m.; Sunday, 1 p.m. to 4 p.m. Closed major holidays. Admission charge.

Boyhood Home of Robert E. Lee
The only man offered command of both opposing armies in a war, Lee lived in this house until 1825 when he enrolled at West Point.

Captain's Row
100 Block of Prince Street
Alexandria, Virginia 22314

When Alexandria was one of the principal ports of entry in the country, some of the ships' captains docked at wharves here making Alexandria their home port and building homes convenient to the river. A good time to walk Captain's Row is after dark when the old fashioned street lights cast shadows on the cobblestone and create an old world atmosphere.

Carlyle House
121 North Fairfax Street
Alexandria, Virginia 22314
703-549-2997

Alexandria's "grandest" home was built in 1752 by Scottish merchant John Carlyle. In the spring of 1755, General Edward Braddock made Carlyle House his Alexandria headquarters. At a meeting in the home's elegant great parlor, he and five Royal governors planned the strategy and funding of the early campaigns of the French and Indian War. Open Tuesday through Saturday, 10 a.m. to 5 p.m.; open Sunday, 1 p.m. to 5 p.m. Admission charge.

Christ Church
Cameron Street
Alexandria, Virginia 22314
703-549-1450

This English country-style church was built between 1767 and 1773 of native brick and stone. George Washington was on the vestry; the church contains his pew. Robert E. Lee was confirmed in the church. Open Monday through Friday, 9 a.m. to 4 p.m.; Saturday, 9 a.m. to 12 noon. Free.

Historic Sites, cont.

George Washington Masonic National Memorial
101 Callahan Drive
Alexandria, Virginia 22301
703-683-2007

The Masonic Temple contains outstanding George Washington memorabilia, including the family Bible and a clock which stopped at the time of his death. Large murals and stained glass windows depict events of Washington's life. The Temple Tower which rises 333 feet above the highest point of the land in Alexandria rewards Baytrippers on a clear day with a magnificent panorama that extends for 20 miles in every direction. Open daily, 9 a.m. to 5 p.m. Free.

The Lee-Fendall House
614 Oronoco Street
Alexandria, Virginia 22314
703-548-1789

More than 37 different Lee's occupied this gracious home at one time or another. It was built on land formerly owned by General "Light Horse Harry" Lee, Robert E. Lee's father. In this house, "Light Horse Harry" wrote the farewell address from the citizens of Alexandria when Washington left Mount Vernon to become first President of the United States. Open daily, 10 a.m. to 4 p.m.; Sunday, 1 p.m. to 4 p.m. Admission Charge.

Mount Vernon Plantation
George Washington Memorial
Parkway
Mount Vernon, Virginia 22121
703-780-2000

George Washington's estate on the Potomac River has a great view of the water, interesting outbuildings (stables, smokehouse, springhouse, icehouse, storehouse), a lovely bowling green, wonderful gardens, the tombs of George and Martha, and the mansion itself. Open March through October, daily, 9 a.m. to 5 p.m.; open November to February, daily, 9 a.m. to 4 p.m. Admission charge.

Woodlawn Plantation
9000 Richmond Highway
Mount Vernon, Virginia 22121
703-780-4000

The rich heritage of Northern Virginia is epitomized by Woodlawn Plantation. Once part of George Washington's Dogue Run Farm, the then retired President gave the estate to his adopted daughter, Eleanor Parke Custis, and his nephew, Lawrence Lewis, as a wedding gift. Open daily, 9:30 a.m. to 4:30 p.m. Closed: Thanksgiving, Christmas, and New Year's Day. Admission charge.

**Frank Lloyd Wright's
Pope-Leighey House**
9000 Richmond Highway
Mount Vernon, Virginia 22121
703-780-4000

In 1938, Frank Lloyd Wright said, "A house of moderate cost is America's most difficult problem,"...and that "people of moderate means are entitled to well-designed homes." You're invited to visit this masterpiece built in 1940. Open daily, 9:30 a.m. to 4:30 p.m. Closed Thanksgiving and Christmas Day. Admission charge.

■ **MISCELLANEOUS**

Torpedo Factory Art Center
105 North Union Street
Alexandria, Virginia 22314
703-838-4565

This refurbished World War I and II plant which formerly produced torpedo parts is now the city's leading tourist attraction and contains the studios of nearly 200 artisans and craftsmen as well as a laboratory and exhibits of one of the nation's largest and oldest urban archeological programs. Open daily, 10 a.m. to 5 p.m. Closed major holidays. Free.

■ MUSEUMS

Gadsby's Tavern Museum
134 North Royal Street
Alexandria, Virginia 22314
703-838-4242

In its heyday in the late 1700's, the Tavern and adjoining hotel were known as the finest hostelry in America. George Washington dined and met with other patriots and danced at his annual birth night ball here. Open Tuesday through Saturday, 10 a.m. to 5 p.m.; Sunday, 10 a.m. to 5 p.m. Fee.

The Lyceum
201 South Washington Street
Alexandria, Virginia 22314
804-838-4994

A graceful example of Greek-revival architecture and now a handsome museum, the Lyceum was established by Quaker-educator Benjamin Hallowell in 1839 as a cultural and scientific center. Open daily, 10 a.m. to 5 p.m.; Sunday, open 1 p.m. to 5 p.m. Free.

Stabler Leadbeater Apothecary Museum
105-107 South Fairfax Street
Alexandria, Virginia 22314
703-836-3713

Founded in 1792, this early pharmacy is now a museum and antique shop. Featuring a colorful collection of hand-blown glass and early medical ware, the shop contains the original furnishings and glassware. Open Tuesday through Saturday, 10 a.m. to 4 p.m.; closed Sunday. Admission charge.

■ PARKS AND GARDENS

The Carlyle House Historic Park
121 North Fairfax Street
Alexandria, Virginia 22314
703-549-2997

A pleasing mix of a Formal Parterre garden, an elegant period summer house, and colorful perennial beds. Much of the gardens have been restored to their original 18th century appearance. Open Tuesday through Saturday, 9 a.m. to 5 p.m.; Sunday, 12 noon to 5 p.m. Admission charge.

City Hall/Market Square
300 King Street
Alexandria, Virginia 22314
703-838-4000

Market Square is in front of City Hall, and it is the center of both old and new Alexandria. It still functions as a weekly outdoor market and once served as a parade ground for colonial troops under the command of General Braddock.

Daingerfield Island
George Washington Memorial Parkway
McLean, Virginia 22101
703-285-2598
703-285-2601

This 106-acre site offers opportunities for hiking, bird watching, organized sports, and picnicking. The Washington Sailing Marina, operated by Guest Services, Incorporated, is located on the north end of the island and provides a full service sailboat marina which includes boat rentals. Open dawn to dusk. Free.

Fort Hunt
C/O National Park Service
George Washington Memorial
Parkway
McLean, Virginia 22101
703-285-2598
703-285-2601

Fort Hunt contains 156 acres for picnicking, biking, and viewing the batteries which guarded the river approach to Washington, D.C. beginning in 1898. The guns were dismantled in 1918. Open daily, dawn to dusk. Free.

Fort Ward Park and Museum
4301 West Braddock Road
Alexandria, Virginia 22304
703-838-4848

Home of a Civil War museum and restored Union fort. Fort Ward is the fifth largest of the 68 forts built to protect Washington, D.C. during the Civil War. Open daily, dawn to dusk. Free.

Mount Vernon Gardens
George Washington Memorial
Parkway
Mount Vernon, Virginia 22121
703-780-2000

Period plants in a garden following George Washington's original design. Tour guides point out that Washington masterfully planned his gardens to allow the vegetable and flower beds to be placed unusually close to the house. Open daily, 9 a.m. to 5 p.m. Admission charge.

Mount Vernon Trail
George Washington Memorial
Parkway
McLean, Virginia 22101
703-285-2598

The Mount Vernon Trail is 17 miles long, and it parallels the Potomac River and George Washington Memorial Parkway from Memorial Bridge to Mount Vernon. The trail is shared by hikers, bikers, and joggers; along the way you can enjoy parks, wildlife habitats, and marshes.

Parks and Gardens, cont.

River Farm Park
7931 East Boulevard Drive
Alexandria, Virginia 22314
703-768-5700

River Farm Park is home to the headquarters of the American Horticultural Society. Many of these gardens are designed just for kids but adults will enjoy the test gardens of the American Dahlia and Iris Societies. Open weekdays, 8:30 a.m. to 5 p.m.; Saturday, 11 a.m. to 4 p.m. Free during the week. Admission charge on weekends.

■ SEASONAL EVENTS

Virginia Scottish Games
3900 West Braddock Road
Alexandria, Virginia 22304
703-549-0205

A weekend of Scottish revelry celebrating Celtic heritage. It's one of the nation's largest Highland Gatherings. Clan societies, world class athletes, dancers, musicians, exhibitors, and thousands of spectators gather for this annual event. Held late July. Admission charge.

Washington's Birthday Parade
221 King Street
Alexandria, Virginia 22314
703-838-4200

Alexandria honors its most famous citizen with a full month of activities held throughout the city. Festivities culminate on the Federal holiday. Free.

Waterfront Festival
North Union Street
Alexandria, Virginia 22314
703-838-4200

In recognition of Alexandria's maritime heritage, the American Red Cross sponsors its annual festival. Among the festivities will be a host of sailing ships, music, rides, crafts vendors, and an abundance of regional food. Held annually, the first weekend in June. Admission charge.

Restaurants

Chadwicks
203 South Strand Street
Alexandria, Virginia 22314
703-836-4442

House specialties include fresh seafood, hamburgers, steaks, salads, and sandwiches; daily specials include homemade soups. Open for lunch and dinner. Credit cards: AE, DC, MC, and V.

The Chart House
One Cameron Street
Alexandria, Virginia 22314
703-684-5080

Inside you will find a lush, tropical decor with windows that look out on the Potomac River. Specialties include steaks, seafood, Prime Rib, and fresh fish with an outstanding salad bar and raw bar. Outdoor deck, fireplace in the lounge. Open for lunch and dinner. Credit cards: AE, CB, D, DC, MC, and V.

The Cruise Ship Dandy
Zero Prince Street
Alexandria, Virginia 22314
703-683-6076

Climate controlled, year round dining while cruising on the Potomac River past the monuments. Open for dinner only and Sunday brunch. Credit cards: MC and V.

The Fish Market
105 King Street
Alexandria, Virginia 22314
703-836-5676

Seven dining rooms, some balcony seating. Seafood is the order of the day here, featuring fresh fish and local seafood. Ragtime piano nightly. Open for lunch and dinner. Credit cards: AE, MC, and V.

Restaurants, cont.

Gadsby's Tavern
138 North Royal Street
Alexandria, Virginia 22314
703-548-1288

Colonial cuisine in a historical landmark with costumed waiters is only a part of what makes Gadsby's a must stop for Baytrippers. Diners can choose from such colonial favorites as Country-cured Ham topped with brown sugar, raisin sauce, and brandied peaches. A Game Pie is also interesting which consists of venison, rabbit, and quail. Open for dinner only; Sunday brunch. Credit cards: AE, DC, MC, and V.

Geranio Restaurante
722 King Street
Alexandria, Virginia 22314
703-548-0088

Dine in a sophisticated, romantic setting featuring Northern Italian cuisine. Open daily for lunch and dinner. Credit cards: AE, DC, MC, and V.

Hard Times Cafe
1404 King Street
Alexandria, Virginia 22301
703-683-5340

The Hard Times Cafe is nothing but good times. Casual dining featuring Texas Chili, Cincinnati Chili, and Vegetarian Chili, along with 31 brands of popular and local beers. Open for lunch and dinner.

IL Porto Restaurant
121 King Street
Alexandria, Virginia 22314
703-836-8833

Specialties here include homemade pastas, seafood, veal, chicken, and some great homemade ice cream. Open daily for lunch and dinner. Credit cards: AE, MC, and V.

Portner's
109 South St. Asaph Street
Alexandria, Virginia 22314
703-683-1776

Enjoy the converted 1883 historic firehouse setting. Specialties include grilled steaks, seafood, pasta, pizza, hamburgers, salad, and sandwiches. Open for lunch and dinner. Credit cards: AE, D, DC, MC, and V.

Potowmack Landing
George Washington Memorial Parkway
Alexandria, Virginia 22314
703-548-0001

Indoor and outdoor dining; Sunday brunch. Specialties include grilled seafood. Their waterfront setting provides a skyline view of nearby National Airport. Watch planes take off and land while you're dining. Open daily for lunch and dinner. Credit cards: AE, CB, D, DC, MC, and V.

The Seaport Inn
6 King Street
Alexandria, Virginia 22314
703-549-2341

River views. There's a fireplace in the 1765 George Washington Tavern Room. House specialties include seafood, beef, veal, and chicken. Open daily for lunch and dinner. Credit cards: AE, CB, DC, MC, and V.

Two-Nineteen
219 King Street
Alexandria, Virginia 22314
703-549-1141

Enjoy New Orleans' Creole cuisine in formal or informal dining rooms or out on the patio. Jazz nightly in the Basin Street Lounge downstairs. Open for lunch and dinner. Credit cards: AE, CB, D, MC, and V.

211

Restaurants, cont.

Union Street Public House
121 South Union Street
Alexandria, Virginia 22314
703-548-1785

Oyster bar, grill room. Specialties include local fish, shell fish, grilled home-smoked meats. Open for lunch and dinner. Credit cards: AE, DC, MC, and V.

The Wharf
119 King Street
Alexandria, Virginia 22314
703-836-2834

Whole Maine lobsters, award-winning Crab Imperial. Also great jazz in the lounge. Open daily for lunch and dinner. Credit cards: AE, D, DC, MC, and V.

Accommodations

■ **BED AND BREAKFASTS**

The Little House
719 Gibbon Street
Alexandria, Virginia 22314
703-548-9654

Princely Bed and Breakfast, Ltd.
819 Prince Street
Alexandria, Virginia 22314
703-683-2159

The Mallard of Old Towne
106 Commerce Street
Alexandria, Virginia 22314
703-548-5618

■ **CAMPING**

Aquia Pines Campground
3071 Jefferson Davis Highway
Stafford, Virginia 22554
703-659-3447

■ HOTELS, MOTELS, AND INNS

**Alexandria Econo Lodge
Old Town**
700 North Washington Street
Alexandria, Virginia 22314
703-836-5100
800-424-4777

Best Western Old Colony Inn
625 First Street
Alexandria, Virginia 22314
703-548-6300
800-235-0115

Comfort Inn Mount Vernon
7212 Richmond Highway
Alexandria, Virginia 22306
703-765-9000
800-433-2546

Courtyard by Marriott Hotel
2700 Eisenhower Avenue
Alexandria, Virginia 22314
703-329-2323
800-428-1105

The Executive Club
610 Bashford Lane
Alexandria, Virginia 22314
703-739-2582
800-535-2582

Guest Quarters Suite Hotel
100 South Reynolds Street
Alexandria, Virginia 22304
703-370-9600
800-424-2900

Holiday Inn Eisenhower Metro
2460 Eisenhower Avenue
Alexandria, Virginia 22314
703-960-3400
800-HOLIDAY

Holiday Inn of Old Town
480 King Street
Alexandria, Virginia 22314
703-549-6080
800-368-5047

Howard Johnson
5821 Richmond Highway
Alexandria, Virginia 22303
703-329-1400
800-I-GO-HOJO

Morrison House
116 South Alfred Street
Alexandria, Virginia 22314
703-838-8000
800-367-0800

Ramada Hotel Old Town
901 North Fairfax Street
Alexandria, Virginia 22314
703-683-6000
800-2-RAMADA

Sheraton Suites Alexandria
801 North St. Asaph Street
Alexandria, Virginia 22314
703-836-4700
800-325-3535

ARLINGTON

■ **BACKGROUND:** Arlington is not a city nor a town; it's a county. Originally, it was part of the District of Columbia. In 1846, it was retroceded to Virginia. The area now known as Arlington County was inhabited by Indians for more than 9,000 years. In 1669, an English ship captain-with land grant in hand-laid claim to a 6,000-acre tract and sold it off to Scotsman John Alexandria for 672 pounds of tobacco. From then on the area flourished with agriculture and tobacco. Arlington connects Washington with five bridges and is a picturesque setting that combines the conveniences of today with the heritage of our past.

Attractions

■ **VISITOR INFORMATION**

Arlington Convention and Visitors' Service
735 South 18th Street
Arlington, Virginia 22202
703-358-5720
800-677-6267

■ **AIRPORTS**

Washington Dulles International Airport
Dulles Access Road
Sterling, Virginia 20041
703-661-2700

Washington National Airport
George Washington Memorial Parkway
Arlington, Virginia 20001
703-661-2700

■ HISTORICAL SITES

Arlington House
West Memorial Bridge
Arlington, Virginia 22211
703-285-2598

The Robert E. Lee Memorial Arlington House is the former home of the Confederate General and Civil War hero. Here in 1861 General Lee wrote the letter resigning his commission from the U. S. Army to fight for his native Virginia. Arlington House is located in the Arlington National Cemetery. Open daily, 9:30 a.m. to 6 p.m. Free. Parking fee.

Arlington National Cemetery
West Memorial Bridge
Arlington, Virginia 22211
703-697-2131

At this famous cemetery, you'll find the Tomb of Unknowns, Kennedy's grave site, and the Arlington House. One of the most moving experiences at Arlington Cemetery is to watch the changing of the guard before the Tomb of the Unknowns. Every hour on the hour, April through September, and every half-hour, April through September, the guard is ceremoniously changed. Open daily, 8 a.m. to 7 p.m. (closes 5 p.m. October through March). Free. Parking fee.

Iwo Jima Statue
Arlington Boulevard
Arlington, Virginia 22211
202-619-7222

The Iwo Jima Statue is dedicated to Marines who have given their lives since 1775. A Marine Corps Color Guard raises the flag at 8 a.m. and lowers it at sunset. Formal ceremonies are held at the Memorial Tuesday between 7 p.m. and 8:30 p.m., mid-May to mid-October. Free.

■ MISCELLANEOUS

Arlington Art Center
3550 Wilson Boulevard
Arlington, Virginia 22201
703-524-1494

Arlington Art Center features changing art exhibits by emerging, local artists. Open 11 a.m. to 5 p.m., Tuesday through Friday, and 1 p.m. to 5 p.m., Saturday and Sunday. Free.

The Pentagon
14th Street Bridge
Arlington, Virginia 22201
703-695-1776

The Pentagon serves as headquarters for the Army, Navy, Air Force, and Joint Chiefs of Staff. The Pentagon is so named because it has five sides. It also has five stories and five separate concentric rings connected by ten corridors. Guided tours are the only way Baytrippers can see the Pentagon. Tours leave from the concourse every half hour from 9:30 a.m. to 3:30 p.m., Monday through Friday. Free.

■ MUSEUMS

Arlington Historic Society Museum
1805 South Arlington Ridge Road
Arlington, Virginia 22202
703-892-4204

This former schoolhouse now features Civil War artifacts, 19th-century kitchenware, ladies fashions through the years, and more about local history. Open Friday and Saturday, 11 a.m. to 3 p.m., and Sunday, 2 p.m. to 5 p.m. Free.

■ PARKS AND GARDENS

Algonkian Regional Park
1600 Potomac View Road
Sterling, Virginia 22170
703-450-4655

A beautiful riverfront park offering a diverse choice of outdoor recreation. Algonkian is scenically situated on the shores of the Potomac River just 30 miles from the Nation's Capital. Open year round, dawn to dusk. Free.

Bon Air Park and Memorial Rose Garden
850 North Lexington Street
Arlington, Virginia 22205
703-358-4747

One of the finest collections of roses. Includes more than 157 varieties, 32 of which have been awarded the American Rose Society's "E" award for Excellence. The Park also includes the Azalea Garden, Ornamental Tree Garden, and Wildflower Area. Open daily, 7 a.m. to 9 p.m. Free.

Claude Moore Colonial Farm at Turkey Run
6310 Georgetown Pike
McLean, Virginia 22101
703-442-7557

Approximately 100 acres are used by a costumed, 18th-century, family to demonstrate a small scale, low-income homestead in Northern Virginia during the late colonial period. Open April 1 through December 20, Wednesday through Sunday, 10 a.m. to 4:30 p.m. Admission charge.

Parks and Gardens, cont.

Great Falls Park
9200 Old Dominion Drive
Great Falls, Virginia 22066
703-759-2915

Flowing from the Piedmont area, near the Nation's capital, the Potomac River builds up force as it falls over a steep, jagged rock wall and flows through a narrow gorge. This dramatic scenery makes the 800-acre Great Falls Park. Open daily, dawn to dusk, except Christmas Day. Admission charge.

Potomac Overlook Park
2845 North Marcey Road
Arlington, Virginia 22207
703-528-5406

This 100-acre park along the Potomac shoreline offers nature trails through towering oaks and tulip poplars, a nature center with archaeological and wild-flower displays, and wonderful views of the Washington, D.C. skyline. Open daily, dawn to dusk. Nature Center open Tuesday through Saturday, 10 a.m. to 5 p.m.; Sunday, 1 p.m. to 5 p.m. Free.

Theodore Roosevelt Island
George Washington Memorial Parkway
Arlington, Virginia 22101
703-285-2598

Three major biological communities make up Roosevelt Island. Marsh, swamp, and upland forest provide a refuge for a variety of native plants and animals. A memorial is located in the northern center of the island which includes a 17-foot bronze statue of the Nation's 26th President. Open daily, 8 a.m. until dark. Free.

Wolf Trap Farm Park
1624 Trap Road
Vienna, Virginia 22182
703-255-1916
703-938-2404

Wolf Trap Farm Park for the Performing Arts and the Barns of Wolf Trap are part of the first National Park solely for the performing arts. The variety of entertainment varies from dance to symphony orchestras to comedies. Open year round. Admission charge.

Restaurants

Chez Froggy
509 South 23rd Street
Arlington, Virginia 22202
703-979-7676

The menu changes daily for both lunch and dinner at this delightful little French restaurant. Offerings include Cold Cucumber Soup with Fresh Dill, Fresh Rainbow Trout Sauteed With Pecans, and the house specialty, Frog Legs. Open Monday through Friday, lunch and dinner; Saturday, dinner only. Credit cards: MC and V.

Gourmet Pizza Deli/
Lost Dog Cafe
5876 Washington Boulevard
Arlington, Virginia 22205
703-237-1552

If you're a pizza or pasta lover, you will enjoy this gourmet shop. House specialties include pizza, spaghetti and meatballs, spaghetti with white clam sauce, lasagna, Eggplant Parmesan, ravioli, Fettucini Parmesan, and Fettucini Primavera. If you like beer with your food, the Lost Dog Cafe now has over 100 kinds. Open daily from 11 a.m. to 10 p.m. Credit cards: MC and V.

Restaurants, cont.

Le Canard
123 Branch Road
Vienna, Virginia 22180
703-281-0070

The attention to detail is what makes Le Canard one of the best restaurants in the country. And the talents displayed by Chef Damien Heaney are remarkable. The chef's selections of fresh fish and crab are all five star. This is a lovely place to have a meal whether you're entertaining clients or relaxing with friends. Open Monday through Friday, lunch and dinner; Saturday and Sunday, dinner only. Credit cards: AE, CB, DC, MC, and V.

The Quarterdeck
1200 North Fort Myer Drive
Arlington, Virginia 22209
703-528-CRAB

There is one thing to note about The Quarterdeck-they specialize in steamed crabs. They come medium, large, or jumbo; by the half dozen or the dozen; hot, fresh, and coated with a delightful seafood seasoning. It is one of my favorite restaurants. I guarantee you're gonna like this spot. Open daily for lunch and dinner. Credit cards: MC and V.

Queen Bee
3181 Wilson Boulevard
Arlington, Virginia 22201
703-527-3444

Vietnamese restaurants have become a rage in Northern Virginia, and the Queen Bee is a great choice. Most raves go to the outstanding grilled dishes. Rated one of *Washingtonian Magazine's* "50 Best." Open daily for lunch and dinner. Credit cards: MC and V.

Red Hot and Blue
3014 Wilson Boulevard
Arlington, Virginia 22201
703-243-1510

The house special in this popular chain of BBQ joints is Smoked Ribs Memphis-style, slathered with sauce. Don't forget to try the onion rings. Open daily, lunch and dinner. Credit cards: MC and V.

The View
1401 Lee Highway
Arlington, Virginia 22209
703-524-6400

The menu is short, the prices are high, but the view is worth the visit. The Sunday brunch is without a doubt first class. Open daily for dinner and Sunday for brunch. Credit cards: AE, DC, MC, and V.

Whitey's
2761 North Washington Boulevard
Arlington, Virginia 22201
703-525-9825

Get away from the sightseeing crowd. Locals believe this is still one of their most popular choices. "Great value" in all American cuisine. With a name like Whitey's, it can't be all bad. Open daily, lunch and dinner. Credit cards: AE, D, MC, and V.

Accommodations

■ BED AND BREAKFASTS

Memory House Bed and Breakfast
6404 North Washington
Boulevard
Arlington, Virginia 22205
703-534-4607

■ HOTELS, MOTELS, AND INNS

Americana Hotel
1400 Jefferson Davis Highway
Arlington, Virginia 22202
703-979-4400

Best Western Arlington Inn and Tower
2480 South Glebe Road
Arlington, Virginia 22206
703-979-4400

Best Western Rosslyn West Park Hotel
1900 North Fort Myer Drive
Arlington, Virginia 22209
703-527-4814

Courtyard by Marriott
1533 Clarendon Boulevard
Arlington, Virginia 22209
703-528-2222

Courtyard Hotel
2899 Jefferson Davis Highway
Arlington, Virginia 22262
703-549-3434
800-312-2211

*Heaven and earth never
agreed better to frame a place
for man's habitation.*

—CAPTAIN JOHN SMITH
1612

Crystal City Marriott Hotel
1999 Jefferson Davis Highway
Arlington, Virginia 22202
703-413-5500

Crystal Gateway Marriott Hotel
1700 Jefferson Davis Highway
Arlington, Virginia 22202
703-920-3230

Days Hotel Crystal City
2000 Jefferson Davis Highway
Arlington, Virginia 22202
703-920-8600

Econo Lodge National Airport
2485 South Glebe Road
Arlington, Virginia 22206
703-979-4100

Holiday Inn Arlington Ballston
4610 North Fairfax Drive
Arlington, Virginia 22203
703-243-9800

**Holiday Inn Washington
Key Bridge**
1850 North Fort Myer Drive
Arlington, Virginia 22209
703-522-0400

Holiday Inn National Airport
1489 Jefferson Davis Highway
Arlington, Virginia 22202
703-521-1600

Key Bridge Marriott
1401 Lee Highway
Arlington, Virginia 22209
703-524-6400

Quality Inn Iwo Jima
1501 Arlington Boulevard
Arlington, Virginia 22209
703-524-5000

Sheraton Crystal City Hotel
1800 Jefferson Davis Highway
Arlington, Virginia 22202
703-486-1111

Sheraton National Hotel
Columbia Pike at Washington
Boulevard
Arlington, Virginia 22204
703-521-1900

Stouffer Concourse Hotel
2399 Jefferson Davis Highway
Arlington, Virginia 22202
703-418-6800

**Washington Arlington
Travelodge**
3030 Columbia Pike
Arlington, Virginia 22204
703-521-5570
800-255-3050

223

POTOMAC RIVER,
MARYLAND SIDE

Washington, D.C. to St. Mary's City

Follow the water....

- Washington, D.C.
- Indian Head
- Port Tobacco
- Cobb Island
- Leonardtown
- St. George Island
- St. Mary's City

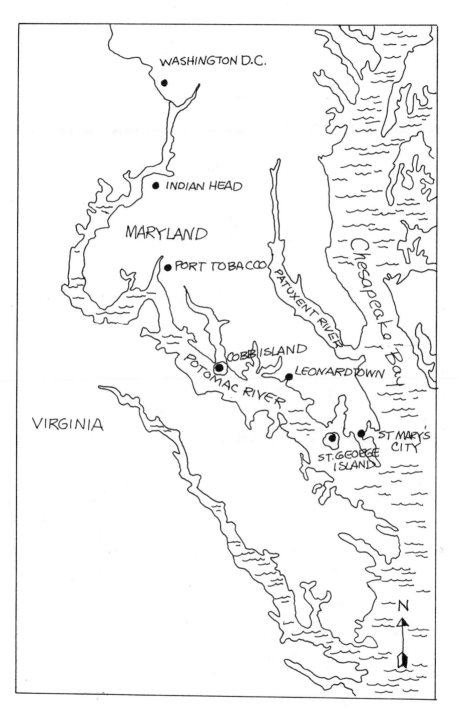

WASHINGTON, D.C.

■ **BACKGROUND:** Washington, D.C. was named in honor of the first President, and it was Washington himself from his Mt. Vernon home who supervised the site selection on the Potomac River. The "federal city" was to be on a square of land 100 miles wide ceded by both Maryland and Virginia. George Washington chose the Frenchman Pierre L'Enfant, who had fought in the Revolutionary War, to draw up the plans for a grid of streets. At the time that the City of Washington was being built, the government offices were based in Philadelphia, and they moved to Washington, the new Capital, in 1800. Just a few short years after that, 1814 to be exact, much of the City of Washington was burned down by the British.

Attractions

■ **VISITOR INFORMATION**

Washington, D.C. Visitors Information Service
1212 New York Avenue, N.W.
Washington, D.C. 20005
202-789-7000

Washington Tourist Information Center
1455 Pennsylvania Avenue, N.W.
Washington, D.C. 20005
202-789-7038

■ **AIRPORTS**

Washington Dulles International Airport
Dulles Access Road
Herndon, Virginia 20041
703-661-2700

Washington National Airport
George Washington Memorial Parkway
Arlington, Virginia 20001
703-661-2700

■ BOAT CRUISES

Spirit of Washington
Pier 4
6th and Water Streets, S.W.
Washington, D.C. 20024
202-554-8000

Cruise aboard Washington's largest entertaining, dining harbor cruise ship. From historical homes to National Monuments, the Spirit will show you Washington's famous Potomac River. Select from fun and sun lunch cruises, evening dinner cruises, or moonlight party cruises. Fee.

■ FISHING

Life Outdoors Unlimited
4708 Sellman Road
Beltsville, Maryland 20705
301-937-0010

Join in the fun and excitement of fishing the historical Potomac River with Ken Penrod and his first-class guides. Learn why so many revere this flowing stretch of water that runs to the nation's capital from its origin, more than 250 miles to the northwest. Call for your schedule and time of departure. Fee.

■ GUIDED SIGHTSEEING TOURS

All About Town, Inc.
519 6th Street, N.W.
Washington, D.C. 20001
202-393-3696

All About Town offers lectured tours on full-size, air conditioned motor coaches to many of Washington's historic sites. Your choices include a deluxe, all-day combination tour. See the government at work. Learn about the three branches-Legislative, Executive, and Judicial. Visit the Smithsonian Museum of American History where you can see Dorothy's ruby slippers. Need more? Call for your scheduled tour. Fee.

Gray Line of Washington, D.C. Tours
Union Station Bus Level
50 Massachusetts Avenue, N.E.
Washington, D.C. 20002
202-289-1995
800-862-1400

Gray Line specializes in tours to suit all your needs. They offer the Sunday Morning Tour, Interior of Public Buildings Tour, Black Heritage Tour, Multi-Lingual Tour, Washington After Dark Tour-oh, there's more! Call for your schedule. Fee.

Holiday Tours of Washington
7308 Highbridge Road
Bowie, Maryland 20715
301-262-3517

Baytrippers, do you want to save money? Holiday Tours of Washington can help you see and visit more places in one or two days than you could see on your own. Lectured tours, free pickup and return from local hotels. Individuals or groups. Open year round. Fee.

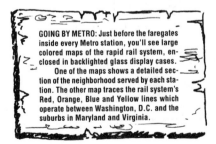

GOING BY METRO: Just before the faregates inside every Metro station, you'll see large colored maps of the rapid rail system, enclosed in backlighted glass display cases.
One of the maps shows a detailed section of the neighborhood served by each station. The other map traces the rail system's Red, Orange, Blue and Yellow lines which operate between Washington, D.C. and the suburbs in Maryland and Virginia.

Oldtown Trolley Tours
5225 Kilmer Place
Hyattsville, Maryland 20781
301-985-3020

Colorful anecdotes, humorous stories, and historical information are combined to help you see more than just the monuments. Board where you like, when you like, and get on and off at the sights that interest you. Open daily, 9 a.m. to 4 p.m. (5 p.m. during the summer). Fee.

Tourmobile Sightseeing, Inc.
1000 Ohio Drive, S.W.
Washington, D.C. 20024
202-554-5100

Experienced narrators will guide you beyond the marble of the monuments to reveal the tales of the men whose lives inspired their construction. This tourmobile stops at 18 of the most visited historic sites. Open daily, 9 a.m. to 6:30 p.m., June 15 through Labor Day; 9:30 a.m. to 4:30 p.m., the remainder of the year. Fee.

Washington Area Mini Bus Tours
5025 13th Place, N.E.
Washington, D.C. 20017
202-526-2049

Guided narrated tours of the Washington area are provided by experienced professionals. Group and individual tours available. Open daily. Fee.

■ HISTORIC SITES

Bureau of Engraving and Printing
14th and C Streets, S.W.
Washington, D.C. 20228
202-874-3019

"The buck stops here." It also starts here. This is where approximately $20 billion is printed every year. This mostly replaces worn or mutilated bills taken out of service. The average dollar lasts about 18 months. Open Monday through Friday, 9 a.m. to 2 p.m. Free.

Historic Sites, cont.

Frederick Douglass Home
1411 W Street, S.E.
Washington, D.C. 20020
202-426-5961

Former home of Frederick Douglass, the famous abolitionist, orator and diplomat. The Visitor Center features a film followed by a half-hour tour. Open daily, April to September, 9 a.m. to 5 p.m., and from October to March, 9 a.m. to 4 p.m. Free.

FBI Headquarters
10th Street and Pennsylvania Avenue, N.W.
Washington, D.C. 20535
202-324-3447

Tour the J. Edgar Hoover Building and check out the "ten most wanted fugitives." Your visit will give you a fascinating look at crime fighting techniques used by the FBI. Open Monday through Friday, 8:45 a.m. to 4:15 p.m. Free.

Folger Shakespeare Library
201 East Capital Street, S.E.
Washington, D.C. 20003
202-544-7077

The library contains the world's largest collection of Shakespeare's printed works along with 260,000 books and manuscripts, of which 100,000 are rare. Open Monday through Saturday, 10 a.m. to 4 p.m. Free.

Library of Congress
1st Street at Independence Avenue, S.E.
Washington, D.C. 20540
202-707-5458

The world's largest library displays the Three Volume Gutenberg Bible and Thomas Jefferson's rough draft of the Declaration of Independence. There are 535 miles of bookshelves in three gigantic buildings. Open Monday through Saturday, 9 a.m. to 5:30 p.m. Call for tour times. Free.

National Geographic Society's Explorers Hall
17th and M Streets, N.W.
Washington, D.C. 20036
202-857-7588
202-857-7689

The National Geographic Society's Explorers Hall is home to many of the interesting items that have made their magazine one of the most popular in the world. Don't miss this exciting collection. Open Monday through Saturday and holidays, 9 a.m. to 5 p.m.; Sunday, 10 a.m. to 5 p.m. Closed December 25. Free.

Pavilion at the Old Post Office
1100 Pennsylvania Avenue, N.W.
Washington, D.C. 20004
202-523-5691 - Tower
202-289-4224

The renovated, historic Old Post Office is Washington's festive market. The atrium offers visitors more than 100 shops, restaurants, food courts, daily entertainment, and a spectacular view of the city from the 315-foot clock tower. Open daily, 8 a.m. to 11 p.m., mid-April to mid-September; 10 a.m. to 5:45 p.m., mid-September to mid-April.

Supreme Court
One First Street, N.E.
Washington, D.C. 20543
202-479-3030

The Supreme Court is the highest court in the land. It's nine Justices, or Judges, decide whether laws are constitutional or not. Baytrippers can attend court sessions which are open to the pubic without a pass. Lectures are offered when the court is not in session. Open Monday through Friday, 9 a.m. to 4:30 p.m. Lectures presented every half-hour, 9:30 a.m. to 3:30 p.m. Closed Federal holidays. Free.

Historic Sites, cont.

Union Station
50 Massachusetts Avenue, N.E.
Washington, D.C. 20002
202-371-9441

This is one of the last of the great train stations. Originally built in 1907, it was recently renovated. The results are a dazzling center where you can dine at 47 different restaurants and eateries, take in a movie (there are nine theaters), and explore nearly 100 shops. The building is open 24 hours a day, although movie theaters, shops, and eateries have shorter, separate hours. Free.

U.S. Capitol
Capitol Hill
Constitution Avenue and
Independence Avenue, N.W.
Washington, D.C. 20515
202-224-3121

Be sure to allow plenty of time when visiting the Capitol where Congress meets; there's a lot to see. Begin your sightseeing of the Capitol in the Rotunda where you can join a free half-hour tour. For starters it is an impressive sight. The Rotunda is 180 feet high and 97 feet across. It is crowned by a nine million pound cast iron dome. Tours daily, every 15 minutes, 9 a.m. to 3:45 p.m. Free.

U.S. Naval Observatory
34th and Massachusetts Avenue, N.W.
Washington, D.C. 20392
202-653-1507
202-653-1541

Baytrippers, don't overlook their Monday night tour. Those lucky enough to obtain passes will get a chance to look through the observatory's largest telescope. Tickets are limited. Open Monday only. Doors open at 7:30 p.m., October 21 to March 31; April 1 to October 20, at 8:30 p.m. Guided tours last 1 1/2 to 2 hours. Free.

White House
1600 Pennsylvania Avenue, N.W.
Washington, D.C. 20500
202-456-7041

The White House has been home to every President except George Washington. He died before it was completed. In 1814, the British set the White House on fire. It was saved when a thunder storm doused the flames. Seven of the 132 rooms are open for review. Open for 20-minute tours, Tuesday through Saturday, 10 a.m. to 12 noon. Limited number of tickets at the Ellipse booth. Distributed from 8 a.m., Memorial Day to Labor Day; the rest of the year, tickets are not required. Enter at the East Gate.

■ MEMORIALS AND MONUMENTS

Jefferson Memorial
South Bank of the Tidal Basin, N.W.
Washington, D.C. 20242
202-426-6821

This memorial for our 3rd President was dedicated in 1943. Inside is a 19-foot bronze statue. The walls are filled with quotes from the Declaration of Independence. Open daily, 8 a.m. to 12 midnight. Free.

Lincoln Memorial
Potomac Park at 23rd Street
South of Constitution Avenue, N.W.
Washington, D.C. 20242
202-426-6841

This is a memorial to our 16th President, Abraham Lincoln. A 19-foot statue overlooks the reflecting pool on the mall. Open daily, 8 a.m. to 12 midnight. Closed Christmas. Tours upon request. Free.

Vietnam Veterans Memorial
Constitution Avenue
Between 21st and 22nd Streets, N.W.
Washington, D.C. 20242
202-634-1568

This modern memorial of black granite is inscribed with names of 58,000 people who died in or became missing during the Vietnam War. Open 24 hours a day. Free.

Washington Monument
Constitution Avenue at 15th Street on the Mall
South of Constitution Avenue, N.W.
Washington, D.C. 20242
202-426-6841

This is the tallest masonry structure in the world-555 feet 5-1/8 inches-and it provides a unique panoramic view of Washington via elevator. Open daily, 9 a.m. to 5 p.m.; April to Labor Day, 8 a.m. to 12 midnight. Free.

■ MISCELLANEOUS

Corcoran Gallery of Art
17th Street and New York
Avenue, N.W.
Washington, D.C. 20006
202-638-3211

This fantastic collection of 18th, 19th, and 20th century American and European art work includes the famous portrait of George Washington by Gilbert Stuart. You'll recognize it, as it's the one depicted on our almighty one dollar bill. Changing exhibits also include photography. Open Tuesday through Sunday, 10 a.m. to 4:30 p.m., and on Thursday until 9 p.m. Admission charge.

The Municipal Fish Wharf
Maine Avenue, S.W.
Washington, D.C. 20024
202-554-5520
202-554-4173

Located along the Southwest waterfront, the municipal fish wharf has an ambience all of its own. As they have for generations, watermen sell fresh crabs, fish, clams, and oysters. Nearby a shoreline promenade leads past marinas and seafood restaurants.

The National Aquarium
Department of Commerce
Building
14th Street and Pennsylvania
Avenues, N.W.
Washington, D.C. 20230
202-482-2825

Established in 1873, the National Aquarium is America's First Aquarium, and it holds over 1,200 specimens from salt and freshwater. It features exhibits that tell you about the animals' habits and habitats. Open daily, 9 a.m. to 5 p.m. Admission charge.

■ MUSEUMS

Anacostia Museum
1901 Fort Place, S.E.
Washington, D.C. 20560
202-357-2700

The museum, located in the historic Anacostia section of Washington, presents exhibitions on the history and culture of African Americans. The Harlem Renaissance, the development of African American churches, and inventions by African slaves and African Americans have been the subjects of exhibitions at the museum. Open daily, 10 a.m. to 5 p.m. Closed Christmas. Free.

Arts and Industries Building
900 Jefferson Drive, S.W.
Washington, D.C. 20560
202-357-2700

The dynamic spirit of America a century ago is recaptured in this, the second oldest Smithsonian building on the Mall. It houses "1876: A Centennial Exhibition," recalling the ambience of the Victorian era by recreating the 1876 Centennial Exhibition held in Philadelphia. Open daily, 10 a.m. to 5 p.m. Closed Christmas. Free.

B'Nai B'Rith Klutznick Museum
1640 Rhode Island Avenue,
N.W.
Washington, D.C. 20036
202-857-6583

Judaic collection on permanent display and special exhibits and programs throughout the year. Open Sunday through Friday, 10 a.m. to 5 p.m. Closed Saturday and on legal and Jewish holidays. Free.

Daughters of the American Revolution Museum
1776 D Street, N.W.
Washington, D.C. 20006
202-879-3254

The museum contains an impressive collection of decorative arts which reflects the artistry and craftsmanship present in America before the Industrial Revolution. Open Monday through Friday, 8:30 a.m. to 4 p.m.; Sunday, 1 p.m. to 5 p.m. Free.

Dolls' House and Toy Museum
5236 44th Street, N.W.
Washington, D.C. 20015
202-244-0024

This museum contains a carefully researched collection of antique dolls' houses, toys, and games, most of them Victorian, and all of them antique. Open Tuesday through Saturday, 10 a.m. to 5 p.m.; Sunday, 12 noon to 5 p.m. Admission charge.

Freer Gallery of Art
Jefferson Drive and 12th Street, S.W.
Washington, D.C. 20560
202-357-2700

The Freer is a museum of Asian art with objects dating from Neolithic times to the early 20th century. The gallery also houses works by late 19th- and early 20th-century Americans, including a major collection of works by James McNeill. Open daily, 10 a.m. to 5 p.m. Closed Christmas. Free.

Hirshhorn Museum and Sculpture Garden
7th Street and Independence Avenue, S.W.
Washington, D.C. 20560
202-357-2700

The museum features the largest public collection in the United States of sculpture by Henry Moore. Other highlights include large sculptures by Rodin, Jetelova, and Matisse. Open daily, 10 a.m. to 5 p.m. Garden open, 7:30 a.m. to dusk. Closed Christmas. Free.

Museums, cont.

Marine Corps Museum
Building 58
Charles Morris Avenue
Washington Navy Yard
9th and M Streets, S.E.
Washington, D.C. 20374
202-433-3840

Many of the exhibits on display here highlight the Marine Corps' role in the Pacific War from 1941 to 1945. On display are uniforms and weapons, even Japanese samurai swords. Open Monday through Saturday, 10 a.m. to 4 p.m. On Sunday and for seasonal hours during the summer, open 12 noon to 5 p.m. Free.

National Air and Space Museum
6th and Independence Avenue, S.W.
Washington, D.C. 20560
202-357-2700

Experience the history of flight, from the plane flown by the daring Wright Brothers to the Apollo 11 Command Module. It's all here in the most visited museum in the world. Highlights include touchable moon rock and Hubble Space Telescope model. Open daily, June 17 through Labor Day, 9:30 a.m. to 7:30 p.m. The rest of the year, 10 a.m. to 5:30 p.m. Free.

National Archives
7th and Constitution Avenue, N.W.
Washington, D.C. 20565
202-501-5000

The National Archives is home to some of the most important documents in American history, including the Declaration of Independence, the Constitution, the Bill of Rights, and the Magna Carta. Open daily, 10 a.m. to 5:30 p.m., April to Labor Day, until 9 p.m. Free.

National Building Museum
401 F Street, N.W.
Washington, D.C. 20001
202-272-2448

The National Building Museum was designed as a memorial to Civil War Veterans. Today it presents exhibits on all aspects of building architecture. The great hall has been the site of many presidential inaugural balls. Open Monday through Saturday, 10 a.m. to 4 p.m., and Sunday, 12 noon to 4 p.m. Free.

National Gallery of Art
6th Street and Constitution Avenue, N.W.
Washington, D.C. 20565
202-737-4215
202-357-2000

One of the finest art museums in the world with extensive collections of Western Europe and American paintings. Open Monday through Saturday, 10 a.m. to 5 p.m.; Sunday, 11 a.m. to 6 p.m. Closed Christmas and New Year's Day. Free.

National Museum of African Art
950 Independence Avenue, S.W.
Washington, D.C. 20560
202-357-2700

This museum is the only museum in the United States dedicated exclusively to the collection, exhibition, and study of the traditional arts of Africa south of the Sahara. Open daily, 10 a.m. to 5 p.m. Closed Christmas. Free.

National Museum of American History
14th Street and Constitution Avenue, N.W.
Washington, D.C. 20560
202-357-2700

From the patent model of Eli Whitney's cotton gin to a Ford Model T, objects on display at the museum embody the Nation's scientific, technological, and cultural heritage. Open daily from June 17 to Labor Day, 9:30 a.m. to 7:30 p.m. The rest of the year, open 10 a.m. to 5:30 p.m. Free.

Museums, cont.

National Museum of Natural History
10th Street and Constitution Avenue, N.W.
Washington, D.C. 20560
202-357-2700

With more than 119 million objects in its research collections, the museum is a fascinating resource on people and their natural surroundings. Visitors can learn about humankind's earliest history and the development of world cultures. There are thousands of specimens of mammals, birds, amphibians, reptiles, insects, sea life, fossils, gems, minerals, rocks, ores, and meteorites. Open daily, 10 a.m. to 5 p.m. Closed Christmas. Free.

National Portrait Gallery/ Museum of American Art
8th and G Streets, N.W.
Washington, D.C. 20001
202-357-2700

The National Museum of American Art and the National Portrait Gallery share the same quarters; they are housed in the historic Old Patent Office-site of Abraham Lincoln's second inaugural reception. More than 30,000 works span 250 years of American art. Open daily, 10 a.m. to 5:30 p.m. Closed Christmas. Free.

Navy Museum
Building 76
Washington Navy Yard
9th and M Streets, S.E.
Washington, D.C. 20374
202-433-4882

The Navy Museum takes a look at the Navy's role in shaping American history. The museum contains a variety of ship models, uniforms, photography, and fine arts displays. Open daily, September to May, 9 a.m. to 4 p.m.; Saturday and Sunday, 10 a.m. to 5 p.m. June to August, week day hours are 9 a.m. to 5 p.m. Free.

Renwick Gallery
17th Street and Pennsylvania
Avenue, N.W.
Washington, D.C. 20560
202-357-2700

Changing exhibitions of 20th-century American crafts, as well as a selection from the permanent collection, are featured at the Renwick Gallery. Open daily, 10 a.m. to 5 p.m. Closed Christmas. Free.

Arthur M. Sackler Gallery
1050 Independence Avenue,
S.W.
Washington, D.C. 20560
202-357-2700

Changing exhibitions of Asian art, drawn from major collections in the United States and abroad, highlight the varied artistic traditions of Asia from ancient times to the present. Open daily, 10 a.m. to 5 p.m. Closed Christmas. Free.

Smithsonian Institution
1000 Jefferson Drive, S.W.
Washington, D.C. 20560
202-357-2700
202-357-2020

The Smithsonian Visitor Center housed in the "Castle," the oldest building in the Smithsonian's 14 museums, is the place to begin your sightseeing tour. Highlights include two orientation theaters featuring a 20-minute filmed overview of the Institution, electronic wall maps, and scale models of Washington's famous monuments. Open daily, 9 a.m. to 5 p.m. Closed Christmas. Free.

Textile Museum
2320 S Street, N.W.
Washington, D.C. 20008
202-667-0441

Founded in 1925, this museum features more than 12,000 exhibitions of historic and contemporary handmade textile arts. Open Monday through Saturday, 10 a.m. to 5 p.m.; Sunday, 1 p.m. to 5 p.m. Admission charge.

Museums, cont.

U.S. Holocaust Memorial Museum
100 Raoul Wallenberg Place, S.W.
Washington, D.C. 20024
202-488-0400

At the Holocaust Museum, you'll find an actual barracks building from Auschwitz and a rare documentary film. A major exhibit, the Tower of Faces, is dedicated to presenting the history of the persecution and murder of millions of Jews and other victims of Nazi tyranny from 1935 to 1945. Open daily, 10 a.m. to 5 p.m. Closed Christmas Day. Admission free but tickets required.

■ NEIGHBORHOODS

There are several neighborhoods that should be on every Baytripper's walking tour. We suggest you put on your walking shoes and get a close-up look at some of Washington's Treasures.

CAPITOL HILL

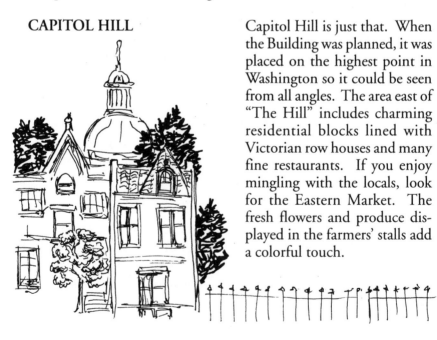

Capitol Hill is just that. When the Building was planned, it was placed on the highest point in Washington so it could be seen from all angles. The area east of "The Hill" includes charming residential blocks lined with Victorian row houses and many fine restaurants. If you enjoy mingling with the locals, look for the Eastern Market. The fresh flowers and produce displayed in the farmers' stalls add a colorful touch.

CHINATOWN

Chinatown is fun and it's full of Chinese treasures, especially great restaurants. The street signs are in both English and Chinese and it's an easy walk. This neighborhood is only eight blocks square.

GEORGETOWN

The Port of Georgetown was founded on the tobacco trade and was an established community 40 years before the founding of Washington. Today it is a special place filled with charm, history, and many shops and restaurants.

ADAMS MORGAN

The Adams Morgan area is a charming, colorful cosmopolitan neighborhood, a Latin-American enclave between Connecticut and Florida Avenues.

■ PARKS AND GARDENS

C&O Canal National Historic Park
11710 MacArthur Boulevard
Potomac, Maryland 20854
301-299-3613
301-299-2026
301-739-4200

The Chesapeake and Ohio Canal stretches 184 miles from Georgetown in N.W. Washington to Cumberland, Maryland. In the summer months, Baytrippers can enjoy mile-long, mule-drawn barge trips. Call for schedule and destination points. Admission charge.

Dumbarton Oaks
1703 32nd Street, N.W.
Washington, D.C. 20007
202-338-8278
202-342-3200

At Dumbarton Oaks, formal gardens span 16 acres with reflecting pools, hidden benches, and shade trees. Flowers blossom from early spring to autumn. Gardens open, 2 p.m. to 5 p.m. daily, April through October. Closed national holidays. Admission charge.

Enid A. Haupt Garden
1000 Independence Avenue, S.W.
Washington, D.C. 20560
202-357-2700

This four-acre garden rests atop the Smithsonian's underground museum, research, and education complex, which houses the Arthur M. Sackler Gallery and the National Museum of African Art. Named for its donor, Enid Haupt, the park-like area features exquisite trees, plants, and flowers. Highlights are saucer magnolias, hybrid tea roses, and 19th-century garden furniture. Open daily, 7 a.m. to 5 p.m. Closed Christmas. Free.

Kenilworth Aquatic Gardens
Anacostia Avenue and Douglas
Street, N.E.
Washington, D.C. 20020
202-426-6905

The aquatic gardens are regarded as one of the Nation's botanical treasures. There are 14 acres of ponds containing more than 100,000 water plants, including some of the rarest and most colorful water lilies known. Open daily, 7 a.m. to 5 p.m. Guided tours, 9 a.m., 11 a.m., 1 p.m., daily. Free.

National Arboretum
3501 New York Avenue, N.E.
Washington, D.C. 20002
202-475-4815

The United States National Arboretum was established by an Act of Congress on March 27, 1927. There are 444 acres of trees, shrubs, and flowering plants, along with a bonsai garden and, my favorite, the spectacular herb garden. Open daily, Monday through Friday, 8 a.m. to 5 p.m.; Saturday and Sunday, 10 a.m. to 5 p.m. (The National Bonsai Collection is open daily, 10 a.m. to 2:30 p.m.) Free.

National Mall
Constitution Avenue and
Independence Avenue, N.W.
Washington, D.C. 20242

The National Mall is a magnificently lavish green park area extending from the U.S. Capitol to the Washington Monument. It's a pleasant two-mile walk, and the pathway is lined on both sides with splendid old elm trees and several of the Smithsonian Institution Museums.

245

Parks and Gardens, cont.

National Zoological Park
3001 Connecticut Avenue, N.W.
Washington, D.C. 20008
202-673-4717

Here are giant pandas, shrews, monkeys, ostriches, ants, and elephants, special programs and demonstrations, unusual gardens, and much, much more. The buildings are open daily, May 1 through September 15, 9 a.m. to 6 p.m. The grounds are open from 8 a.m. to 8 p.m. The rest of the year the buildings are open, 9 a.m. to 4:30 p.m., and the grounds, 8 a.m. to 6 p.m. Free.

Potomac Park
1100 Ohio Drive, S.W.
Washington, D.C. 20242
202-426-6700

Washington's Potomac Park is divided into two sectors—East Potomac Park and West Potomac Park. The southern tip of East Potomac Park is Hains Point. A fountain that rises from the river shoots its 100-foot spray to the sky. Also, there are more than 2,500 feet of bicycle paths. The area is a favorite spot for joggers. West Potomac Park offers such attractions as lovely views of the Potomac River, the Lincoln and Jefferson Memorials, Constitution Gardens, the reflecting Pool, and the Tidal Basin ringed by Washington's renowned Cherry Trees. Open year round. Free.

**Rock Creek Park and
Nature Center**
5200 Glover Road, N.W.
Washington, D.C. 20008
202-426-6829
202-426-6832

Rock Creek Park consists of 1,750 acres of woodland park that snakes through the heart of Washington. Here you can rent a horse for a guided trail ride, take a bike ride, jog, picnic, or visit the Nature Center with exhibits on the native forest. Nature Center, open daily; hours, 8:30 a.m. to 5 p.m. Free.

U.S. Botanic Garden
1st Street and Maryland Avenue,
S.W.
Washington, D.C. 20515
202-225-7099

These National Gardens feature an exotic jungle and a tropical rain forest. Perhaps the most spectacular exhibit is the world-famous orchid collection which, each week, displays more than 200 blooming varieties from its total of 10,000 plants. Open daily, 9 a.m. to 5 p.m. Closed Christmas. Free.

Washington National Cathedral
Massachusetts and Wisconsin
Avenues, N.W.
Washington, D.C. 20016
202-537-6200

The gardens of Washington National Cathedral are highlighted by the Bishop's Garden. A garden with "many rooms," it was built originally as the private garden for the Bishop. My favorite room is the "Herb bed and the Sundial." An old English sundial rests atop a 13th century Gothic Capital discovered in monastery ruins near Rheims Cathedral in France. Open daily. Free.

■ SEASONAL EVENTS

Cherry Blossom Festival and Parade
Washington, D.C.
202-646-0366

Washington's fabled cherry blossoms draw hundreds of thousands of spectators each spring. This two-week event celebrates the Japanese cherry trees. Late March to early April. Call for schedule. Free.

Easter Egg Roll
1600 Pennsylvania Avenue, N.W.
Washington, D.C. 20500
.202-456-2200

The annual Easter Egg Roll is held on the White House lawn and is open to children aged eight and under, accompanied by an adult. Eggs and entertainment are provided. Held the Monday following Easter, 10 a.m. to 2 p.m. Free.

Folklife Festival
National Mall, N.W.
Washington, D.C. 20242
202-357-2700

Sponsored by the Smithsonian Institution. More than one million visitors attend this popular festival of American Folklife. Highlights are the ethnic foods, the music, and creative crafts. Held the end of June. Call for schedule. Free.

Ford's Theater
511 10th Street, N.W.
Washington, D.C. 20004
202-426-6924

This is the red brick theater where John Wilkes Booth shot President Abraham Lincoln on Friday, April 14, 1865. Ford's is a performing theater; professional shows appear throughout the year. Open daily, 9 a.m. to 5 p.m., and Sunday, 9 a.m. to 2 p.m. Free.

Kennedy Center
2700 F Street, N.W.
Washington, D.C. 20566
202-467-4600

A living memorial to the late President, the center has five theatres and is home to the American Film Institute, the Washington Opera, and the National Symphony. Open daily, 10 a.m. to 1 p.m. Every 15 minutes, there are 40-minute tours. Free.

Arena Stage
6th Street and Main Avenue, S.W.
Washington, D.C. 20024
202-488-3300

"Theater in the round," it's one of the best in town. Arena Stage presents an entertainment mix of dramas, comedies, and musi"Theater in the round," it's one of the best in town. Arena Stage presents an entertainment mix of dramas, comedies, and musicals. Open seasonally. Call for schedule. Admission charge.

Carter Barron Amphitheater
16th Street and Colorado Avenue, N.W.
Washington, D.C. 20008
202-426-6837
202-426-0486

Outdoor theater is performed under the stars and by the stars in this 4,000-seat, outdoor complex. Open seasonally. Admission charge.

National Theatre
1321 Pennsylvania Avenue, N.W.
Washington, D.C. 20005
202-628-6161
800-233-3123

Broadway plays are presented in a richly decorated and beautifully renovated theatre dating from 1835. Open spring, fall, and winter. Call for schedule. Admission charge.

Washington Opera
207 F Street, N.W.
Washington, D.C. 20566
202-416-7851
202-416-7800
800-87-OPERA

A night at the opera? Why not! If you want tickets for opening night or any night, we suggest you purchase tickets early. Open year round. Call for schedule. Admission charge.

Independence Day Celebration
202-789-7000
202-619-7222

The spectacular fireworks display draws up to 100,000 people, so come early and stay late. Events begin at 10 a.m. on the west steps of the U. S. Capitol and conclude at the Washington Monument grounds. Held on the 4th of July. Free.

Laurel Race Course
Route 198 and Race Track Road
Laurel, Maryland 20275
301-725-0400
800-638-1859

"They're off." The thrill of thoroughbred racing at its finest is alive and well at this state-of-the-art track. Open seasonally. Admission charge.

Adams Morgan Day
202-789-7000

Celebrate the culture, heritage, and food of the community along 18th Street, Columbia Road, and Florida Avenue in one of D.C.'s unique neighborhoods. Held early September. Free.

Smithsonian Kite Festival
15th Street on the Mall
Washington, D.C. 20242
202-357-3244

This is the "Rose Bowl" of kite festivals. If it's a nice day, you can expect 10,000 people to attend this event. Flyers of all ages gather to compete for prizes and trophies. This two-day event is held on the Washington Monument Grounds in late March. Free.

Washington Boat Show
9th Street and New York
Avenue, N.W.
Washington, D.C. 20005
202-371-42001

If you like boats, you'll love the Washington Boat Show. Over 700 boats on display at the Washington Convention Center make this the largest mid-Atlantic boat show-over 9 acres of boats and accessories-held in mid-February. Admission charge.

Washington Bullets
USAIR Arena
One Harry S. Truman Drive
Landover, Maryland 20785
301-622-3865

"It ain't over 'til the fat lady sings." Enjoy the excitement and magic of N.B.A. basketball. Forty home games are played at the USAIR Arena. Seasonal, November through April. Admission charge.

Washington Capitals
USAIR Arena
One Harry S. Truman Drive
Landover, Maryland 20785
301-386-7000

The fast and exciting game of hockey is at its best with the "Caps." You won't want to miss the action. Season runs from October through May. Admission charge.

Washington Warthogs
USAIR Arena
One Harry S. Truman Drive
Landover, Maryland 20785
301-499-3000

Get your kicks all summer long with the fast-paced indoor soccer league. The Warthogs are wonderful! Don't miss 'um. Seasonal-June to mid-September. Admission charge.

Restaurants

Here is a list of some of Washington's most popular restaurants. As in any major city, the big selection and variety of styles of cuisines to be enjoyed are staggering. We have grouped our selections into the neighborhood in which they can be found. Bon appetite!

■ CAPITAL HILL

Hawk N' Dove
329 Pennsylvania Avenue, S.E.
Washington, D.C. 20002
202-543-3300

Housed in a unique old building on Capital Hill, Hawk N' Dove features a limited menu with cheeseburgers, chili, and soups being the most popular. Bass Ale is on tap. The setting is one of dark wood and signs of the time. Open daily, lunch and dinner. Credit cards: AE, DC, MC, and V.

■ DOWNTOWN

Brickskeller
1523 22nd Street, N.W.
Washington, D.C. 20037
202-293-1885

the Brickskeller's infamous
"BRICKBURGER"
a hamburger with
Bacon·Salami·onion·sharp cheese
Lettuce·Slaw·French fries
5.50

The Brickskeller features "The World's Largest Selection of Beer." You open the medieval-looking wooden door and walk down a short stairway lined with pictures of old American breweries and a collection of coasters. You can begin your meal with a down home Louisiana Po Boy and finish with an Eastern Shore Crab Loaf. Open Monday through Friday, lunch and dinner; Saturday and Sunday, dinner only. Credit cards: AE and DC.

El Bodegon
1637 R Street, N.W.
Washington, D.C. 20009
202-667-1710

El Bodegon serves authentic continental Spanish dishes. Wine is poured directly from porrons to mouth and spirited flamenco dancers add to your good times. Open Monday through Friday for lunch and dinner; Saturday, dinner only. Credit cards: AE, C, MC, and V.

Irongate Inn
1734 N Street, N.W.
Washington, D.C. 20036
202-737-1370

The Irongate Inn is a quiet and intimate restaurant that has earned a good reputation. If you are trying Middle Eastern food for the first time, I suggest you try the "Arabian Knight's Platter." It's an exciting combination meal that's sure to please. Open daily for lunch and dinner. Credit cards: AE, C, CB, DC, MC, and V.

John Mandi's Market Inn
200 E Street, S.W.
Washington, D.C. 20024
202-554-2100

The "Market Inn" is known as "The Lobster House of Washington" and it's in this very restaurant that I enjoyed the "best lobster I've ever eaten." You can get just about any kind of fish or shellfish your heart desires. It's all here with over 100 varieties of seafood daily. Open Sunday through Thursday, lunch and dinner. Closed Monday, Tuesday, and Wednesday. Credit cards: AE, CB, DC, MC, and V.

Restaurants, cont.

Old Ebbitt Grill
675 15th Street, N.W.
Washington, D.C. 20005
202-347-4801

Established in 1856, Old Ebbitt Grill is the oldest bar in Washington with a prime downtown location. It's very popular with the local yokels, as well as the political powerful. Open for breakfast, lunch, and dinner. Credit cards: AE, DC, MC, and V.

The Palm
1225 19th Street, N.W.
Washington, D.C. 20005
202-293-9091

First-class steaks, lobsters, and hearts of palm salad. Once inside, ask for Joe LeVaca. He's the waiter who will turn your lunch or dinner into a special event. Open for lunch and dinner, Monday through Friday. Open for dinner only, Saturday and Sunday. Credit cards: AE, DC, MC, and V.

Trader Vic's
16th and K Streets, N.W.
Washington, D.C. 20036
202-347-7100

Trader Vic's is located in the Capital Hilton Hotel and continues to be a favorite of locals and tourists alike. Chinese entrees are the favorite dishes, and the tropical drinks with those strange sounding names are sure to please. Open Monday through Saturday. Closed Sunday. Credit cards: AE, CB, DC, MC, and V.

■ GEORGETOWN

Nathan's Restaurant
3150 M Street, N.W.
Washington, D.C. 20007
202-338-2000

Nathan's is located at the intersection of Wisconsin and M Streets in historic Georgetown. It's dark inside, and it can be a madhouse at times. Nathan's is Georgetown with a Georgetown crowd and a great place to stop for people watching. Open lunch and dinner. Credit cards: AE, CB, DC, MC, and V.

Old Europe
2434 Wisconsin Avenue, N.W.
Washington, D.C. 20007
202-333-7600

Authentic German cuisine in an authentic German setting. The walls are covered with ornately framed, old-fashioned paintings. The food is as steady and respectable as the restaurant's reputation promises. Enjoy your meal with a German beer and you'll believe you're in old Europe. Open Monday through Saturday, lunch and dinner; Sunday, dinner only. Credit cards: AE, CB, DC, MC, and V.

Sea Catch
Canal Square
1054 31st Street, N.W.
Washington, D.C. 20007
202-337-8855

Overlooking the C&O Canal, this beautifully restored building houses some of the finest seafood preparation that Washington has to offer. Patrons can enjoy the unique raw bar which features a variety of shell fish and fish smoked on the premises. Open Monday through Saturday. Closed Sunday. Credit cards: AE, DC, MC, and V.

255

Restaurants, cont.

Tony and Joe's Seafood Place
3000 K Street, N.W.
Washington, D.C. 20007
202-944-4545

Located on the banks of the Potomac River with views of the Kennedy Center. Here you'll find all types of fresh fish and seafood dishes sure to please. Open daily, lunch and dinner. Credit cards: AE, DC, M, MC, and V.

■ SOUTHWEST WATERFRONT

Gangplank
600 Water Street, S.W.
Washington, D.C. 20024
202-554-5000

Baytrippers can walk the gangplank, or should we say "Welcome Aboard." This popular eaterie floats in some very historic waters. Specialties include salmon pot pie and grilled mahi mahi. Look for daily specials; open daily for lunch and dinner. Credit cards: AE, DC, MC, and V.

Hogate's Seafood Restaurant
800 Water Street, S.W.
Washington, D.C. 20024
202-484-6300

Hogate's has been a Washington tradition for over 50 years. House specialties are mostly seafood. My favorite is the mariner's platter. Don't forget to order the "Rumbuns." They are worth the visit. Open daily for lunch and dinner. Credit cards: C, CB, D,

Le Rivage
1000 Water Street, S.W.
Washington, D.C. 20024
202-488-8111

Le Rivage has a wonderful waterfront location with a view of the Washington Monument and the marina complex. Classic French food is served in a nice casual setting inside or out. Open daily, Monday through Friday, lunch and dinner; Saturday and Sunday, dinner only. Credit cards: AE, CB, DC, MC, and V.

Phillips Flagship
900 Water Street, S.W.
Washington, D.C. 20024
202-488-8495
202-488-8515

Located on the southwest waterfront overlooking the Washington Channel, Phillips is the perfect place to feast on local seafood. Go early-the lines are sometimes long. Open daily for lunch and dinner. Credit cards: AE, C, DC, MC, and V.

Pier 7 Inn
650 Water Street, S.W.
Washington, D.C. 20024
202-554-2500

Thoughts of my visit recall large, mildly spiced crab cakes with a pleasant aftertaste. The cole slaw was rich and creamy, and the oven fries, crisp and hot. Open daily, lunch and dinner. Credit cards: DC, MC, and V.

Accommodations

Washington has millions of visitors each year. Baytrippers who plan to spend a night, a week, or a month in the city should not do so without a reservation. Our listing includes many price ranges from camping to very expensive. Take a moment to call for a price range that suits you.

■ BED AND BREAKFASTS

Bed and Breakfast Accommodations, Ltd.
Box 1011
Washington, D.C. 20005
202-328-3510

Bed and Breakfast League
Sweet Dreams and Toast
P.O. Box 9490
Washington, D.C. 20016
202-363-7767

Adams Inn
1744 Lanier Place, N.W.
Washington, D.C. 20009
202-745-3600

Mrs. Jay's Bed and Breakfast
2951 Upton Street, N.W.
Washington, D.C. 20008
202-364-0228
800-949-3581

■ CAMPING

Cherry Hill Park
9800 Cherry Hill Road
College Park, Maryland 20740
301-937-7116

■ HOTELS, MOTELS, AND INNS

Allen Lee Hotel
2224 F Street, N.W.
Washington, D.C. 20037
202-331-1224

Best Western/Center City
1201 13th Street, N.W.
Washington, D.C. 20005
202-682-5300
800-458-2817

Best Western/Downtown
724 Third Street, N.W.
Washington, D.C. 20001
202-842-4466
800-242-4831

Capital Hilton Hotel
16th and K Streets, N.W.
Washington, D.C. 20036
202-393-1000
800-HILTONS

Channel Inn Hotel
650 Water Street, S.W.
Washington, D.C. 20024
202-554-2400
800-368-5668

Comfort Inn/Downtown
500 H Street, N.W.
Washington, D.C. 20001
202-289-5959
800-234-6423

Days Inn/Connecticut Avenue
4400 Connecticut Avenue, N.W.
Washington, D.C. 20008
202-244-5600

Days Inn/Downtown
1201 K Street, N.W.
Washington, D.C. 20005
202-842-1020
800-562-3350

Dupont Plaza Hotel
1500 New Hampshire Avenue, N.W.
Washington, D.C. 20036
202-483-6000
800-421-6662

Georgetown Suites
1000 29th Street, N.W.
Washington, D.C. 20007
202-298-1600
800-298-1688

Harrington Hotel
11th and E Streets, N.W.
Washington, D.C. 20004
202-628-8140
800-424-8532

Holiday Inn/Central
1501 Rhode Island Avenue, N.W.
Washington, D.C. 20005
202-483-2000
800-HOLIDAY

Hotels, Motels, and Inns cont.

Holiday Inn/Crowne Plaza
775 12th Street, N.W.
Washington, D.C. 20005
202-737-2200
800-HOLIDAY

Holiday Inn/Georgetown
2101 Wisconsin Avenue, N.W.
Washington, D.C. 20007
202-338-4600
800-465-4329

Holiday Inn/Thomas Circle
1155 14th Street, N.W.
Washington, D.C. 20005
202-737-1200
800-HOLIDAY

Howard Johnson Lodge
2601 Virginia Avenue, N.W.
Washington, D.C. 20037
202-965-2700

Latham Hotel/Georgetown
3000 M Street, N.W.
Washington, D.C. 20007
202-726-5000
800-368-5922

Quality Hotel/Downtown
1315 16th Street, N.W.
Washington, D.C. 20036
202-232-8000
800-368-5689

Ramada Inn/Downtown
1430 Rhode Island Avenue, N.W.
Washington, D.C. 20005
202-462-7777
800-368-5690

Windsor Inn
1842 16th Street, N.W.
Washington, D.C. 20009
202-667-0300

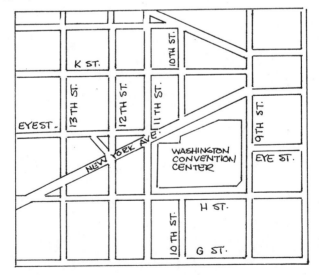

FINDING AN ADDRESS

The U.S. Capitol is the geographic center of Washington's streets. The city is divided into four quadrants—Northwest, Northeast, Southwest and Southeast. The dividing lines of each quadrant are North Capitol Street, South Capitol Street, East Capitol Street and the Mall, radiating like the spokes of a wheel from the Capitol itself.

North-South streets are numbers. East-west streets are letters in alphabetical order *(there are no J, X, Y and Z streets)*. Diagonal streets with state names, such as Rhode Island and Pennsylvania, are avenues. Circles and squares occur at the intersections of diagonal avenues and numbered and lettered streets.

As one moves away from the downtown area, streets follow in alphabetical order with two-syllable names *(Belmont, Chapin, Clifton)* and then three-syllable names *(Allison, Buchanan, etc.)* and finally streets named after flowers and trees *(Aspen, Butternut, Chestnut)* reaching out to the Washington-Maryland border in Upper Northest and Northeast.

Always check the quadrant indicator of a local address *(e.g., NW, NE, SW, SE)* before setting out since visitors will find that 500 C Street for instance can be found in four different locations, in the NW, NE, SW and SE quadrants of the nation's capital.

Jefferson Memorial

INDIAN HEAD

■ **BACKGROUND:** Legend has it that an Indian brave from across the Potomac River in Virginia fell in love with an Indian Princess who was promised to a brave from the Algonquian tribe. The girl's father told them to forget it-that she was already promised. But they continued to see each other. The Chief chopped off the brave's head and stuck it on a pole to warn other Indians that the girl was taken and to stay away. Well, you can believe the legend or not, but I can't think of a better story on how the name for this town was selected.

Attractions

■ **VISITOR INFORMATION**

Charles County Tourism
Route 6
Port Tobacco, Maryland 20677
301-934-9305
800-766-3386

■ **HISTORIC SITES**

Fort Washington
Fort Washington Road
Fort Washington, Maryland
20744
301-763-4600

The Fort is an outstanding example of an early 19th-century coastal defense. It was designed to withstand attack by wooden naval vessels armed with smoothbore artillery. Its high masonry walls, gun positions, dry moat, and drawbridge illustrate some of the principles of military science and architecture used during our Nation's early life. Open daily from 7:30 a.m. to dark. Admission charge.

■ PARKS AND GARDENS

The National Colonial Farm
3400 Bryan Point Road
Accokeek, Maryland 20607
301-283-4201

The National Colonial Farm is a recreation of a middle class, Southern Maryland tobacco plantation of the mid-18th century. Open Tuesday through Sunday, 10 a.m. to 5 p.m. Closed Monday and major holidays. Admission charge.

Parks and Gardens, cont.

Oxon Run Farm
Oxon Hill Road
Oxon Hill, Maryland 20745
301-839-1177

Old-fashioned farm with pens and pastures for common farm animals. Many varieties of vegetables are grown in the garden; why the cows are even milked by hand. Open daily, dawn to dusk. Free.

Smallwood State Park and Smallwood Retreat
Route 224
Rison, Maryland 20658
301-743-7613

The park is of interest for two reasons-one, the nature trail that takes you along the Matawoman Creek Parkland, and the second is a historic 18th century home that's been restored. The house was owned by William Smallwood, the namesake of the park and a prominent Maryland leader of the Revolutionary War era. Open daily, 8 a.m. to sunset. House open, 12 noon to 5 p.m., weekends and holidays, May to September. Free.

Restaurants

Marsh Hall
Marshall Hall Road
Bryans Road, Maryland 20616
301-283-5438

We've been coming to this friendly roadside spot for years, sure each time that the impeccably fresh seafood will be as good as on our last visit. My suggestion is to try the steamed crabs, the crab cakes, and the soft shell crab sandwich. Open Wednesday through Sunday for dinner only. Credit cards: DC, MC, and V.

Mick's Quail Inn
63 Glymont Road
Indian Head, Maryland 20640
301-743-3666

Mick's offers a dinner buffet, salad, and dessert bar. Menu includes crab, shrimp, seafood, and chicken. Open daily, lunch and dinner. Credit cards: AE, DC, MC, and V.

Accommodations

■ CAMPING

Goose Bay Marina
9365 Goose Bay Lane
Welcome, Maryland 20693
301-934-3812
301-932-0885

Smallwood State Park
Route 224
Rison, Maryland 20658
301-743-7613

■ HOTELS, MOTELS, AND INNS

Indian Head Inn
Highway 210
Indian Head, Maryland 20640
301-743-5405

PORT TOBACCO

■ **BACKGROUND:** Port Tobacco first existed as the Indian settlement of Potopaco, colonized by the English around 1634. Port Tobacco became a major seaport during the 1600's with the European ships bringing much needed goods to the colonies and returning with large hogsheads of tobacco.

Attractions

■ **VISITOR INFORMATION**

Charles County Tourism
Route 6
Port Tobacco, Maryland 20677
301-934-9305
800-766-3386

■ **HISTORIC SITES**

Charles County Courthouse
Chapel Point Road
Point Tobacco, Maryland 20677
301-932-5882
301-934-4313

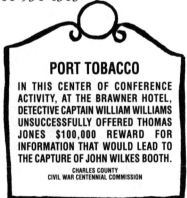

PORT TOBACCO

IN THIS CENTER OF CONFERENCE ACTIVITY, AT THE BRAWNER HOTEL, DETECTIVE CAPTAIN WILLIAM WILLIAMS UNSUCCESSFULLY OFFERED THOMAS JONES $100,000 REWARD FOR INFORMATION THAT WOULD LEAD TO THE CAPTURE OF JOHN WILKES BOOTH.

CHARLES COUNTY
CIVIL WAR CENTENNIAL COMMISSION

The present courthouse, a reconstruction, is furnished as a 19th century courtroom. Upstairs is the Charles County Museum of Port Tobacco, with exhibits on tobacco and the archeological finds of historic Port Tobacco. Open June through August, Thursday through Sunday, 12 noon to 4 p.m. Open July 4; closed other Federal holidays. Open April through May, September through mid-December, Saturday and Sunday only, 12 noon to 4 p.m. Closed January through March. Admission charge.

Mount Carmel Monastery
Mitchel Road
La Plata, Maryland 20646
301-934-1654

Founded by four Carmelite nuns on October 15, 1790, the Mount Carmel Monastery was the first convent in Colonial America. Two of the convent buildings have been restored. Open daily, 9 a.m. to 5 p.m. Free.

Thomas Stone National Historic Site
6655 Rosehill Road
Port Tobacco, Maryland 20677
301-934-6027

A plantation called Habre de Venture, owned by Thomas Stone. He was a well-respected lawyer who voted for and signed the Declaration of Independence. Open from 9 a.m. to 5 p.m., Wednesday through Sunday, September to May; and daily during June, July, and August. Closed Christmas and New Year's Day. Free.

■ MUSEUMS

The Piscataway Indian Museum
Country Lake Drive
White Plains, Maryland 20695
301-782-7622
301-372-1932

This museum attempts to educate the non-Indian public to the diversity of people who are known by the term "American Indian." Exhibits cover tribal structures, Indian art, lodging construction, and the locations of Indian communities. Live Indian art presentations of historical as well as present-day significance can be experienced at their semi-annual pow wows on the first weekend of June and the third weekend of September. Open Tuesday and Thursday, 12 noon to 4 p.m., and Sunday from 1 p.m. to 4 p.m. Free.

Museums, cont.

Surratt House Museum
9110 Brandywine Road
Clinton, Maryland 20735
301-868-1121

Built in 1852 as a middle class plantation home, this structure served as a post office and as a tavern. In the fall of 1864, the Surratt Family House became entangled in a plot to kidnap President Abraham Lincoln. This plot turned to assassination on April 14, 1865. Today the museum presents a variety of programs focusing on the fascinating web of the Lincoln Conspiracy. Open Thursday and Friday, 11 a.m. to 3 p.m.; Saturday and Sunday, 12 noon to 4 p.m. Admission charge.

■ **PARKS AND GARDENS**

Doncaster Forest
Route 6
Doncaster, Maryland 20640
301-934-2282

This woodland is heavily forested with poplar, sweet gum, white oak, and pine and is used primarily to demonstrate scientific forest management. Doncaster affords excellent hiking, hunting, and picnicking. Open daily, sunup to sundown. Free.

Myrtle Grove Wildlife Management Area
Route 225
La Plata, Maryland 20646
301-743-5161

With 834 acres for hunting, a gun range, fishing, and hiking, part of Myrtle Grove is a water impoundment for waterfowl. During their fall migratory period, great numbers of ducks and geese stop here. Open daily, dawn to dusk. Free.

Restaurants

Captain Billy's Crab House
Popes Creek Road
Newburg, Maryland 20664
301-932-4323

Captain Billy welcomes you to try his seafood platter. It includes crab cake, fried shrimp, oysters, catch of the day, and, if the season is right, soft shell crab. Open daily for lunch and dinner. Credit cards: MC and V.

Captain John's Seafood Restaurant
Route 254
Cobb Island, Maryland 20625
301-259-2315

Captain John's is one of the best when it comes to preparing the famous blue crab. I've eaten in over 400 seafood restaurants-I should know. You won't be disappointed! Open daily for breakfast, lunch, and dinner. Credit cards: MC and V.

Casey Jones
Route 6
La Plata, Maryland 20646
301-932-6226

"Casey Jones was a railroad man" and this is a railroad restaurant sitting next to the train tracks in downtown La Plata. The chef's specials include baked flounder, grilled salmon and delicious pasta. Open daily for lunch and dinner. Credit cards: AE, MC, and V.

Dexter's BBQ Pit
Route 6 West at Chapel Point Road
Port Tobacco, Maryland 20677
301-934-0672

Dexter's BBQ Pit is famous for the close-trimmed, marinated, smoked, hand-pulled, good tasting barbecue that's prepared here. Baytrippers can choose from a slab of ribs or a chicken/rib combo to piled high sandwiches of pork or beef with hot or mild sauce-it's good! Open Wednesday through Sunday for lunch and dinner.

Restaurants, cont.

Loredo's Restaurant
Route 301
White Plains, Maryland 20695
301-932-8667

If you love Mexican food, you'll love Loredo's. Steaks and seafood are also served. The atmosphere is casual and comfortable. Open daily for lunch and dinner. Credit cards: D, MC, and V.

Robertson's Crab House
Popes Creek Road
Newburg, Maryland 20664
301-934-9236

Many people travel to Robertson's just for the Maryland steamed crabs, seasoned and cooked in the home-style method famous for more than 50 years. I can't wait to return. Will I see you there? Open Memorial Day through Labor Day; closed January and February. Open weekends only in March and April. Lunch and dinner.

Shymansky's Restaurant
Route 254
Cobb Island, Maryland 20625
301-259-2881
301-259-2221

Open for many, many years, this waterside restaurant located at the bridge to Cobb Island is a favorite of the locals. The menu is extensive but I go here for cream of crab soup and crab cakes. Open daily for breakfast, lunch, and dinner. Credit cards: MC and V.

Accommodations

■ CAMPING

Aqua-Land Campground
U.S. Route 301, South
Newburg, Maryland 20664
301-259-2575

Port Tobacco Campground
1137 Shirley Boulevard
Port Tobacco, Maryland 20677
301-932-1407

■ HOTELS, MOTELS, AND INNS

Best Western
6900 Crain Highway
La Plata, Maryland 20646
301-934-4900

Holiday Inn Hotel
St. Patrick's Drive
Waldorf, Maryland 20603
301-645-8200

Days Inn
Highway 301, North
Waldorf, Maryland 20603
301-932-9200

Knights Inn
Highway 301, South
Waldorf, Maryland 20603
301-932-5090

Econo Lodge/La Plata
U.S. Highway 301, South
La Plata, Maryland 20646
301-934-1400

Super 8 Motel
Highway 301, South
La Plata, Maryland 20646
301-934-3465

Econo Lodge/Waldorf
Business Park Drive
Waldorf, Maryland 20601
301-645-0022

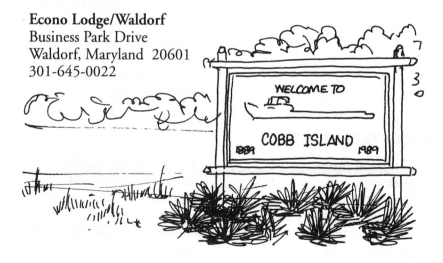

LEONARDTOWN

■ **BACKGROUND:** The first name for Leonardtown was Seymourtown. It was named in 1652 by the Provincial Governor of the State, John Seymour. The name was changed to Benedict Leonardtown in the late 17th century.

Attractions

■ **VISITOR INFORMATION**

St. Mary's County Economic and Community
Development
Route 245
Leonardtown, Maryland 20650
301-475-4411
800-327-9023

■ **BOAT RENTALS**

Quade's Store
Route 239
Bushwood, Maryland 20618
301-769-3903

Are you looking for a great way to get away? Try the small boat rentals at Quade's Store. Light tackle and bait are available if you would like to try your hand at fishing on the Wicomico River. Open seasonally, 7 a.m. to 6 p.m. Fee.

■ **MISCELLANEOUS**

**Maryland International
Raceway**
Route 234
Budd's Creek, Maryland 22610
703-368-8445
301-449-RACE

Be there as the smoke clears to watch the speed and hear the thunder of championship drag racing. Open March through November. Call for schedule. Admission charge.

■ MUSEUMS

Old Jail Museum
11 Courthouse Drive
Leonardtown, Maryland 20659
301-475-2467

See exhibits of county artifacts and memorabilia. A lady's cell is displayed. Now home of the St. Mary's County Historical Society. Open Tuesday through Saturday, 10 a.m. to 4 p.m. Closed Sunday and Monday.

St. Clement's Island/Potomac River Museum
Bayview Road
Colton's Point, Maryland 20626
301-769-2222

Located at Colton's Point, the Potomac River Museum traces history of the area and life along the Potomac River through archaeological exhibits and current events. On the Island, a cross marks the landing of the first Maryland colonist in 1634 and celebrates the first Roman Catholic Mass in English-speaking America. Open March 25 to Memorial Day: weekdays, 9 a.m. to 4 p.m.; weekends, 12 noon to 4 p.m.; October through March 24, Wednesday through Sunday, 12 noon to 4 p.m. Free.

■ PARKS AND GARDENS

St. Mary's River State Park
Chancellor's Run Road
Cosoma Road
Leonardtown, Maryland 20659
301-872-5688

St. Mary's River State Park is located at the northern end of the St. Mary's River watershed. The park shows a wide range of habitats from wooded acres and fields to swamps and small streams. A favorite attraction is the St. Mary's Lake, a trophy bass lake. Open daily, dawn to dusk. Free.

■ SEASONAL EVENTS

Annual Blessing of the Fleet
St. Clement's Island
Colton's Point, Maryland 20626
301-769-2222

This is the commemoration of the landing of the first settlers in Maryland on St. Clement's Island. Free boat rides to the island are given from Colton's Point. Points of interest: exhibits, seafood, celebration of the mass. Early October, 10 a.m. to 5 p.m. Admission charge.

St. Mary's County Oyster Festival
Route 5/St. Mary's County Fairgrounds
Leonardtown, Maryland 20650
301-863-5015

National Oyster Shucking Contest, oyster cook-off contest, oysters served every style, Southern Maryland stuffed ham sandwiches, music, exhibits. Mid-October at Fairgrounds in Leonardtown. Admission charge.

Restaurants

Sunset Bar and Grill
Route 520
Bushwood, Maryland 20618
301-769-9892

Located in the former site of the T's Cove Restaurant, the Sunset Bar and Grill features a popular all-you-can-eat buffet. Along with Maryland's #1 steamed crabs, you get corn on the cob, hush puppies, and cole slaw. Open daily for lunch and dinner.

Ye Olde Restaurant
415 Washington Street
Leonardtown, Maryland 20650
301-475-3020

Ye Olde Restaurant is located in the old movie theater, on the Square in downtown Leonardtown. Traditional starters include Soup du Jour. Choices for dinner include baked stuffed chicken breast, stuffed shrimp, fried seafood platter, and prime rib au jus. Open daily for breakfast, lunch, and dinner. Credit cards: D, MC, and V.

Accommodations

■ CAMPING

La Grande Estate Camping
Route 5
Leonardtown, Maryland 20650
301-475-8550

St. Patrick's Creek Campground
Abell Road
Abell, Maryland 20606
301-769-4099

■ HOTELS, MOTELS, AND INNS

Leonardtown Motel
Washington Street
Leonardtown, Maryland 20650
301-475-3011

ST. GEORGE ISLAND

■ **BACKGROUND:** St. George Island was founded in 1634 and is rich in history and folklore. This island in the Potomac River was invaded by the British several times during the Revolutionary War and the War of 1812. It is now a summer resort known for its crabs and cool summer breezes.

Attractions

■ **VISITOR INFORMATION**

St. Mary's County
Economic and Community Development
Route 245
Leonardtown, Maryland 20650
301-475-4411
800-327-9023

■ **BOAT CRUISES**

Dee of St. Mary's
Box 134
Piney Point, Maryland 20674
301-994-2245
301-994-0897

Captain Jack Russell sails his classic skipjack, the "Dee of St. Mary's," from St. George Island anytime the weather's good. Group charters up to 24 people. Featured are environmental tours of the St. Mary's and the Patuxent Rivers. Also enjoy crab feasts during the hot summer months and oyster roasts in the fall. Seasonal. Fee.

■ CRABBING/FISHING

Piney Point Pier
Route 249
Piney Point, Maryland 20674

Located immediately before the bridge to St. George Island, this is a 100-foot fishing and crabbing pier with picnic area. Open year round. Free.

St. George Island Pier
Route 249
St. George Island, Maryland 20674

Located at the end of Route 249, this island hideaway is a hot spot for sport crabbing and a great place to watch local watermen unload their daily catch. Open year round. Free.

■ HISTORIC SITES

Piney Point Lighthouse
Lighthouse Road
Tall Timbers, Maryland 20690
301-769-2222

The Piney Point Lighthouse was built in 1836 and is unique in its classic tower design. A newly completed walkway takes you around the grounds and down to the Potomac River. Open, dawn to dusk. Free.

■ MISCELLANEOUS

Harry Lundeberg School of Seamanship
Route 249
Piney Point, Maryland 20674
301-994-0010

The largest training facility for deep sea merchant seafarers in the United States. A museum includes a unique collection of historic maritime documents, as well as old sailing vessels of the Chesapeake Bay. Open 9 a.m. to 5 p.m., the first Sunday of each month. Free.

Restaurants

Cedar Cove Inn
Route 249
Valley Lee, Maryland 20692
301-994-1814
301-994-1155

Cedar Cove Inn is located at Cedar Cove Marina, looking out at Herring Creek. Everything here is laid back and casual. A limited menu lists sandwiches, soups, and salads. Open seasonally for breakfast, lunch, and dinner. Credit cards: MC and V.

Evan's Seafood Restaurant
Route 249
St. George Island, Maryland 20674
301-994-2299

Evan's sits in the middle of this tiny, narrow island, surrounded by tall sheltering pines. Open since 1963, it has become one of the most outstanding and well-known restaurants in the state. Specialties: fresh Maryland seafood! Open Tuesday through Friday, dinner only; Saturday, lunch and dinner. Closed Monday. Credit cards: AE, MC, and V.

The Reluctant Navigator
Tall Timbers Road
Tall Timbers, Maryland 20690
301-994-1508

Located at Tall Timbers Marina, the Reluctant Navigator relies on a strong local following, as well as the boating crowd that seeks out the restaurant in the summer. Look for fresh crab dishes on the menu and you won't be disappointed. Open for breakfast, lunch, and dinner. Seasonal. Credit cards: MC and V.

Swann's Restaurant
Route 249
Piney Point, Maryland 20674
301-994-0774

Take a step back in time with the old world charm that offers casual dining inside or out on a scenic deck. Look for fresh seafood, fabulous prime rib, and a super salad bar. Open daily for breakfast, lunch, and dinner.

Accommodations

■ **BED & BREAKFASTS**

Potomac View Farm
Tall Timber Road
Tall Timbers, Maryland 20690
301-994-0418
301-994-1508

■ **CAMPING**

Camp Merryelande
Camp Merryelande Road
St. George Island, Maryland
20674
800-382-1073

Take It Easy Campground
Route 249
Callaway, Maryland 20620
301-994-0494

Dennis Point Campground
Windmill Point Road
Drayden, Maryland 20630
301-994-2288

■ **HOTELS, MOTELS, AND INNS**

Swann's Hotel
Route 249
Piney Point, Maryland 20674
301-994-0774

ST. MARY'S CITY

■ **BACKGROUND:** The first settlers to this part of Maryland arrived in the "Ark" and "Dove" on the 25th of March, 1634. The land they purchased from the Indians included the village of Yaocomico, which they renamed St. Maries. St. Maries City served as the capital of Maryland until 1694. At that time it was moved to Annapolis. Today's St. Mary's has been relatively undisturbed by development and is thus a favorite of history buffs and archaeologists.

Attractions

■ **VISITOR INFORMATION**

St. Mary's County Economic and Community Development
Route 245
Leonardtown, Maryland 20650
301-475-4411
800-327-9023

St. Mary's Visitor Center
39 Rosecroft Road
St. Mary's City, Maryland 20686
800-SMC-1634

■ **BEACHES**

Elm's Public Beach
Forest Road
Dameron, Maryland 20628
301-475-4571

Located on the Chesapeake Bay. Pavilion, field for team sports, picnic tables, swimming. Open weekends only. Free.

■ BOAT CHARTERS

Scheible's Fishing Center
23 Wynne Road
Ridge, Maryland 20680
301-872-5185

If you're not a fishing veteran or you're unfamiliar with fishing techniques used for trolling and chumming for blues or bottom jigging for seatrout, don't be discouraged. Experienced guides are available for your convenience and fishing enjoyment. Scheible's Fishing Center has everything you need for a day of fishing or crabbing on the Chesapeake Bay. Open daily during season. Call for your schedule. Fee.

■ BOAT CRUISES

Smith Island Cruises
Box 41
Rhodes Point, Maryland 21824
410-425-2771

Smith Island is Maryland's only inhabited island accessible exclusively by boat. Comprised of three separate villages, namely Ewell, Tylerton, and Rhodes Point. History has recorded that Capt. John Smith sailed up the Chesapeake in the year 1608, came ashore here, and gave this island his name. Upon departing from Point Lookout State Park, your cruise will take a relaxing one hour and 40 minutes before entering the historic Isle of Smith. Your tour departs daily, Memorial Day through Labor Day, and weekends only during the month of September. Leaves at 10 a.m. and returns at 4 p.m. Admission charge.

■ HISTORIC SITES

Historic St. Mary's City
Route 5
St. Mary's City, Maryland 20686
301-862-0990
800-SMC-1634

St. Mary's City is a National Historic Landmark and Maryland's first capital (1634-95), an 800-acre, outdoor history museum. Attractions include the replica of the square-rigged Maryland Dove, one of the two ships that brought the first settlers and supplies from England. You'll also find the reconstructed State House of 1676, the Godiah Spray Tobacco Plantation, archaeological excavations, Farthering's Ordinary (a 17th century inn exhibit and modern restaurant), the Margaret Brent Memorial Gardens, and a visitor center with an archaeological exhibit hall. Guided walking tours are provided, and museum exhibits are open from March 25 through the last weekend in November, Wednesday through Sunday, 10 a.m. to 5 p.m. Admission charge.

■ PARKS AND GARDENS

Point Lookout State Park
Route 5
Scotland, Maryland 20687
301-872-5688

Point Lookout State Park is located at the southern tip of St. Mary's County at the confluence of the Chesapeake Bay and the Potomac River. It is the site of Fort Lincoln, an earthen fort built by Confederate prisoners. Two monuments honor the 3,364 Confederate dead from the prison camp. The visitors' center contains a Civil War Museum. You'll also discover a boat ramp, swimming, fishing, picnicking, a playground, and much, much more. Park open year round. Visitors' center and Civil War Museum open weekends, May through September. Open daily. Admission charge.

■ SEASONAL EVENTS

Maryland Days Weekend
Route 5
St. Mary's City, Maryland 20686
301-475-4411
800-327-9022

Traditionally, Maryland Days Weekend is the State's first major outdoor festival. This regional showcase includes Indian exhibits, archaeology exhibits, music, food, arts and crafts, and Civil War encampments. Two days, mid-March, 10 a.m to 5 p.m., Saturday and Sunday. Admission charge.

Stuffed Ham
Corned ham stuffed with a dressing made of kale, cabbage, celery, onions and seasonings

A Southern Maryland tradition

Seasonal Events, cont.

Militia Weekend
Route 5
St. Mary's, Maryland 20686
800-327-9023
301-475-4411

The historic Maryland capital city comes alive with a 17th century military encampment, musket and pike drills, tactical demonstrations, swordplay, pageantry, and crafts. Mid-June, two days. Admission charge.

Restaurants

Farthing's Arbor
Route 5
St. Mary's City, Maryland 20686
301-862-0990

Lunch is served to guests seated on 17th-century benches and tables by costumed waitresses. Menu items include fresh salads, sandwiches, pumpkin muffins, and garden vegetables. Open, April through August, Wednesday through Sunday. Lunch only.

Scheible's Crab Pot
23 Wynne Road
Ridge, Maryland 20680
301-872-5185

Home of some of the best fishing in the entire Chesapeake Bay. Point Lookout offers the angler more species of fish, and Scheible's offers more ways to cook them than any restaurant in the state. Entrees include crab cakes, soft shell crab, and the day's catch, fried or broiled. Open for breakfast, lunch, and dinner, May through October.

Southridge Restaurant
Route 5
Ridge, Maryland 20680
301-872-5151

Family dining in a relaxed, friendly atmosphere featuring crab cakes, steaks, soups, and salad bar. Open for lunch and dinner daily. On Sunday, breakfast buffet, lunch, and dinner. Credit cards: AE, MC, and V.

Spinnaker's Restaurant
Miller's Wharf Road
Ridge, Maryland 20680
301-872-4340

Located at the Point Lookout Marina. Keep in mind when you dine here that all meals are prepared to order; the use of fresh herbs highlights your dinner. Specialty dishes of poultry, fresh local seafood, beef, and lamb are prepared. Open, Thursday through Sunday, dinner only; Memorial Day to Labor. Credit cards: D, DC, MC, and V.

Accommodations

■ **BED AND BREAKFASTS**

Old Kirk House
Route 5
Scotland, Maryland 20687
301-872 '.093

St. Michael's Manor
Route 5
Scotland, Maryland 20687
301-872-4025

■ **CAMPING**

Point Lookout State Park
Route 5
Scotland, Maryland 20687
301-872-5688

Seaside View Campground
Seaside View Road
Ridge, Maryland 20680
301-872-4141

■ **HOTELS, MOTELS, AND INNS**

Scheible's Motel
23 Wynne Road
Ridge, Maryland 20680
301-872-5185

BLUEFISHING CAPITAL
SCHEIBLE'S
FISHING CENTER
RESTAURANT • MOTEL
NEXT RIGHT AT INTERSECTION

PATUXENT RIVER
Lexington Park to Solomons Island

Follow the water....

- Lexington Park
- Benedict
- Upper Marlboro
- Broomes Island
- Solomons Island

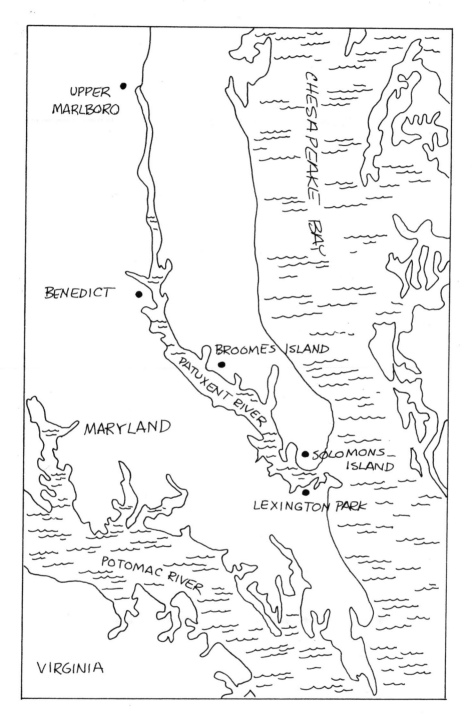

UPPER MARLBORO

CHESAPEAKE BAY

BENEDICT

BROOMES ISLAND

PATUXENT RIVER

MARYLAND

SOLOMONS ISLAND

LEXINGTON PARK

POTOMAC RIVER

VIRGINIA

LEXINGTON PARK

■ **BACKGROUND:** The first name for Lexington Park was Jarboes-ville. The name was taken from John Jarboe, one of Maryland's early French pioneers. In 1942, the Federal Government built a multi-million dollar naval air flight center and the name was changed to Lexington Park, commemorating the World War II aircraft carrier, the U.S.S. LEX-INGTON. Today this area is a haven for sport fishermen and recreational boating enthusiasts. Anyone with a keen interest in flying will marvel at the sight of the Blue Angels performing at the air flight center.

Attractions

■ **VISITOR INFORMATION**

St. Mary's County Chamber of Commerce
6260 Waldorf-Leonardtown Road (Route 5)
Mechanicsville, Maryland 20659
301-884-5555

■ **HISTORIC SITES**

Cecil's Mill Historic District
Indian Bridge Road
Great Mills, Maryland 20634
301-994-1510

Cecil's Mill Historic District includes a Christmas country store and the old mill. Listed in the National Register of Historic Places, Cecil's Flour Mill (circa 1900) and Cecil's General Store still remain and are open to sell locally-made arts and crafts. Open Friday and Saturday, mid-March through October 31; open daily November 30 through December 23. Free.

Sotterley Mansion
Jones Wharf Road
Hollywood, Maryland 20636
301-373-2280

This is a working, colonial plantation (circa 1717) graced with architectural beauty and a magnificent setting along the Patuxent River. The mansion contains period furnishings, a Chinese chippendale staircase, and other hand-carved wood works. Open daily June through October (closed Mondays). Tours begin at 11 a.m., with the last tour at 4 p.m. Tours available by appointment only in April, May, and November. Admission charge.

■ MUSEUMS

Navy Air Test and Evaluation Museum
Route 235 and Shangri-La Drive
Lexington Park, Maryland
20653
301-863-7418

The nation's only museum dedicated to testing and evaluation of naval aircraft; early photographs, vintage scale models, and full scale planes are on display. Astronauts `Glenn, Shepard, Schirra, and Carpenter received test pilot training here. Open year round. Hours in July to September 30, 10 a.m. to 5 p.m., Tuesday through Saturday, and noon to 5 p.m. on Sunday. Hours in October to June 30, 11 a.m. to 5 p.m., Tuesday through Saturday, and noon to 5 p.m. on Sunday. Closed Monday. Free.

Restaurants

The Belvedere
Route 235
Lexington Park, Maryland
20653
301-863-6666

The Belvedere offers a wide variety of seafood; house specialty, prime rib. Open breakfast, lunch, and dinner. Credit Cards: AE, DC, MC, and V.

Drift Inn Seafood
Drift Inn Road
Oraville, Maryland 20659
301-884-3470

Leonard Copsey opens his Inn only three days a week but his method of preparing crabs is one of the best the Bay has to offer. So, don't pass him by. Open April to November. Friday, dinner only; Saturday and Sunday, lunch and dinner.

Hill's Halfway House
5300 Three Notch Road
Mechanicsville, Maryland
20659
301-884-3287
301-932-6887

Hills' reputation rests with its food, say owners Billy and Linda, and that seems like a supremely logical decision. There are daily specials but my favorite is the Halfway House Platter-roast beef, stuffed ham, fried chicken breast, crab cake, baked potato, and tossed salad with rolls and butter. It sounds good, doesn't it? Open daily; breakfast, lunch, and dinner. Credit cards: AE, CB, D, DC, MC, and V.

Restaurants, cont.

Lenny's Restaurant
280 Three Notch Road
California, Maryland 20619
301-373-2965

Lenny's has served the public since 1952 and presents itself as a sharp, well-run restaurant with a full range of seafood specialties. Of special note is the Bar-B-Q Sandwich and the Southern Maryland stuffed ham. Open daily; breakfast, lunch, and dinner. Credit cards: AE, CB, MC, and V.

Sandgates Inn
Sandgates Road
Mechanicsville, Maryland
20659
301-373-5100

Oysters-on the half shell, steamed, or in a stew...these are just a couple of the treats that Sandgates offers you. Others are hot and spicy steamed crabs and delicious soft crab sandwiches. Open daily for lunch and dinner.

Accommodations

■ **BED AND BREAKFAST**

Myrtle Point
Patuxent Boulevard
California, Maryland 20619
301-862-3090

■ **HOTELS, MOTELS, AND INNS**

Belvedere Motor Inn
Route 235
Lexington Park, Maryland 20653
301-863-6666

Patuxent Inn
Route 235
Lexington Park, Maryland 20653
301-862-4100

Lord Calvert Motel
Route 235
Lexington Park, Maryland 20653
301-863-8131

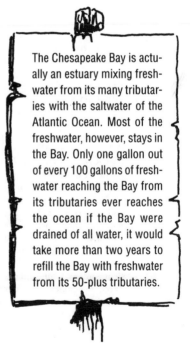

The Chesapeake Bay is actually an estuary mixing freshwater from its many tributaries with the saltwater of the Atlantic Ocean. Most of the freshwater, however, stays in the Bay. Only one gallon out of every 100 gallons of freshwater reaching the Bay from its tributaries ever reaches the ocean if the Bay were drained of all water, it would take more than two years to refill the Bay with freshwater from its 50-plus tributaries.

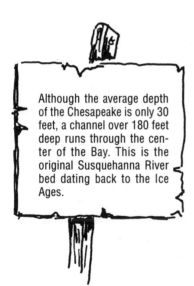

Although the average depth of the Chesapeake is only 30 feet, a channel over 180 feet deep runs through the center of the Bay. This is the original Susquehanna River bed dating back to the Ice Ages.

BENEDICT

- **BACKGROUND:** In 1695, it was known as Benedict-Leonard Town. The name was shortened in 1747 to Benedict-Town. Today, however, it's just Benedict. Both names honored Benedict Leonard Calvert, the Fourth Lord Baltimore. Benedict was one of the first designed ports established by the 1683 Act for Advancement of Trade, and it was from this port that the British marched on Washington, D.C. and burned the Capital. Today Benedict draws families with children or diners looking for great seafood.

- **VISITOR INFORMATION**

   Charles County Tourism
   Route 6 West
   Port Tobacco, Maryland 20677
   301-870-3388
   800-SO.MD.FUN

   "Booth and David Herold arrived at Dr. Mudd's home at 4 a.m. April 15. Dr. Mudd examined Booth's leg, had a splint made for him and had both him and Herold retire to an upstairs bedroom as Booth was in no condition to travel. They left between 2 and 4 p.m. that afternoon (Holy Saturday). Herold was unable to rent a carriage for their departure. They left by their own horses, down the plantation road back of Dr. Mudd's home and crossed over the Zachiah Swamp. They were next seen sitting on Brice's Chapel steps (this place is off Piney Church Road). Their next siting was at Col. Samuel Cox's home at Bel Alton, Md. Several days later they crossed the Potomac into Virginia and were captured at Garrett's Farm near Port Royal, in Virginia. It has been said Booth and Herold were about six miles off their plotted courses, all due to Booth's injury and his need for a doctor.

   Dr. Mudd did not know the real identity of his visitors (Tyler and Tyson) nor did he know that President Lincoln was assassinated the night before. Dr. Mudd was tried and convicted by a Military Court for setting Booth's leg and harboring him for a few hours. He was sent to Fort Jefferson Prison, Dry Tortugas Island, Fla. for life, June 29, 1865. He was pardoned and released by President Andrew Johnson, Feb. 8, 1869 and returned home 20 March 1869. Five children were born after he returned home: Henry, Stella, Edward, Rose DeLima and Nettie. He died Jan. 10, 1883, at the age of 49. He never regained his health as he contacted yellow fever while caring for the sick at the island prison."

   From: A History of the Role Charles County Played in the Civil War.

Attractions

■ CRABBING/FISHING

Shorter's Pier
Patuxent Avenue
Benedict, Maryland 20612
301-274-3284

If you would like to try your hand at catching the famed blue crab, give Shorter's Pier a try. It's fun! Fee.

■ HISTORIC SITES

Dr. Samuel A. Mudd House
Route 232/
Dr. Samuel Mudd Road
Gallant Green, Maryland 20601
301-743-3837
301-645-6870

Had John Wilkes Booth not injured his leg in his assassination of President Abraham Lincoln, Dr. Samuel A. Mudd would have remained an anonymous figure in America's history. The doctor, unaware of the assassin's act, set Booth's leg and housed him for several hours. Booth then continued on his way through Charles County into Virginia, where Federal troops finally caught him. The restored home of Dr. Mudd is now furnished with period pieces. Costumed docents retrace the infamous evening. Open March through November, weekends only, noon to 4 p.m. Admission charge.

■ MISCELLANEOUS

Tobacco Auctions
Route 5
Hughesville, Maryland 20659
301-870-3388

Spring in Charles County signals the opening of the tobacco auctions, at which farmers sell their previous year's crop. Auctioneers, buyers, and sellers amble down aisles of elbow-piled high tobacco with auctioneers selling a burden, which weighs about 200 pounds, within five seconds. Four of the State's seven tobacco warehouses are located in Charles County. Visitors are welcome to watch the auction. Open mid-March through April, Monday to Thursday. Doors open at 9 a.m. Free.

From an early time tobacco was marketed by consignment to a particular London or outport merchant who handled a planter's crop from the time it reached England until it was sold. The merchant received the bills of lading, ordered the cargo unloaded, paid the customs duty, carted the hogsheads to warehouses, sorted the leaf into several grades, and sold it in the market at the most advantageous price. From the time the crop left the Chesapeake until it was finally sold, it remained the property of the planter, being transported, unloaded, and stored at his risk. The consignment merchant merely served as an agent, receiving his remuneration in the form of a commission, usually two and a half or three per cent of the sale price. After depositing the net proceeds of the sale of the tobacco to the planter's account, the merchant sent him a notification of his balance. Against this credit the planter drew from time to time by means of a short note called a bill of exchange, a forerunner of the modern check.

From: Tobacco Coast by Arthur Pierce Middleton, Ph.D.
The Mariner's Museum, Newport News, VA. 1953.

Restaurants

Chappelear's Restaurant
Patuxent Avenue
Benedict, Maryland 20612
301-274-9828

Chappelear's presents casual waterfront dining. The rear porch sits out over the water. All dinners include two vegetables, hot rolls with butter, and salad. Open daily for lunch and dinner.

Ray's Bar and Grill
Desoto Landing Road
Benedict, Maryland 20612
301-274-3733

Ray's is a down home type of place where the locals like to hang out. The kitchen presents such specials as seafood platters and homemade crab cakes. Open for lunch and dinner.

Shorter's Place
Patuxent Avenue
Benedict, Maryland 20612
301-274-3284

Shorter's Place dates back to the 1930s and still maintains a following that returns year after year. Specials include a combination seafood platter and steamed oysters. Open daily for lunch and dinner.

Accommodations

■ HOTELS, MOTELS, AND INNS

Charlotte Hall Motel
Route 5
Charlotte Hall, Maryland 20622
301-884-3172

UPPER MARLBORO

■ **BACKGROUND:** Upper Marlboro is the seat of Prince George's County. It was named "Upper" to differentiate it from Lower Marlboro. The name for both came from John Churchill, the first Duke of Marlborough (1650-1722), the hero of the battle of Blenheim. Marlborough was very popular throughout the colonies. Today you can find manor houses, historic churches, tobacco fields, and cultural museums with artifacts of bygone eras.

Attractions

■ **VISITOR INFORMATION**

Calvert County Tourism
Route 2/4
Prince Frederick, Maryland 20678
800-331-9771

Prince George's County Visitors Bureau
9475 Lottsford Road
Landover, Maryland 20785
301-925-8300

■ **HISTORIC SITES**

Darnall's Chance
14800 Governor Oden Bowie Drive
Upper Marlboro, Maryland 20772
301-952-8010

Darnall's Chance was constructed in the late 17th or early 18th century. It was the home of Daniel Carroll, who signed the U.S. Constitution, and his brother, John Carroll, the first bishop of the Roman Catholic Church in America. The original building is considered to be the oldest building still standing in Prince George's County. Open Sundays, noon to 4 p.m. Admission charge.

■ HISTORIC TOWN

Lower Marlboro
Route 262
Lower Marlboro, Maryland
20736

Browse through one of the oldest towns in Maryland. This settlement, once a British port, saw the building of one of the first schools in Maryland, the Marlboro Academy. A ferry service, which crossed the Patuxent River, was established early here, and later there was a steamboat wharf. Several 18th century homes are still part of the community.

■ MISCELLANEOUS

Prince George's Equestrian Center
14955 Pennsylvania Avenue
Upper Marlboro, Maryland
20772
301-952-7990

As early as 1750, horse races were held at this track. The County owns the track which serves as an equestrian center. Special events are held here every weekend from April through November, featuring horse shows, county fairs, and concerts. Admission charge.

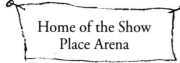

Home of the Show
Place Arena

Tobacco Auctions
Old Marlboro Pike, Route 725
Upper Marlboro, Maryland
20772
301-782-4594

Tobacco is a major cash crop in Southern Maryland. Across the countryside, fields of the "green gold" ripen as they did in the days of the plantations. Every spring buyers from around the world flock to keep time to the auctioneer's song in a pageant which has changed little over the centuries. Open mid-March through April, Monday to Thursday,. Doors open at 9 a.m. Free.

■ PARKS AND GARDENS

Merkle Wildlife Sanctuary
11704 Fenno Road
Upper Marlboro, Maryland
20772
301-888-1410

This sanctuary was named after Edward Merkle, an active conservationist who devoted much of his life to protecting wild animals and the natural environment. In 1932, he introduced Canada geese to the western shores of Maryland, and thousands of geese now migrate here each winter. The visitor center provides opportunities for nature exploration and study. Open 10 a.m. to 4 p.m., Tuesday through Sunday. Free.

Patuxent River Park
1600 Croom Airport Road
Upper Marlboro, Maryland
20772
301-627-6074

The Patuxent River Park offers access to Maryland's vast natural resources with nearly 6,000 acres devoted to hiking, boating, camping, canoeing, horseback riding, fishing, and observation. The park is open at 8 a.m. and closes approximately one hour before dark. Free.

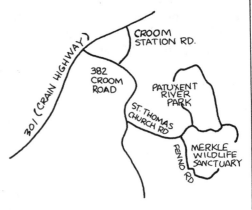

Restaurants

Big Daddy's B.B.Q.
Route 408
Wayson's Corner, Maryland
20774
410-741-0008

"All Meat Slow Cooked on a Wood Fire". If you like your ribs hand-rubbed in special seasonings and herbs, then cooked to perfection, I know you're going to love this carry out. Open daily for lunch and dinner.

Penwick House Restaurant
Route 4 South
Dunkirk, Maryland 20754
410-257-7077
301-855-5388

This country inn, filled with Victoriana, serves the finest of Maryland Tidewater cuisine. Open for lunch and dinner. Credit cards: AE, MC, and V.

Rip's Country Inn
3809 North Crain Highway
(Route 301)
Mitchellville, Maryland 20716
301-805-5901

Rip's has been serving thick steaks, prime rib, and the best of Maryland's seafood for many years. These specialties, plus a distinctive salad, are served in an atmosphere that is "handsome but unpretentious." Open daily for breakfast, lunch, and dinner. Credit cards: AE, D, DC, MC, and V.

Accommodations

■ HOTELS, MOTELS, AND INNS

Andrews Field Motel
9109 Marlboro Pike
Upper Marlboro, Maryland
20772
301-599-6000

Rips Motel
3809 North Crain Highway
(Route 301)
Mitchellville, Maryland 20716
301-805-5901
301-805-5900

Forest Hills Motel
2901 Crain Highway
Upper Marlboro, Maryland
20772
301-627-3969

BROOMES ISLAND

■ **BACKGROUND:** Broomes Island gets its name from John Brome. In 1851 he was granted "Bromes Manor," a 2000-acre tract. Descendants changed the name to its present Broome. The British attacked the Brome Plantation in 1814 and burned it to the ground. After the Civil War, Broomes Island was established as a fishing settlement. Today visitors search out tranquility, hospitality and great seafood.

Attractions

■ **VISITOR INFORMATION**

Calvert County Tourism
Route 2/4
Prince Frederick, Maryland 20678
800-331-9771

■ **HISTORIC SITES**

Port Republic School No. 7
3100 Broomes Island Road
Port Republic, Maryland 20676
410-586-8232
410-586-0482

Restored one-room school house authentically preserved with historic memorabilia. Open Memorial to Labor Day, 2 p.m. to 4 p.m., Sunday only. Free.

■ **MUSEUMS**

Jefferson Patterson Park and Museum
Route 265
St. Leonard, Maryland 20685
410-586-0050
410-586-0055

The Jefferson Patterson Park and Museum is an archaeological and environmental preserve with 512 acres of rolling pasture, woodland, and agricultural fields and 2_ miles of waterfront on the scenic Patuxent River and St. Leonard Creek. Open April 15 through October 1, 10 a.m. to 5 p.m., Wednesday through Sunday. Free.

■ PARKS AND GARDENS

Battle Creek Cypress Swamp Sanctuary
Grays Road
Prince Frederick, Maryland
20678
410-535-5327

Step back in time to a primordial world at Battle Creek Cypress Swamp Sanctuary. This 100-acre nature sanctuary contains the northernmost stand of Bald Cypress Trees in the United States, and a walk through the grounds recalls the time some 100 thousand years ago when a large part of Maryland was covered with swamps and saber-toothed tigers and mammoths roamed the landscape. Open year round, except closed every Monday, and on Thanksgiving, Christmas, and New Year's Day. Hours in April through September 30, 10 a.m. to 5 p.m., Tuesday through Saturday, and 1 p.m. to 5 p.m. on Sunday. October through March 31, closed at 4:30 p.m. Free.

BALD CYPRESS
Stop for a moment and look up. Towering 50 to 100 feet over your head is the majestic bald cypress, the most abundant tree of the swamp. Bald cypress has a flared base (for stability) and feathery needles (leaves) which are shed in the fall. Peculiar knobby projections poking through the mud are called "knees" and are extensions of the root system. The knees help brace the cypresses against high winds and may help provide oxygen to the submerged roots.

NATURE CENTER

Parks and Gardens, cont.

The Calvert Homestead
4555 Sixes Road
Prince Frederick, Maryland
20678
410-535-3786
410-535-5393

The Calvert Homestead is a small flower and herb farm that features a complete line of the highest quality hand-crafted brooms an original tobacco wreaths and ornaments. The greenhouse is filled with fresh herbs, scented geraniums and perennials. Open daily Monday through Fridays, 8 a.m to 6 p.m. Call before you come on weekends. Free.

■ SEASONAL EVENTS

Celtic Festival
10515 Mackell Road
St. Leonard, Maryland 20685
410-855-9479
410-257-9003

The Festival includes traditional highland games and dances, Celtic music, arts and crafts, as well as food and information on the rich Celtic experience. Late April. Admission charge.

Restaurants

Old Field Inn
485 Main Street
Prince Frederick, Maryland
20678
410-535-1054
301-855-1054

This old Victorian home was converted into a restaurant. The front rooms have old-fashioned fireplaces which add to the quiet dining atmosphere. Specialties include Veal Wellington, chicken of the day, and salmon parmesan. Open Tuesday through Sunday for lunch and dinner. Credit cards: AE, D, and V.

Stoney's Seafood House
Oyster House Road
Broomes Island, Maryland
20615
410-586-1888

Stoney's is a drop-in kind of seafood place on the shores of Island Creek. Seafood chowder is a specialty as are the "fresh catches" which could include a variety of local Patuxent River fish. Also featured is crab soup, crab cakes, and cooked-to-order steamed crabs layered with Stoney's secret spices. Open daily for lunch and dinner. Credit Cards: MC and V.

Accommodations

■ CAMPING

Matoaka Beach Cabins
Box 124
Calvert Beach Road
St. Leonard, Maryland 20685
410-586-0269

Patuxent Campsites
Box 832 Williams Wharf Road
Prince Frederick, Maryland 20678
410-586-9880

SOLOMONS ISLAND

■ **BACKGROUND:** Solomons Island was originally called Bourne's Island (1680), then Summerville's Island (1740). It became known as Solomons Island because of Isaac Solomon's oyster packing facilities here. Shipyards developed to support the island's fishing fleet. The feigned bug-eye sailing crafts were built here in the 19th century. The deep-protected harbor has been a busy marine center ever since. In the War of 1812, Commodore Joshua Barney's flotilla sailed from here to attack British vessels on the Chesapeake Bay. Whether you come for seafood or sightseeing, boating or browsing, hiking or history, Solomons has something for everyone.

Attractions

■ **VISITOR INFORMATION**

Calvert County Tourism
Route 2/4
Prince Frederick, Maryland 20678
800-331-9771

■ **BOAT CHARTERS**

Bunky's Charter Boats, Inc.
Box 379, Main Street
Solomons, Maryland 20688
410-326-3241

Thirteen charter boat fleet, rental boats. Open seven days, 6 a.m. to 8 p.m. Seasonal. Fee.

James Sport Fishing Charters
Calvert Marina
Solomons Island, Maryland 20688
410-798-0607
800-322-4039

Captain Glenn James offers the ultimate Chesapeake Bay fishing trip. Leave from Solomons Island and fish the Lower Bay on day one. Stay overnight at Somers Cove Motel in Crisfield, and then fish Tangier Sound on the second day. Seasonal. Fee.

Solomons Charter Captains
Box 831
Solomons Island, Maryland
29688
410-326-2670

For sports fishing enthusiasts, Solomons has one of the largest charter boat fleets on the Chesapeake. Licensed captains offer full and half-day fishing trips. For your day on the Bay, let an experienced captain steer you to the perfect spot to angle for the plentiful blues, trout, drum, flounder, and bass. Seasonal. Fee.

■ BOAT CRUISES

Wm. B. Tennison
14200 Solomons Island Road
Solomons, Maryland 20688
410-326-2042

The Calvert Marine Museum offers cruises aboard the oldest Coast Guard-licensed, passenger vessel on the Chesapeake Bay. Sail busy Solomons inner harbor; see Solomons Island and the Chesapeake Biological Laboratory. Cruise past the United States Naval Recreation Center at Point Patience, and pass underneath the Governor Thomas Johnson Bridge. These cruises are held May through October. This one-hour cruise departs at 2 p.m. on Wednesday through Sunday. Admission charge.

■ BOAT RENTALS

Solomons Boat Rentals
Solomons Island Road
Solomons, Maryland 20688
410-326-4060

William Stewart offers Bay-trippers a chance to have fun on the Bay, sail, cruise, fish, crab, or water ski. All types of boats are offered. Call for weekly specials. Fee.

■ MISCELLANEOUS

**Calvert Cliffs Nuclear Power
Plant**
Route 2/4
Lusby, Maryland 20657
410-260-4673

An exhibit built inside a working tobacco barn that in part dates back to 1818. The visitors center has been transformed to let you "walk through the ages." Outside an award-winning overlook gives you an unparalleled view of the Chesapeake Bay with the Nuclear Power Plant spread on its shore before you. Open from 10 a.m. to 4 p.m. every day except major holidays. Free.

■ MUSEUMS

Calvert Marine Museum
14200 Solomons Island Road
Solomons Island, Maryland
20688
410-326-2042

The rich maritime history and diversity of life found in the Chesapeake Bay come alive in this unusual museum in Solomons. Here you'll find boats, models, paintings, wood carvings, aquariums, and fossils. Outdoor exhibits include a boat basin and a recreated salt marsh. You can also visit the restored Drum Point Lighthouse, one of the last of its kind on the Chesapeake. Nearby the J.C. Lore Oyster House features a boatbuilding exhibit and artifacts of the local seafood industry. Open daily 10 a.m. to 5 p.m. Closed major holidays. Admission charge.

■ PARKS AND GARDENS

Calvert Cliffs State Park
Route 2/4
Lusby, Maryland 20657
301-888-1622
301-888-1410

On the western side of the Chesapeake Bay, the Calvert Cliffs dominate the shore for 30 miles. These cliffs were formed over 15 million years ago. There are 13 miles of marked foot trails for hiking in the Park, and Baytrippers may hunt for fossils on the open beach, though no digging or climbing is allowed. Open April through October, 8 a.m. to 6 p.m. Free.

Flag Ponds Nature Park
Route 2/4
Lusby, Maryland 20657
410-535-5327
410-586-1477

Here on 327 acres you are surrounded by the beauty the Chesapeake Bay area has to offer. Baytrippers will discover a wide variety of native wildlife including muskrat, otter, white-tailed deer, turkey, fox, and the majestic Pileated Woodpecker. The flora ranges from the venerable hardwood trees to the native Blue Flag Iris, which gives Flag Ponds Nature Park its name. Open from 10 a.m. to 6 p.m. daily, from Memorial Day through Labor Day. Admission charge.

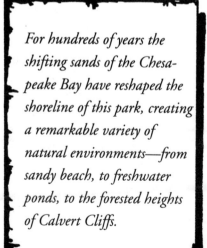

For hundreds of years the shifting sands of the Chesapeake Bay have reshaped the shoreline of this park, creating a remarkable variety of natural environments—from sandy beach, to freshwater ponds, to the forested heights of Calvert Cliffs.

Flag Ponds Nature Park offers three miles of gentle hiking trails, observation platforms overlooking two ponds, a wetlands boardwalk, a beach and fishing pier on the Chesapeake Bay, and a visitor's center with wildlife exhibits.

- ## SEASONAL EVENTS

Patuxent River Appreciation Days
Main Street
Solomons Island, Maryland 20688
410-326-3719
410-326-2042

Baytrippers take note! There will be boat rides, lighthouse tours, entertainment, a wood carving display, fossil collecting, arts and crafts, and a parade. Held early October, it runs from 10 a.m. to 5 p.m. on Saturday and Sunday. Free.

A Solomons Christmas
Main Street
Solomons Island, Maryland 20688

Annual Solomons Christmas walk. It's a festive Solomons Island open house weekend. The merrymaking includes a candlelight walk, boat light parade, live nativity scene, breakfast with Santa, refreshments, and good cheer. The first weekend in December. Fee.

Restaurants

Bowen's Inn
Solomons Island Road
Solomons, Maryland 20688
410-326-9814

Calvert County has been called "the charm of the Chesapeake" and nowhere is this more evident than at this waterfront inn. When we asked the waiter what's cooking now, we were told that the crab soup had just come off the fire and the crab cakes were freshly made. We selected both, and the results were mighty good. Open daily, lunch, and dinner. Credit cards: MC and V.

Lunch & Dinner

China Harbor
77 Charles Street
Solomons, Maryland 20688
410-326-6888

China Harbor offers "casual dining with a taste of the Orient". Delicious authentic Chinese cuisine is served in a delightful waterfront dining room. Open Thursday through Sunday. Dinner only.

Dry Dock Restaurant
C Street
Solomons, Maryland 20688
410-326-4817

Zahniser's Dry Dock Restaurant has it all-fine food and drink and a spectacular view. House specialties include shrimp bisque, shrimp scampi, grilled salmon, flounder and crab Florentine, scallops, spiced shrimp, crab cakes, and soft-shell crabs. Open Monday through Saturday, dinner only; Sunday, brunch and dinner. Closed Tuesday during the off season. Credit cards: AE, C, MC, and V.

The Frying Pan
Route 765
Lusby, Maryland 20657
410-326-1125

The Frying Pan restaurant offers delicious, home-cooked meals "just like mom used to make." House specialties include liver and onions, baked chicken, spaghetti and meatballs and much, much more. Open daily for breakfast, lunch, and dinner.

311

Restaurants, cont.

Lighthouse Inn
Patuxent Avenue
Solomons, Maryland 20688
410-326-2444

Inside you gaze through a two-story wall of glass that overlooks the harbor. The "Skipjack Bar," the Inn's most unusual feature, was modeled from an actual oyster boat. House specialties include steamed clams, crab cocktail, clams casino, cream of crab soup, catch of the day, stuffed flounder, fried shrimp, and crab imperial. Open daily for lunch and dinner. Credit cards: MC and V.

The Maryland Way
Routes 2/4
Solomons, Maryland 20688
410-326-6311

This restaurant is part of the Solomons Holiday Inn Hotel Conference Center and Marina. If you stop here for dinner, I suggest you try the hot sampler. Here oysters casino, oysters Rockefeller, clams casino, clams Rockefeller, and mussels are featured. It's a great way to sample the Bay's bounty. Open daily, breakfast, lunch, and dinner. Credit cards: AE, CB, D, DC, MC, and V.

The Naughty Gull
499 Lore Street
Solomons, Maryland 20688
410-326-4855

The Naughty Gull Restaurant sits in a cove shaded by pine trees. Daily offerings include crab cake platter, shrimp scampi, surf & turf, stuffed shrimp, crab imperial. Open daily for lunch and dinner. Credit cards: MC and V.

Restaurants, cont.

Solomons' Pier Restaurant
Solomons Island Road
Solomons, Maryland 20688
410-326-2424

All seating is highlighted by the breathtaking view of the sunset and the spectacular span of the Thomas Johnson Bridge. House specialties include the seafood platter, stuffed shrimp, steamed seafood dinner, crab fluff, clams on the half-shell, clams casino, steamed oysters, crab cakes, and crab imperial. Open daily for lunch and dinner. Credit cards: AE, C, MC, and V.

Vera's White Sands
White Sands Drive
Lusby, Maryland 20657
410-586-1182

Oh, there are white sands at Vera's, but there is also much, much more. The surroundings look like the set of a Hollywood studio. The thatched room is jammed full of treasures that Vera has brought back from her travels around the world. House specialties include stuffed shrimp, crab imperial, and the catch of the day. Open for dinner only, Tuesday through Saturday; Sunday, open for lunch and dinner. Credit cards: C, MC, and V.

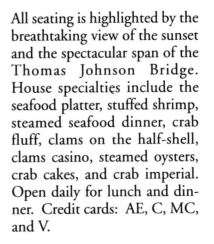

Accommodations

■ BED AND BREAKFAST

Back Creek
A and Calvert Streets
Solomons Island, Maryland 20688
410-326-2022

By-the-Bay
Calvert Street
Solomons Island, Maryland 20688
410-326-3428

Davis House B&B
Charles and Malthby Streets
Solomons Island, Maryland 20688
410-326-4811

■ HOTELS, MOTELS, AND INNS

Bowen's Inn
Solomons Island Road
Solomons, Maryland 20688
410-326-9814

Holiday Inn Hotel
155 Holiday Drive
Solomons, Maryland 20688
410-326-6311

Comfort Inn
Lore Street
Solomons, Maryland 20688
410-326-6303
800-228-5150

SOLOMON'S ISLAND

ORIGINALLY CALLED BOURNE'S (1680).
THEN SOMERVELL'S ISLAND (1740). IT
BECAME KNOWN AS SOLOMON'S ISLAND
BECAUSE OF ISAAC SOLOMONS' OYSTER
PACKING FACILITIES HERE. SHIPYARDS
DEVELOPED TO SUPPORT THE ISLANDS
FISHING FLEET. THE FAMED 'BUGEYE'
SAILING CRAFT WERE BUILT HERE IN THE
19th CENTURY. THE DEEP, PROTECTED
HARBOR HAS BEEN A BUSY MARINE CENTER
EVER SINCE. IN THE WAR OF 1812,
COMMODORE JOSHUA BARNEY'S FLOTILLA
SAILED FROM HERE TO ATTACK BRITISH
VESSELS ON THE CHESAPEAKE BAY.

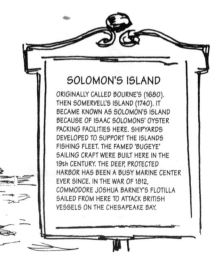

ANNAPOLIS

Chesapeake Beach to Annapolis

Follow the water....

- Chesapeake Beach
- North Beach
- Rose Haven
- Deale
- Shady Side
- Galesville
- Edgewater
- Annapolis

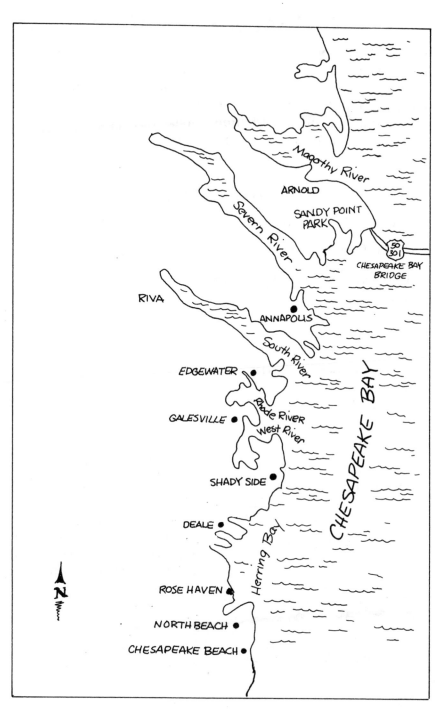

CHESAPEAKE BEACH

■ **BACKGROUND:** Chesapeake Beach was named and incorporated by the Maryland Assembly in 1894. The town became a bustling resort in the early 1900s. Trains brought politicians and their lady friends. They were joined by thousands of others who had come to enjoy sandy beaches and a picturesque waterfront. Today Chesapeake Beach is undergoing great changes-new condos, sidewalks, and a new town center.

Attractions

■ **VISITOR INFORMATION**

Calvert County Tourism
Routes 2 and 4
Prince Frederick, Maryland 20678
800-331-9771

Chesapeake Beach Town Hall
8200 Bayside Road
Chesapeake Beach, Maryland
20732
410-257-2230

■ **BEACHES**

Breezy Point
5230 Breezy Point Road
Chesapeake Beach, Maryland
20732
301-855-1243 ext. 225

Breezy Point Beach has a lot to offer. My favorite is the half mile of sandy beach on the Chesapeake Bay with netted swimming area and the beautiful shaded picnic area. Open daily, May 31 to September 1. Admission charge.

■ BOAT CHARTERS

Rod 'N Reel Charters
Mears Avenue
Chesapeake Beach, Maryland
20732
301-855-8450
800-233-2080

Chesapeake Beach is the "Charter Fishing Capital of Maryland." Large parties are accommodated. Baytrippers can enjoy six-hour trips, eight-hour trips, or experience the thrill of fishing from a headboat. Private charters are welcome. Open seasonally. Call the Dockmaster for your schedule and departure times. Fee.

Seaside Charters
Harbor Road
Chesapeake Beach, Maryland
20732
301-855-4665

Depart from Fishing Creek for a day on the Bay. The Bay is plentiful with bluefish, rockfish, and flounder; and Seaside Charters offer tackle and bait, along with the knowledge of how to land the "big ones". Half-day trips and all-day trips available. Call for departure times. Fee.

■ MUSÉUMS

Chesapeake Beach Railway Museum
Mears Avenue
Chesapeake Beach, Maryland 20732
410-257-3892

The Chesapeake Beach Railway Museum captures some of the history and charm of the early days. Memories of the railroad/resort era evoke surges of nostalgia. It's ironic that the trains which transported the people also brought the cars that replaced the train. Open daily, May through September, 1 p.m. to 4 p.m. Open weekends only, April and October, 1 p.m. to 4 p.m. Winter, open by appointment. Admission charge.

■ PARKS AND GARDENS

Bay Front Park
Route 261
Chesapeake Beach, Maryland
20732
410-257-2230

A delightful park awaits Baytrippers who are in search of a wonderful way to enjoy the beautiful Chesapeake Bay. Walk the Timber Walkway, fossil hunt, fish, or swim (no lifeguards). Open daily, sunup to sundown. Free.

Chesapeake Beach Water Park
4079 Creekside Drive
Chesapeake Beach, Maryland
20732
410-257-1404

Up a lazy river on the ole Creekside, rent yourself a tube and slide, slide, slide. Young and old alike will take delight in this state of the art water park. This is a family friendly place that is suited to all ages and all levels of swimming ability. Open seasonally Memorial Day to Labor Day. Admission charge.

■ SEASONAL EVENTS

Founder's Day Celebration
Mears Avenue
Chesapeake Beach, Maryland
20732
410-257-2735

A lineup of old fashioned fun and games will please everyone who makes the trek to this Calvert County hamlet. The Antique Car Run features over 100 vintage automobiles. Also on track will be Dixieland and school bands, as well as a calliope, clowns, and master magicians. Founder's Day is the perfect time to discover Chesapeake Beach. Annual mid-May event. Free.

Restaurants

Abner's Seaside Crabhouse
Harbor Road
Chesapeake Beach, Maryland
20732
410-257-3689

"Famous since 1963," Abner's has a reputation for preparing good steamed crabs. Open daily for lunch and dinner. Credit cards: MC and V.

Lagoons Island Grille
8416 Bayside Road
Chesapeake Beach, Maryland
20732
410-257-7091

A recent lunch at Lagoons revealed its warm, warm country colors, island music and small island touch. I love my seafood and was impressed by the seafood puff stew. Open daily for lunch and dinner. Credit cards: MC and V.

Rod 'N Reel Restaurant
Mears Avenue
Chesapeake Beach, Maryland
20732
410-257-2735

This restaurant can accommodate a large number of diners. A Bay sampler includes such specials as crab cake, crab imperial, and soft shell crab platters. Open daily for lunch and dinner; breakfast on weekends includes Sunday brunch. Credit cards: AE, M, and V.

The Sea Breeze
8132 Bayside Road
Chesapeake Beach, Maryland
20732
410-257-6126

The Sea Breeze has a complete menu featuring Italian cuisine along with seafood, prime rib, and steaks. Open daily for breakfast, lunch, and dinner. Credit cards: MC and V.

Smokey Joe's Grill
Mears Avenue
Chesapeake Beach, Maryland
20732
410-257-2427

A bottle of beer, a batch of BBQ'd baby back ribs, and a Bay view. Open weekdays for dinner only; weekends for lunch and dinner.

Wesley Stinnett's
8617 Bayside Road
Chesapeake Beach, Maryland
20732
410-257-6100

Famous for home-cooked, country style meals. Specials include boneless chicken breasts, fried chicken, and swordfish fixed any way you want it. Open daily for breakfast, lunch, and dinner. Credit cards: MC and V.

Accommodations

■ **BED AND BREAKFASTS**

Tidewater Treasures
7315 Bayside Road
Chesapeake Beach, Maryland
20732
410-257-0785

■ **CAMPING**

Breezy Point
5230 Breezy Point Road
Chesapeake Beach, Maryland
20732
410-257-2561

NORTH BEACH

■ **BACKGROUND:** North Beach has had a strong and colorful history. In 1924, it boasted Victorian hotels, rooming houses, and a grand pier that extended 200 feet into the Bay. Excursion boats brought visitors from Baltimore, and a busy trolley ran between North Beach and the neighboring resort, Chesapeake Beach. A decline began with the Great Depression. In a vain attempt to revive tourism, gambling was legalized, and the town's hotels and restaurants gave way to the casinos and taverns. Gambling continued until 1968. Today redevelopment of the town is in progress, and new condominiums and retail shops have opened.

Attractions

■ VISITOR INFORMATION

Town Hall
8916 Chesapeake Avenue
North Beach, Maryland 20714
410-257-9618

■ BEACHES

North Beach Public Beach
Bay Avenue
North Beach, Maryland 20714
410-257-9618

Families and friends flock to this bayside beach to sun and swim. Open daily, year round. Free.

■ CRABBING/FISHING

North Beach Fishing Pier
Bay Avenue
North Beach, Maryland 20714
410-257-9618

The North Beach Baywalk spans ten blocks, with the main pier stretching out 200 feet into the Bay. Excellent crabbing and fishing. Open daily, sunup to sundown. Free.

■ SEASONAL EVENTS

North Beach Days Festival
8916 Chesapeake Avenue
North Beach, Maryland 20714
410-257-9618

The tiny town of North Beach swells to over 10,000 people who come for crabs, beer, music, food, and fun for the whole family. Held annually in late August. Free.

Restaurants

Neptune's Seafood Pub
8800 Chesapeake Avenue
North Beach, Maryland 20714
410-257-7899

Mussels with garlic is just one of the house specials. Chef and owner Bil Shockley is a graduate of the Culinary Institute of America. You will enjoy his seafood delights in a pub-like atmosphere. Open daily for lunch and dinner. Credit cards: MC and V.

Accommodations

■ BED AND BREAKFASTS

Westlawn Inn
9200 Chesapeake Avenue
North Beach, Maryland 20714
410-257-1069

ROSE HAVEN

■ **BACKGROUND:** Archaeological studies suggest that the Rose Haven area was occupied primarily during the summer months by small groups from an Indian tribe which returned intermittently from about 400 A.D. to 900 A.D. Here they built wigwams, used shell money, made grooved stone axes, and net-marked pottery. Their fondness for oysters and clams is evidenced today by the numerous shells found in their refuse pits and large shell heaps along the shores. Hence, the Indian name "Chesapeake," which meant "Great Shellfish Bay." Most of the artifacts uncovered at Rose Haven are now under study at the Maryland Geological Survey Lab in Baltimore. Additional artifacts are on exhibit in Merryman Hall at Johns Hopkins University.

Attractions

■ **VISITOR INFORMATION**

**Annapolis and Anne Arundel County
Visitors Bureau**
26 West Street
Annapolis, Maryland 21401
410-280-0445

■ **BOAT CHARTERS**

Lucky Duck
7149 Lake Shore Drive
Rose Haven, Maryland 20714
410-257-2927

Captain J.F. Rupp offers fishing trips tailored to your special interests. Full-day trips and half-day trips leave the Herrington Harbor dock at 6:30 a.m. All you have to do is show up. Call for schedule. Fee.

Restaurants

Herrington on the Bay
7149 Lake Shore Drive
Rose Haven, Maryland 20714
410-741-5101
301-855-8435

House specialties include baked stuffed shrimp, catch of the day, fried flounder, broiled scallops, crab cakes, crab imperial, fried oysters, sauteed soft shell crabs, shrimp scampi, stuffed baked avocado, stuffed flounder, and cream of crab soup. Open seasonally for lunch and dinner. Credit cards: C, MC, and V.

Accommodations

■ **HOTELS, MOTELS, AND INNS**

Herrington Inn
7149 Lake Shore Drive
Rose Haven, Maryland 20714
410-741-5100

DEALE

■ **BACKGROUND**: Deale's chief activity is fishing—both commercial and charter. Businesses are clustered around the small Rockhold Creek Bridge. Deale sits on a broad peninsula formed by Rockhold Creek, Herring Bay, and Parker's Creek. Since the village was founded in the late 1700s, thousands of boats have lined Rockhold Creek. They are now served by many marinas dotting the shoreline.

Attractions

■ **VISITOR INFORMATION**

Annapolis and Anne Arundel County
Visitors Bureau
26 West Street
Annapolis, Maryland 21401
410-280-0445

■ **BOAT CHARTERS**

Chesapeake Bay Sports Fishing
and Charters
5935 Rockhold Creek Road
Deale, Maryland 20751
410-867-4101
800-675-4103

All-inclusive fishing trips with hundreds of available boats to choose. Call Captain Larry Thomas. Seasonal. Fee.

■ **BOAT CRUISES**

Chesapeake Bay Adventures
5935 Rockhold Creek Road
Deale, Maryland 20751
410-867-4101
800-394-4101

During your cruise, you will experience the daily life on the Bay, see watermen harvest their catches live, and enjoy the picturesque shoreline with its diverse wildlife and historic waterfront towns. Knowledgeable and experienced guides share their environmental views and facts of nature. Seasonal. Fee.

■ **SEASONAL EVENTS**

South County Festival
389 Deale Road
Tracy's Landing, Maryland
20779
410-867-4343
410-867-3129

Highlights of this annual festival include live entertainment, Civil War re-enactments, Indian demonstrations, pony rides, face painting, and food, food, food. Held in mid-May. Free.

Restaurants

Happy Harbor Inn
533 Deale Road
Deale, Maryland 20751
410-867-0949

Home of the
Deale Water Taxi
410-867-0949

This restaurant is located on the water at the foot of Rockhold Creek Bridge. Offerings include homemade crab cakes on a bun and special seafood dinners. Open daily for breakfast, lunch, and dinner.

Skipper's Pier
6158 Drum Point Road
Deale, Maryland 20751
410-867-7100

A white cockatoo named Bucktail will greet you at this popular restaurant on the water. Skipper's Pier features home-cooked food, fresh seafood specials, and great steamed crabs. Open for lunch and dinner daily; breakfast, weekends. Credit cards: MC and V.

Accommodations

■ **BED AND BREAKFASTS**

Makai Pierside Bed and Breakfast
5960 Vacation Lane
Deale, Maryland 20751
410-867-0998
410-261-9580

SHADY SIDE

■ **BACKGROUND:** A tiny bayside community, off the beaten path. Shady Side was once a steamboat stop. Before the post office opened in 1886, the town's name was Sedgefield, named after the sedge grass found in marshy areas.

Attractions

■ **VISITOR INFORMATION**

Annapolis and Anne Arundel County Visitors Bureau
26 West Street
Annapolis, Maryland 21401
410-280-0445

■ **MUSEUMS**

Captain Salem Avery House
1418 E.W. Shady Side Road
Shady Side, Maryland 20764
410-867-4486

Built around 1860 on the banks of the West River. Cap'n. Avery, a Long Island fisherman, came to the area to make his living from the abundant Chesapeake Bay. The museum protects, documents, and illustrates the history and tradition of this unique corner of Southern Maryland. Open, Sunday only, 1 p.m. to 4 p.m. Free.

Restaurants

Bay View Inn
Cedarhurst on the Bay
Shady Side, Maryland 20764
410-867-7373

Take a shore drive in the country and dine in a 200-year-old manor house. Regular menu features veal, steaks, seafood, and poultry. Prime rib is served on weekends. Closed Tuesday. Open for lunch and dinner daily; Sunday for brunch and dinner. Credit cards: AE, MC, and V.

Snug Harbor Inn
1484 Snug Harbor Road
Shady Side, Maryland 20764
410-867-0911

Snug Harbor Inn is a single-story building that has always been a bar and graduated to a fine dining spot over the last few years. During a recent visit I enjoyed some of the best stuffed soft shell crabs that I've ever eaten. The fresh crabs were packed with a crab cake mixture, then dipped in a batter, and fried to perfection. The result was a crispy crunchy crab that had me wishing for more. I can't wait to return. Open daily for lunch and dinner. . Credit cards: MC and V.

GALESVILLE

■ **BACKGROUND:** You'll find luscious food, lively people, and leisurely shopping. Galesville has, the locals say, one main road, one traffic light, and hundreds of boat slips. The town has barely changed over the past 50 years.

Attractions

■ **VISITOR INFORMATION**

Annapolis and Anne Arundel County
Visitors Bureau
26 West Street
Annapolis, Maryland 21401
410-280-0445

■ **FISHING PIERS**

The Memorial Pier
Riverside Drive
Galesville, Maryland 20765

Crabbing hot spot. Stalking the blue crab or learning "how to be a chicken-necker" will leave you happy as a clam. Open dawn to dusk. Free.

Restaurants

Inn at Pirates Cove
Riverside Drive
Galesville, Maryland 20765
410-867-2300

House specialties include broiled shellfish platter, lobster tail, shrimp, scallops, oysters on the half shell, and cream of crab soup. Open daily for lunch and dinner. Credit cards: AE, MC, and V.

Steamboat Landing
4850 Riverside Drive
Galesville, Maryland 20765
410-867-4600

Steamboat Landing prides itself on daily, innovative specials, as well as traditional Maryland favorites. Dine inside, or ask for outdoor seating on their spacious, wraparound deck. Closed Monday. Open daily for lunch and dinner. Credit cards: AE, MC, and V.

Top Side Inn
Riverside Drive
Galesville, Maryland 20765
410-867-1321

Breakfasts on the weekend overlooking the river are always a treat. Other specialties are the delightful homemade soups-vegetable crab, cream of crab, and clam chowder. Open daily for lunch and dinner; breakfast available on weekends. Credit cards: AE, C, MC, and V.

Accommodations

■ BED AND BREAKFASTS

Casablanca Yacht Bed and Boat
4801 Riverside Drive
Galesville, Maryland 20765
410-261-5959

■ HOTELS, MOTELS, AND INNS

Inn at Pirates Cove
4801 Riverside Drive
Galesville, Maryland 20765
410-867-2300

EDGEWATER

■ **BACKGROUND**: Edgewater was once better known as London Town, a once-thriving seaport village covering about 100 acres on the southern shore of the South River. It provided a stopping place and ferry service for travellers making the journey between Williamsburg and Philadelphia. George Washington, Thomas Jefferson, and Francis Scott Key noted making the crossing here.

Attractions

■ **VISITOR INFORMATION**

Annapolis and Anne Arundel County
Visitors Bureau
26 West Street
Annapolis, Maryland 21401
410-280-0445

■ **BOAT RENTALS**

American Powerboat School
2820 Solomon's Island Road
Edgewater, Maryland 21403
410-721-7517

Powerboating, fishing, sailing— one call does it all!! The most unique fleet on the Bay offers ski boats, sportboats, cruisers, motorboats, and trawlers. Rentals/charters, excursions, and instruction. Vacation packages. Open daily, April through October. Fee.

■ HISTORIC SITES

**Londontown Publik House
and Gardens**
839 Londontown Road
Edgewater, Maryland 21037
410-222-1919

Sitting atop a knoll by the South River, an 18th-century brick house offers visitors a sense of the lifestyle of our colonial settlers. This structure was once home to William Brown, a planter and cabinetmaker of his day. Eight acres adjoining the Publik House have been planted to preserve and enhance their natural beauty. Visitors may wander through spring walks massed with daffodils, azaleas, magnolias, wildflowers, and ferns. Native trees, shrubs, and flowers have been given special emphasis throughout the garden, and daylilies blooming in profusion offer magnificent displays in the summer. Open Tuesday through Saturday, 10 a.m. to 4 p.m.; Sunday, noon to 4 p.m. Closed major holidays and on weekends, November 15 to March 15. Admission charge.

GAZEBO GARDEN

Restaurants

Hayman's Crab House
3105 Solomon's Island Road
Edgewater, Maryland 21037
410-956-5656

Open since 1971, this well-known, full-service restaurant and seafood market features soft shell crab, imperial crab, crab meat salad, steamed crabs, and Mrs. Hayman's crab soup. Open daily for lunch and dinner. Credit cards: AE, MC, and V.

Lou's Woodlawn Restaurant
145 Mayo Road
Edgewater, Maryland 21037
410-956-5115

The country buffet features a variety of old-time favorites and offers all you can eat from 5 a.m. to 9 p.m. on Tuesday through Saturday. Selections include fried chicken, BBQ'd ribs, fish, spaghetti, lasagna, vegetables, casseroles, homemade soup, and salad bar items. Open daily for lunch and dinner. Credit cards: MC and V.

Accommodations

■ **BED AND BREAKFASTS**

Riverwatch
145 Edgewater Drive
Edgewater, Maryland 21037
410-974-8152

Facts About Your Chesapeake Bay

The Chesapeake Bay is America's largest estuary, one of the last major healthy ones. An estuary is a mixture of a river and the sea, more precisely defined as a semi-enclosed body of water which has a free connection with the open sea and within which sea water is measurably diluted by fresh water from land drainage.

Also, the Bay is an ecosystem—a unit in which all four of the earth's major components—air, land, living things and water—are continuously interacting.

Vital Statistics

Length — 195 miles.
Width — Ranges from 3 to 22 miles.
Depth — Average is 21 feet. Deepest area is 174 feet off Bloody Point at the southern end of Kent Island.
Area — 3,237 square miles.

A total of 46 principal rivers and streams flow into the Chesapeake, some of the chief rivers being the Susquehanna, the Northeast, the Elk, the Bohemia, the Sassafras, the Bush, the Gunpowder, the Middle, the Back, the Patapsco, the Choptank, the Patuxent, the James, the Rappahannock, the York, the Honga, the Nanticoke, the Wicomico, the Pocomoke and the Potomac.

The tributaries of the Bay drain an area of 64,000 square miles in New York, Pennsylvania, Virginia, West Virginia, Delaware, and Maryland.

Technically, the Chesapeake is the southern extremity of the Susquehanna River Valley. It was flooded by ocean water when sea level rose as a result of melting glaciers. The Chesapeake is approximately 10,000 years old, very young geologically speaking.

As a drowned valley estuary, the Chesapeake differs from the fjords of Norway and estuaries of the Pacific northwest which were scoured out of the land by glaciers, bays like San Francisco created by earthquakes and other violent land shifts and water areas such as Biscayne Bay in Miami and Sinepuxent Bay in Ocean City formed by development of barrier reefs.

Source: Maryland Department of
Natural resources, Annapolis, MD.

ANNAPOLIS

■ **BACKGROUND:** During the 1700s, Annapolis was the seat of Maryland's colonial government. It became a wealthy and cultured town, made prosperous by its location on the Severn River, its busy port, and neighboring productive farms. Baltimore Harbor later replaced the Severn as a transport center, and Annapolis lost its status as a major port. Port or not, the City remained an important political and military center, and in 1845, the Naval Academy was established along the Severn. Annapolis presently occupies three peninsulas and encompasses four tidewater creeks, giving this small City 16 miles of beautiful waterfront.

Attractions

■ **VISITOR INFORMATION**

Annapolis and Anne Arundel County Visitors Bureau
26 West Street
Annapolis, Maryland 21401
410-280-0445

Greater Annapolis Chamber of Commerce
152 Main Street
Annapolis, Maryland 21401
410-268-7676

Harbor Master
City Dock
Annapolis, Maryland 21041
410-263-7973

■ **AIRPORTS**

Baltimore-Washington International Airport
Baltimore, Maryland 21240
410-859-7111

■ BEACHES

Bay Ridge Beach
Herndon Avenue
Annapolis, Maryland 21403
410-269-0858
301-261-2298

Bay Ridge Beach is located on the Chesapeake Bay and offers sandy beaches, swimming pools, a bathhouse, and a picnic grove. Open Memorial Day to Labor Day, daily, 10 a.m. to 6:30 p.m. Admission charge.

■ BOAT CHARTERS

"Samuel Middleton" Fishing Charters
2 Market Space
Annapolis, Maryland 21401
410-263-3323

Depart the historic City Dock of Annapolis for a day on the Bay aboard "Samuel Middleton," a vintage bay-built fishing boat. Have your catch prepared for dinner at the Middleton Tavern, if you wish. Half days are available. Call for schedule. Fee.

■ BOAT CRUISES

Old man in the sea gotcha down? Come to town, and learn powerboating, sailing, or the tricky art of wind surfing.

AYS Sailing School
7416 Edgewood Road
Annapolis, Maryland 21403
410-267-8181

Full-service charter and sailing instruction facility offering captained and bareboat charters on sailboats 28 to 46 feet long. Charter certification courses offered every weekend on the Chesapeake Bay from Annapolis. Fee.

Boat Cruises, cont.

Adventures Afloat
921 Boucher Avenue
Annapolis, Maryland 21403
410-268-8398

Since 1979, the Chesapeake Bay's exclusive guided and captained yacht service specialist. Join Capt. Paul Foer on a sailing vacation, for dinner cruises, floating parties, or for a vacation escape. Full-day, evening, and weekend cruises, or longer. Power and sail up to 150 guests. Fee.

The Annapolis Sailing School
601 Sixth Street
Annapolis, Maryland 21403
410-267-7205

Headquarters of America's oldest and largest sailing school. "Try Sailing" for two hours, daily, noon to 2 p.m. Offering basic, live-aboard cruising, as well as sailing vacations for beginners and old salts alike. Special seven-day package provides unique, fun-filled vacations. Boat rentals available. Open daily. Fee.

Chesapeake Marine Tours
Slip 20, City Dock
Annapolis, Maryland 21403
410-268-7600

"Don't miss the boat." You can cover the waterfront with Chesapeake Marine Tours. Let them provide you with a perspective of Annapolis that you can never see from shore. Boards from and returns to the City Dock. You can choose from a variety of tours including a 40-minute, narrated cruise of Annapolis harbor, the U.S. Naval Academy, and Severn River. Also, you can plan an all-day cruise to historic St. Michael's. Open daily, 9 a.m. to 5 p.m. Admission charge.

Chesapeake Sailing School
7074 Bembe Beach Road
Annapolis, Maryland 21403
410-269-1594

In addition to 12 years of teaching thousands of adults and children (from age six), Chesapeake Sailing School charters sailboats from 22 to 43 feet. Open daily, 9 a.m. to 5 p.m. Fee.

Jiffy Water Taxi
Slip 20, City Dock
Annapolis, Maryland 21403
410-263-0033

Take the taxi to waterfront restaurants on Spa and Back Creeks. Departs City Dock for Back Creek on the hour. Departs Back Creek for City Dock 20 minutes past the hour, if called before the hour. Open daily, mid-May to Labor Day; Monday to Thursday, 10 a.m. to midnight; Friday, 10 a.m. to 1 a.m.; Saturday, 9 a.m. to 1 a.m.; and Sunday, 9 a.m. to midnight. Fee.

Schooner Woodwind
301 4th Street
Annapolis, Maryland 21403
410-267-6333

Baytrippers, during your visit to Annapolis, take a refreshing break from the usual land tour and experience the delights of boating on the Chesapeake Bay. Climb aboard the Schooner "Woodwind," sailing four times daily from the Annapolis Marriott Dock. Call for schedule of departure. Admission charge.

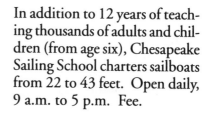

■ BOAT RENTALS

Quiet Waters Park Boat Rentals
Hillsmere Drive
Annapolis, Maryland 21401
410-267-5976

Add a special treat to your visit to Annapolis. Come to Quiet Waters Park Boat Rentals on Harness Creek just off the South River. Rent the new solar-powered, electric, inboard sailboat or a pedal boat, row boat, or canoe. Open daily, April to September, 10 a.m. to dusk. Fee.

Sport Boat Rentals
80 Compromise Street
Annapolis, Maryland 21401
410-268-6551

Join the fun on the Bay. Rentals featuring unsinkable 15-foot and 17-foot sport motorboats. Open daily, 8 a.m. to dusk. Fee.

Wind Surfing Unlimited
1598A Whitehall Road
Annapolis, Maryland 21401
410-757-8008

A vacation's the perfect time to wind surf. Lessons and rentals are available. Open daily, 9 a.m. to 5 p.m. Fee.

■ GUIDED SIGHTSEEING TOURS

A walking tour of historic Annapolis is well worth making so that you don't miss attractions. Here are several agencies that conduct tours of the historic inns, government buildings, and old houses.

Historic Annapolis Foundation Tours
Old Treasury Building
State Circle
Annapolis, Maryland 21401
410-267-8149

Covers the historic district and Naval Academy. Tours by reservation offered year round. Fee.

Maryland State House Tours
Hostess Desk
State House
Annapolis, Maryland 21401
410-974-3400

Tour of first floor public rooms. Open year round except Christmas Day. Lasts 20 minutes. Free.

Naval Academy Guide Service
USNA-Ricketts Hall
Annapolis, Maryland 21402
410-293-3363

Guided walking tours of the Naval Academy feature the history of the Academy's buildings, museums, and grounds. And if you plan ahead, check out the Naval Academy's noon meal formation, where the brigade of midshipmen, attired in their dress uniforms, assemble in front of Bancroft Hall for inspection. Open daily, Monday through Saturday, 10 a.m. to 4 p.m. and Sunday from 12:30 p.m. to 4 p.m. Group tours by reservation year round. Tours depart every half hour. Fee.

Three Centuries Tours of Annapolis
48 Maryland Avenue
Annapolis, Maryland 21404
410-263-5401

Walk Annapolis with "the Colonials" on an informative and entertaining tour of the historic district and U.S. Naval Academy. Allow two hours. Open daily, April through October 31, 9:30 a.m. and 1:30 p.m.; November 1 through March, Saturday only, 10:30 a.m. and 2:30 p.m. Fee.

■ HISTORIC SITES

Charles Carroll House
109 Duke of Gloucester Street
Annapolis, Maryland 21401
410-263-2969

This 1721 structure was the birthplace of Charles Carroll of Carrollton, the only Roman Catholic to sign the Declaration of Independence. Open the third Sunday of each month, 9:30 a.m. to 4:30 p.m. Free.

Chase-Lloyd House
22 Maryland Avenue
Annapolis, Maryland 21401
.410-263-2723

Takes you back in time to the City's golden age. This Georgian townhouse was built in 1769 by Samuel Chase, a signer of the Declaration of Independence. The house is noted for its fine interior detail. Open Tuesday through Saturday, 2 p.m. to 4 p.m. Admission charge.

Governor's Mansion
State and Church Circles
Annapolis, Maryland 21401
410-974-3531

The house, styled as a mid-Victorian brick structure topped with a mansard roof, was completed in 1876. Baytrippers are guided through seven recently renovated public rooms highlighted by beautiful antiques and vintage oriental rugs. Open by appointment, 10 a.m. to 2 p.m., Tuesday through Thursday. Free.

Hammond-Harwood House
19 Maryland Avenue
Annapolis, Maryland 21401
410-269-1714

The Hammond-Harwood House, a national, historic landmark, is an outstanding example of American colonial architecture. Built in 1774 as a town residence for Mathias Hammond, a lawyer and planter, it was the last work of its renowned architect, William Buckland. The building, with its carved entrance, formal gardens, and elegant scale, is a testament to Buckland's talent and skill. Open November through March, Tuesday through Saturday, 10 a.m. to 4 p.m.; Sunday, 1 p.m. to 4 p.m. Open April to October, Tuesday through Saturday, 10 a.m to 5 p.m.; Sunday, 2 p.m. to 5 p.m. Closed Monday, New Year's Day, Thanksgiving, and Christmas. Tours are given on the hour. Admission charge.

Historic Sites, cont.

Maryland State Archives
150 Rowe Boulevard
Annapolis, Maryland 21401
410-974-3914

Home of Maryland's Hall of Records, a historical research facility and repository for documents, records, and maps. Changing exhibits, publications, and Maryland items in lobby. Open daily, Monday through Saturday, 8:30 a.m. to 4 p.m. Free.

Maryland State House
State Circle
Annapolis, Maryland 21401
410-269-3400

The Maryland State House is the oldest state capital in the United States in continuous use. Construction of the original building began in 1772. In 1902, a new section was added to house the modern chambers of the Maryland Senate and House of Delegates. The Treaty of Paris was ratified here, officially ending the American Revolution. On the grounds stands an ancient cannon from the Arc and the Dove, the ships that brought Maryland's first settlers in 1634. Open daily, 9 a.m. to 5 p.m. No tours Thanksgiving, Christmas, or New Year's Day. Free.

Tobacco Price House
4 Pinkney Street
Annapolis, Maryland 21401
410-267-8149

Typical of the warehouses that clustered around the Annapolis City Dock during the 18th century, this small, restored building contains exhibits of implements used in Maryland's tobacco trade. Open by appointment. Admission charge.

William Paca House
186 Prince George Street
Annapolis, Maryland 21401
410-267-6656

Bold and beautiful is the restored home of William Paca, a signer of the Declaration of Independence and revolutionary period Governor of Maryland. Built between 1763 and 1765, the five-part residence boasts a stalwart central block, and wings-all starkly simple and strikingly handsome. Open, Tuesday through Saturday, 10 a.m. to 4 p.m.; Sunday and holidays, noon to 4 p.m. Closed Monday, Thanksgiving, and Christmas. Admission charge.

■ MISCELLANEOUS

**William Preston Lane, Jr.
Memorial Bridge**
Routes 50 and 301
Annapolis, Maryland 21401
410-757-6000

This magnificent span, offering a panoramic view of the Bay, opened on July 30, 1952. It's affectionately known as "the Bay Bridge." It's best to find out when the bridge is clogged with traffic on holiday weekends, so that you can plan your travel to avoid long delays. Toll.

**Pennsylvania Dutch Farmer's
Market**
2472 Solomon's Island Road
Annapolis, Maryland 21401
410-573-0770

Most of the produce is grown in Lancaster County by the Pennsylvania Dutch. Visitors will enjoy the delights made from recipes handed down through the generations which use unprocessed milk and homemade butter, candies, and cheese. Also on the premises is the Fisherman's Cove, an exciting seafood market specializing in all of the Chesapeake Bay's bounty. Open Thursday, 10 a.m. to 6 p.m.; Friday, 9 a.m. to 6 p.m.; and Saturday, 9 a.m. to 3 p.m. Closed major holidays.

■ MUSEUMS

**Banneker-Douglass Museum of
Afro-American Life**
84 Franklin Street
Annapolis, Maryland 21401
410-974-2894

The museum portrays the historical life and cultural experience of African-Americans in Maryland. View African-American arts and crafts. Open Tuesday through Friday, 10 a.m. to 3 p.m.; Saturday, noon to 4 p.m. Free.

Barge House Museum
133 Bay Shore Avenue
Eastport, Maryland 21403
410-268-1802

This community museum, a project of the Eastport Historical Society, focuses on their 127-year-old neighborhood. Changing exhibits include one centered on the glass factory that was a large part of the community around the turn of the century. Open by appointment. Free.

Shiplap House Museum
18 Pinkney Street
Annapolis, Maryland 21401
410-267-8149

Built in 1715, this former tavern is one of the oldest surviving structures in the City. Inside are exhibits on taverns and archaeology. Open daily, 11 a.m. to 4 p.m. Free.

United States Naval Academy Museum
118 Maryland Avenue
Annapolis, Maryland 21402
410-267-2108
410-267-2109

Housed in Preble Hall, the exhibits include more than 50,000 items documenting the history of the Navy and Marine Corps. Perhaps chief among these is the Henry Huddleston Rogers Collection, considered one of the world's finest collections of ship models. Open daily, Monday through Saturday, 9 a.m. to 5 p.m., and Sunday, 11 a.m. to 5 p.m. Closed Thanksgiving, Christmas, and New Year's Day. Free.

Museums, cont.

Victualling Warehouse and Maritime Museum
77 Main Street
Annapolis, Maryland 21402
410-268-5576

The Warehouse Museum includes displays about Annapolis businesses-imports, exports, shipbuilding, sail-making, etc. There's also background on the site's importance during the Revolution, when it supplied the Maryland Navy and the Continental Army with food. Open 11 a.m. to 4:30 p.m., daily, all week during spring and summer; Thursday through Sunday, other months. Free.

■ PARKS AND GARDENS

William Paca Garden
186 Prince George Street
Annapolis, Maryland 21401
410-267-6656
410-263-5553

William Paca's garden design is a unique and early example of landscape in the natural or picturesque style which was at the height of fashion when William Paca visited England in 1761. Now William Paca's garden once again flourishes. Surrounded by a stone and brick wall, the elegant formal terraces, falls, and natural beauty of the wilderness gardens are as they were in the beginning. Open, Monday through Saturday, 10 a.m. to 5 p.m. Closed on Thanksgiving and Christmas. Admission charge.

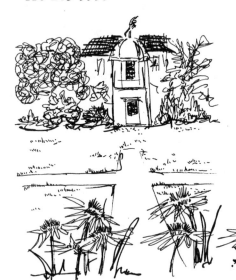

Quiet Waters Park
Hillsmere Drive
Annapolis, Maryland 21401
410-222-3600

Quiet Waters Park features turn-of-the-century fun. Also includes skating, biking, nature walks, and fitness trails. Visitors can fish at the South River overlook promenade that commands a wonderful view of the South River. Open, dawn to dusk. Admission charge.

Sandy Point State Park
800 Revell Highway
Annapolis, Maryland 21401
410-974-2772
410-757-1841

Visit this park any time of the year. It has beaches, marshes, views of the Bay Bridge, and out-of-the-way little trails. On any given day, there's a good chance that ducks on the water will far outnumber any human visitors. Open daily, 6 a.m. to 9 p.m. Admission charge.

Helen Avalynne Tawes Garden
Department of Natural
Resources
Building 580
Taylor Avenue
Annapolis, Maryland 21401
410-974-3717

This six-acre, cultivated garden features pleasant ponds and recreates the various natural communities of Maryland. Open, sunup to sundown, daily. Free.

■ SEASONAL EVENTS

Annapolis Rotary Crab Feast
Rowe Boulevard
Annapolis, Maryland 21404
410-841-2841

World's Largest Crab Feast nearing half-century tradition. Attracts visitors throughout the globe. Serving heaping trays of succulent Chesapeake Bay crabs, crab soup, hot buttered corn, and non-seafood selections for one admission fee. Held the last Friday in July at the Navy-Marine Corps Memorial Stadium off Rowe Boulevard. Admission charge.

Annapolis Spring Boat Show
Annapolis Yacht Basin
Box 4997
Annapolis, Maryland 21403
410-268-8828

The Chesapeake's largest spring boat show features new and used powerboats and sailboats, plus all the new boating, fishing, and skiing equipment, accessories, and services needed to kick off the long boating season on the Bay. Held next to the last weekend in April. Admission charge.

Annapolis United States Powerboat Show
Annapolis City Dock
and Harbor
Box 4997
Annapolis, Maryland 21403
410-268-8828

Unquestionably the largest in-water powerboat show in the world. Held in mid-October. Admission charge.

**Annapolis United States
Sailboat Show**
Annapolis City Dock
and Harbor
Box 4997
Annapolis, Maryland 21403
410-268-8828

For more than two decades, the Annapolis sailboat show has dominated the international sailboat market as the industry's most important show for introducing new boats and products to the public and trade alike. Held in early October, annually. Admission charge.

Chesapeake Appreciation Days
1805A Virginia Street
Annapolis, Maryland 21401
410-269-6622
800-421-9176

An outdoor festival to honor the working watermen of the Bay. Exhibits of arts and crafts, live music, and Maryland seafood are featured. This event is produced to showcase all things Maryland. The highlight of the weekend is the Skipjack Races. These boats come from the last existing sailing fleet which harvests oysters. Held at Sandy Point State Park on the last weekend in October. Admission charge.

Chesapeake Bay Bridge Walk
26 West Street
Annapolis, Maryland 21401
410-268-8687

The Bridge Walk is an annual event not to be missed. Hiking across the span (4.3 miles) is the only way to truly appreciate the beauty of the Bay and Bridge. Park at the Naval Academy on Rowe Boulevard. Shuttle buses will take you to and from the bridge. Held in early May. Free.

Christmas Parade of Lights
Annapolis Harbor and Spa Creek
410-267-8986
410-263-0415

The spirit of Christmas lights up the water. Big sailboats, small sailboats, large powerboats, and small powerboats compete for awards in this Annual Parade of Lights which cruises down Spa Creek. Held the second Saturday in December, 6 p.m. to 10 p.m. Free.

Maryland Renaissance Festival
Box 315
Crownsville, Maryland 21032
410-266-7304
800-296-7304

The Maryland Renaissance Festival is a 22-acre English village alive with more than 200 performers, 8 stages, a 5,000-seat jousting arena, 148 craft shops, and 48 food and beverage facilities. More than 200,000 customers are enthralled annually at Maryland's premier outdoor event. Held late August through early October, Saturday and Sunday only, and Labor Day Monday. Admission charge.

Maryland Seafood Festival
One Annapolis Street
Annapolis, Maryland 21401
410-268-7682

This event features delicious Maryland seafood dishes prepared and sold by various civic, church, and charitable organizations. In addition to the seafood, visitors enjoy continuous live music and entertainment, exhibits, beach and water activities, and much, much more. Held on the first full weekend in September. Admission charge.

354

Mid-Atlantic Wine Festival
Box 2983
Annapolis, Maryland 21401
410-280-3306

This event which occurs at Sandy Point State Park features wine from all of Maryland's vineyards, beer from local micro-breweries and brew-pubs, traditional Maryland good food, and arts and crafts. Held mid-July. Call for schedule. Admission charge.

Restaurants

Annapolis is home to many fine restaurants which offer a wide variety of cuisines and ambience. We couldn't list all the restaurants, but here are some of the favorites.

Buddy's Crabs and Ribs
100 Main Street
Annapolis, Maryland 21401
410-626-1100

Offerings include BBQ'd ribs, fresh crabs, crab cakes, soft shell crabs, steak, and an outstanding view of the downtown Harbor. Open daily for lunch and dinner. Credit cards: AE, C, MC, and V.

Cafe Normandie
185 Main Street
Annapolis, Maryland 21401
410-263-3382

Crepes are the signature dish at Cafe Normandie, and if you love seafood the way I do, you will enjoy the "Annapolis Crepe" which features shrimp, scallops, and mushrooms bounded with creamy lobster sauce. Open daily for breakfast, lunch, and dinner. Credit cards: AE, MC, and V.

Calvert House Inn
2444 Solomon's Island Road
Annapolis, Maryland 21401
410-266-9210

Enjoy fresh fish, crab cakes, or steak. Open daily for lunch and dinner. Credit cards: AE, MC, and V.

Restaurants, cont.

Cantler's Riverside Inn
Forest Beach Road
Annapolis, Maryland 21403
410-757-1467

Jimmy Cantler's Riverside Inn has become an institution over the years for its delicious steamed clams, shrimp, and crabs. Specials offered daily. On unique waterfront setting overlooking Mill Creek. Open daily for lunch and dinner.

Carrol's Creek Cafe
410 Severn Avenue
Eastport/Annapolis, Maryland
21403
410-263-8102

House specialties include Crab Meat Remick, BBQ'd shrimp, catch of the day, crab salad, and soft shell crabs. Open daily for lunch and dinner; Sunday for brunch and dinner. Credit cards: AE, MC, and V.

The Chart House
300 Second Street
Annapolis, Maryland 21403
410-268-7166

The restaurant and lounge overlook the Annapolis harbor. You'll find steaks, seafood, and an extensive salad bar. Open for lunch and dinner weekends; for dinner only weekdays; for brunch also on Sunday. Credit cards: AE, DC, MC, and V.

Davis Pub
400 Chestnut Avenue
Eastport/Annapolis, Maryland
21403
410-268-7432

It's fun! I promise you'll like it here. Crab cakes and home-cooked food fill the menu. Open daily for lunch and dinner; Sunday for brunch and dinner. Credit cards: AE, C, MC, and V.

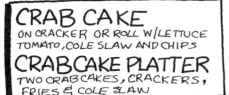

CRAB CAKE
ON CRACKER OR ROLL W/LETTUCE
TOMATO, COLE SLAW AND CHIPS
CRABCAKE PLATTER
TWO CRABCAKES, CRACKERS,
FRIES & COLE SLAW

BEST CRAB CAKES

Fred's Restaurant
2348 Solomon's Island Road
Annapolis, Maryland 21401
410-224-2386

Fred's serves up one of the best crab cakes in town. Don't miss them. Closed Monday. Open daily for lunch and dinner. Credit cards: AE, C, CB, DC, MC, and V.

Harbor House
87 Prince George Street
Annapolis, Maryland 21401
410-268-0771

House specialties include bouillabaisse, fisherman's platter, and oysters Rockefeller. Dine on the terrace. Harbor House evokes the mood of open-air cafes of Europe. Open daily for lunch and dinner. Credit cards: AE, DC, MC, and V.

Marmaduke's Restaurant
301 Severn Avenue
Eastport/Annapolis, Maryland
21403
410-269-5420

Marmaduke's offers casual dining, home-cooked meals, and a piano bar. Open daily for lunch and dinner. Credit cards: AE, C, MC, and V.

McGarvey's Saloon and Oyster Bar
City Dock
Annapolis, Maryland 21401
410-263-5700

American saloon food and raw bar. Open daily for lunch and dinner; Saturday and Sunday also open for brunch. Credit cards: AE, MC, and V.

Restaurants, cont.

Middleton Tavern
2 Market Space
Annapolis, Maryland 21401
410-263-3323

House specialties include oysters on the half shell, smoked blue fish, crab imperial, crab cakes, and seafood crepes. Enjoy the authentic colonial fireside setting or visit the outdoor cafe overlooking the City Dock. Home of the "oyster shooter." Open daily for lunch and dinner; Sunday for brunch and dinner. Credit cards: MC and V.

Mum's Grill
136 Dock Street
Annapolis, Maryland 21401
410-263-3353

Located in the favorite local neighborhood, Mum's Grill features casual dining overlooking the City Dock. Open daily for breakfast, lunch, and dinner. Credit cards: AE, MC, and V.

O'Brien's Oyster Bar & Restaurant
113 Main Street
Annapolis, Maryland 21401
410-268-6288
410-269-0099
301-261-2100

O'Brien's is emerging as one of Annapolis's top restaurants. It's a reputation well earned. Recently recognized as the winner of The Maryland Seafood Cookoff for the "best cream of crab soup." Serves regional cuisine along with innovative pasta and vegetable dishes. Open daily for lunch and dinner. Credit cards: D, MC, and V.

Pussers Landing Restaurant
80 Compromise Street
Annapolis, Maryland 21401
410-626-0004

My visit was timed with the U.S. Sailboat Show. Along with my daily issue of admiralty rum, I slurped down a dozen oysters on the half shell and a heaping bowl of Maryland crab and corn chowder. The results were mighty good. Open daily for breakfast, lunch, and dinner. Credit cards: AE, CB, D, DC, MC, and V.

Rams Head Tavern
33 West Street
Annapolis, Maryland 21401
410-268-4545

Beyond a sometimes crowded bar area, there are several small rooms for dining, as well as an outdoor beer and luncheon garden. The menu is inexpensive and clever. For example, there is shepherd's pie, Mexican lasagna, or Santa Fe chicken. And you can wash it all down with the beer brewing traditions of 27 countries (160 beers). Open daily for lunch and dinner. Credit cards: AE, MC, and V.

The Treaty of Paris
16 Church Circle
Annapolis, Maryland 21401
410-263-2641
800-847-8882

The *New York Times* says it best: "Tucked just below street level in the 1772 inn, this gracious landmark offers food that combines French and Colonial American influences with fresh Maryland seafood." Open daily for breakfast, lunch, and dinner. Credit cards: AE, C, CB, DC, MC, and V.

Accommodations

The area's hotels, inns, and bed and breakfast accommodations will delight you with their attractive surroundings.

■ **BED AND BREAKFASTS**

Annapolis Bed and Breakfast
235 Prince Street
Annapolis, Maryland 21401
410-269-0669

College House Bed and Breakfast
One College Avenue
Annapolis, Maryland 21401
410-263-6124

The Arc and Dove
149 Prince George Street
Annapolis, Maryland 21401
410-268-6277

Courtyard Bed and Breakfast
166 Duke of Glouchester Street
Annapolis, Maryland 21401
410-263-5593

Casa Vahia
262 King George Street
Annapolis, Maryland 21401
410-268-3106

Gibson's Lodging
110 Prince George Street
Annapolis, Maryland 21401
410-268-5555

The Charles Inn
74 Charles Street
Annapolis, Maryland 21401
410-268-1451

Hunter House
154 Prince George Street
Annapolis, Maryland 21401
410-626-1268

Chesapeake Lighthouse B&B
1423 Sharps Point Road
Annapolis, Maryland 21401
410-757-0248

Magnolia House
210 King George Street
Annapolis, Maryland 21401
410-268-3477

Chez Amis Bed and Breakfast
85 East Street
Annapolis, Maryland 21401
410-263-6631

Maryrob Bed and Breakfast
243 Prince George Street
Annapolis, Maryland 21401
410-268-5438

Prince George's Inn
232 Prince George Street
Annapolis, Maryland 21401
410-263-5418

Shaw's Fancy
161 Green Street
Annapolis, Maryland 21401
410-268-9750

William Page
8 Martin Street
Annapolis, Maryland 21401
410-626-1506

■ HOTELS, MOTELS, AND INNS

Academy Motel
200 Revell Highway
Annapolis, Maryland 21401
410-757-2222

Annapolis Marriott/Waterfront
80 Compromise Street
Annapolis, Maryland 21401
410-268-7555

Annapolis Ramada Hotel
173 Jennifer Road
Annapolis, Maryland 21401
410-266-3131
800-351-9209

Comfort Inn Motel
200 Revell Highway
Annapolis, Maryland 21401
410-757-8500

Econo Lodge
591 Revell Highway
Annapolis, Maryland 21401
410-974-4440
800-446-6900

Econo Lodge
2451 Riva Road
Annapolis, Maryland 21401
410-224-4317

Historic Inns of Annapolis
16 Church Circle
Annapolis, Maryland 21401
410-263-7777

Holiday Inn
210 Holiday Court
Annapolis, Maryland 21401
410-224-3150
800-HOL-IDAY

Howard Johnson
170 Revell Highway
Annapolis, Maryland 21401
410-757-1600

Loew's Annapolis Hotel
126 West Street
Annapolis, Maryland 21401
410-263-7777

BALTIMORE

Baltimore to Elkton

Follow the water....

- Baltimore
- Havre de Grace
- North East
- Elkton

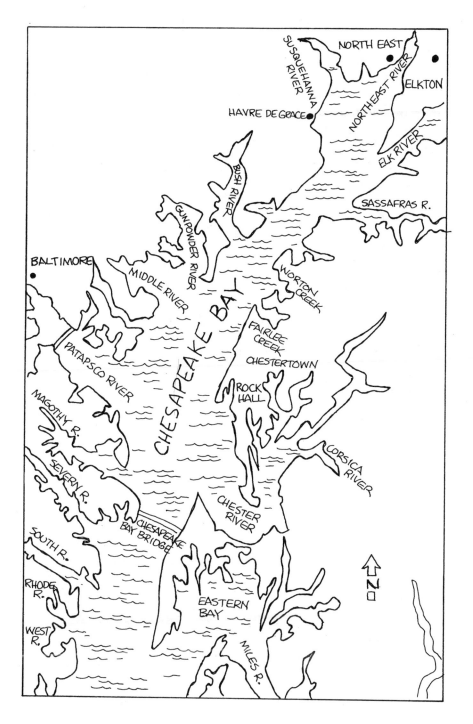

BALTIMORE

■ **BACKGROUND:** Baltimore's long maritime history stretches back to early Indian camps on the shores through the late 20th century revitalization of its harbor. The Baltimore story includes some of the most important and fascinating events of America's past. From 25 houses in the early 1700s, Baltimore grew to become the industrial and transportation capital of the nation by the mid-1800s. The "Star-Spangled Banner" was written in this City, and the Baltimore and Ohio Railroad (the first public railroad in the country) was established here. The city fell under military occupation during the Civil War, suffered the great fire of 1904, and was inundated by the horrendous floods of 1868 and 1972. Through it all, Baltimore rose to become a great industrial and port city. Baltimore takes its name from a small port in the south of Ireland on the River Ilan. The word "Baltimore" means "Town of the great house" in Gaelic.

Attractions

■ **VISITOR INFORMATION**

Amtrak
1500 North Charles Street
Baltimore, Maryland 21201
410-539-2112
1-800-872-7245

**Baltimore Area Convention
  and Visitors Association**
100 Light Street
Baltimore, Maryland 21202
410-659-7300
800-343-3468

Baltimore Area Visitors Center
300 West Pratt Street
Baltimore, Maryland 21201
410-837-4636
800-282-6632

Baltimore Mass Transit
410-539-5000

■ **AIRPORT**

**Baltimore-Washington
International Airport**
Baltimore, Maryland 21240
410-859-7100

■ **BOAT CRUISES:** One way to enjoy Baltimore's waterfront is to take advantage of the cooling breezes on one of the many boat cruises offered in the Inner Harbor.

Bay Lady/Lady Baltimore
301 Light Street
Baltimore, Maryland 21202
410-347-5552
410-727-3113

Cruise—sample the sea, relax, and enjoy the timeless pleasure of travelling on water. Take part in the festivities or escape to the quiet romance of an open deck. Watch the Baltimore Harbor whisk by. Share some fun time, some family time, and some friend-filled time aboard "the ladies." It's like an ocean cruise right in Baltimore Harbor. The Bay Lady is a 600-passenger showboat that features live music. The Lady Baltimore offers trips to Annapolis and St. Michaels, with time for touring and browsing. In addition, various theme cruises are offered. Admission charge.

Chesapeake Charter Tour and Travel
418 East 31st Street
Baltimore, Maryland 21218
410-467-7778

See Baltimore from the water aboard a 60-foot luxury yacht. Enjoy a daily lunch cruise, evening cocktail cruise, or a wonderful sightseeing cruise. This unique service offers extraordinary views of the city. Admission charge.

Boat Cruises, cont.

Clipper City
2501 Boston Street
Baltimore, Maryland 21224
410-575-7930
410-539-6277

Ride the wind to capture the spirit and adventure of a time long ago. Few vessels can match the grandeur or inspire the awe created by the majestic clipper ships of the late 19th century. The Clipper City is unique. She is a replica of an 1854 topsail schooner and is the largest tall ship licensed to carry passengers in the United States. Private charters, corporate charters, convention service, dockside parties, and wedding receptions are available. Admission charge.

Harbor Boating
301 Light Street
Baltimore, Maryland 21202
410-547-0090

Try your feet on these paddle boat rentals. It's a unique way to see the inner harbor. Admission charge.

Maryland Tours, Inc./
Baltimore Patriot
P.O. Box 147
Royal Oak, Maryland 21662
410-685-4288

The British tried it and failed, but now you can land at Fort McHenry. The Fort McHenry and Fells Point shuttle service departs from the Inner Harbor every half hour from 11 a.m. through 5:30 p.m.; Memorial Day through Labor Day. The Baltimore Patriot offers special features such as a 1 1/2 hour narrated cruise of the ever-changing scene at the Baltimore Inner Harbor. Admission charge.

Schooner Nighthawk Cruises
1715 Thames Street
Baltimore, Maryland 21231
410-327-SAIL

Afternoon sail, pirate sail, moonlight sail, midnight mystery cruise, brunch sail, and private charters available for companies, groups, clubs, parties, weddings. Admission charge.

Skipjack Minnie V.
831 South Bond Street
Baltimore, Maryland 21231
410-522-4214

Cruise aboard historic working vessels from the Chesapeake Bay oyster fleet. Six narrated, 1 1/2 hour trips daily, weekends and holidays, spring through fall. Additional trips Tuesday through Friday, mid-June to Labor Day. Departs from Harborplace. Admission charge.

Water Taxi
1615 Thames Street
Baltimore, Maryland 21231
410-547-0090
800-658-8947

So much to see, so little time. Get your "see legs" the water taxi way. The water taxi is an economical service which can make it possible to see more of the many attractions around the Baltimore waterfront. Tickets are good for unlimited use on the day of purchase. Admission charge.

■ GUIDED SIGHTSEEING TOURS

About Town Tours
Ten Fox Hill Court
Perry Hall, Maryland 21128
410-592-7770

Specializing in group tours of Baltimore, Washington, and Annapolis. Fee.

American Tours and Tour Guides
P.O. Box 5686
Baltimore, Maryland 21210
410-235-6484

Customized historic tours for individuals and small groups. Fee.

Baltimore Rent-a-Tour
3414 Philips Drive
Baltimore, Maryland 21208
410-653-2998

Narrated Baltimore tours. Theme excursions, shopping trips, or insomniac tours—customized for your group of 30 or more. Bus transportation. Fee.

Packages Plus Incorporated
P.O. Box 7
Annapolis Junction,
Maryland 20701
410-776-8377
800-759-6784

Complete tour packaging for Baltimore, Washington, Annapolis, and the mid-Atlantic states. Fee.

■ HISTORIC SITES

The Carroll Mansion
800 East Lombard Street
Baltimore, Maryland 21202
410-396-3523

Patriot Charles Carroll of Carrollton, Maryland, wintered here during the last 12 years of his life, managing his estates and investments and receiving visitors who came to meet this "Relic of the Revolution" and signer of the Declaration of Independence. The mansion's rooms, richly furnished, testify to the elegant lifestyle of the period. Open Tuesday through Sunday, 10 a.m. to 4 p.m. Admission charge.

The 1840 House
800 East Lombard Street
Baltimore, Maryland 21202
410-396-3523
410-396-3279

The household of wheelwright John Hutchinson and his family is meticulously recreated to simulate life in 1840 Baltimore. Children and adults can experience a variety of dramatic and participatory programs designed to stimulate senses, involve the emotions, and entertain the mind. Furnishings are reproductions to encourage hands-on participation. Seasonal hours. Admission charge.

Historic Sites, cont.

Fort McHenry
East Fort Avenue
Baltimore, Maryland 21230
410-962-4299

Fort McHenry National Monument and Historic Shrine is world-famous as the birthplace of the American national anthem. The successful defense of this star-shaped fort by American forces during a British attack on September 13 and 14, 1814 inspired Frances Scott Key to pen the words of the "Star-Spangled Banner." Following the Battle of Baltimore, the fort never again came under attack; however, it remained an active military base for many years. During the Civil War, the fort was a Union camp used for the detention of Confederate soldiers. During World War I, it was the site of a 3,000-bed army hospital. In 1925, it became a national park. Open daily, Memorial Day to Labor Day, 9 a.m. to 8 p.m.; other days, 9 a.m. to 5 p.m. Closed Christmas Day. Admission charge.

Fort McHenry National Monument & Historic Shrine Relive the glory of this star-shaped fort where, in 1814, America's successful defense against the British inspired Francis Scott key to write The Star Spangled Banner.

H. L. Mencken House
1524 Hollins Street
Baltimore, Maryland 21223
410-396-7997

This stately 19th century row house overlooking Union Square was the home of Henry Louis Mencken, "the sage of Baltimore," for more than 68 years. It has been restored with Mencken's original furniture and many of his personal belongings. See a delightful audiovisual presentation on the life of Baltimore's famous journalist and literary and social critic. Open Wednesday and Sunday, 10 a.m. to 5 p.m. Admission charge.

Mount Clare Mansion
Carroll Park
1500 Washington Boulevard
Baltimore, Maryland 21230
410-837-3262

The 1754 home of the Barrister Charles Carroll is the oldest mansion in the City of Baltimore. It has been authentically restored with original Carroll pieces. Open Tuesday through Saturday, 11 a.m. to 4 p.m.; Sunday 1 p.m. to 4 p.m. Admission charge.

9 Front Street
Shot Tower Park
Baltimore, Maryland 21202
410-837-5424

This circa 1790 federal townhouse was restored by the Women's Civic League to house its headquarters and tourist information center. It includes kitchen and garden. Open Tuesday through Saturday, 10 a.m. to 4 p.m.; Sunday noon to 4 p.m. Free.

Historic Sites, cont.

Shot Tower
801 East Fayette Street
Baltimore, Maryland 21202
410-837-5424

The Shot Tower was constructed in 1828, 36 years before the outbreak of the Civil War, to make small caliber lead bullets. At over 215 feet high, it was constructed with well over 1 million bricks. The structure was built from the inside out, without the use of exterior bracing. Open daily 10 a.m. to 4 p.m. Free.

■ HISTORIC TOWNS

Ellicott City, Maryland

One thing to be noted about Ellicott is that marble was quarried here that was used to build the US Capital, Washington Monument, and the Library of Congress. Granite quarried here was also used in the construction of the Baltimore and Ohio Railroad. Another claim to Ellicott City's fame is that it was the finishing point for that famous race between the steam engine, Tom Thumb, and a horse-drawn carriage.

■ MISCELLANEOUS

Baltimore Zoo
Swan Drive
Baltimore, Maryland 21217
410-366-LION
410-396-7102

Follow your instincts for the unusual to the Baltimore Zoo. You can wander for hours among 150 acres of aviaries, open-air exhibits, Victorian gazebos and displays, beautiful lakes, and lush walkways. Admire the ruffle of formal "penguin-wear" at feeding time. Witness the grace and intelligence of the elephant, the largest living land mammal. Travel to the banks of the mighty Nile, the African plains, and other wildlife wonderlands all in an afternoon. Open 10 a.m. to 4:30 p.m. daily, with extended hours during the summer. Admission charge.

Miscellaneous, cont.

Harborplace
Inner Harbor
Pratt and Light Streets
Baltimore, Maryland 21201
410-332-4191

Baltimore's Inner Harbor has become one of the East Coast's top tourist attractions. The brainchild of the Rouse Company, Harborplace consists of two glass-enclosed, two-story pavilions overlooking the Inner Harbor. At ground level, the Light Street Pavilion features a colonnade market highlighted by purveyors of produce, seafood, and quick-counter eateries. You'll also discover a two-story, sky-lit trading hall for baked goods and gourmet foods. On both floors of the Light Street Pavilion, enjoy a variety of small eateries. On the second floor, you'll find a colorful bazaar filled with an array of crafts and gifts. The adjacent Pratt Street Pavilion features two stories of small specialty shops offering merchandise from clothing and sportswear to housewares and gifts. In both pavilions, restaurants and cafes with harborside terraces offer food and drink as well as splendid views of the harbor. Open Monday through Saturday, 10 a.m. to 10 p.m.; and Sunday 12 a.m. to 8 p.m.

Lexington Market
400 West Lexington Street
Baltimore, Maryland 21201
410-685-6169

Treat your senses to a delicious variety of international delights. More than 140 merchants sell fresh seafood, produce, meats, delicatessen items, baked goods, sweets, and more. Open Monday through Saturday, 8:30 a.m. to 6:30 p.m.; closed Sunday. Free.

Lightship Chesapeake
Pier 3, Pratt Street
Baltimore, Maryland 21202
410-396-3854

The Lightship Chesapeake began as a floating lighthouse. It was anchored in coastal waters where other types of navigation aids were impractical. Light ships mark major shipping channels and harbor entrances. A welcome sight to ships' captains for many years, these vessels were easily identified by their bright red hulls. The name of their duty station was painted on the side in large white letters and on the beacon lantern atop the mainmast. Climb aboard for a self-guided tour. Open daily except Tuesday and Wednesday. Admission charge.

Miscellaneous, cont.

National Aquarium in Baltimore
Pier 3/501
East Pratt Street
Baltimore, Maryland 21202
410-576-3810

The National Aquarium in Baltimore is one of the largest and most sophisticated aquariums in the U.S. In its spectacular, seven-level, one million gallon structure, over 5,000 creatures swim about. This is a fascinating recreation facility for young children and adults as well as an exciting center of marine research and education. If you've been here before, come again to see the new Marine Mammal Pavilion, with its daily presentations featuring dolphins and whales. (Call for times.) Open summer, May 15 to September 15, Monday through Thursday, 9 a.m. to 5 p.m., Friday through Sunday 9 a.m. to 8 p.m. In winter, open September 15 to May 15, daily 10 a.m. to 5 p.m. and Fridays 10 a.m. to 8 p.m. Discounts October 1 to March 27. Call for times of daily marine mammal presentations. Admission charge.

Pier 6 Concert Pavilion
Pier 6, Pratt Street
Baltimore, Maryland 21202
410-625-4230

The Inner Harbor is blessed with the sound of music now that the new 2,000 seat music pavilion has come to Pier 6. This unique structure is the largest of its kind in the United States and represents a first in urban entertainment centers. Symphony, pop, and jazz are featured throughout the summer season. Admission charge.

Pride of Baltimore II
Pier 3, Pratt Street
Baltimore, Maryland 21202
410-539-1151

Like the clipper and privateers of the past, who established Baltimore's reputation as a seaport and commercial center, the Pride of Baltimore II demonstrates the twin spirits of adventure and enterprise that still characterize Baltimore today. The Pride is Baltimore's goodwill tallship ambassador to ports around the world. Open for tours when in port. Free.

377

Miscellaneous, cont.

Top of the World Trade Center
Pier 2, Pratt Street
Baltimore, Maryland 21202
410-837-4515

The Top of the World Trade Center is the marketplace for international trade in one of the largest ports in the United States. Seeming to rise right out of the harbor, the 30-story World Trade Center is a beautiful pentagonal vision of concrete and glass. It boasts a magnificent view of not only the Inner Harbor, but all of Baltimore City. The observation deck on the 27th floor houses a creative and informative display about Baltimore's famous people, neighborhoods, and, of course, the port itself. It gives you a bird's eye view of downtown and is the perfect place to get acquainted before a tour of the Inner Harbor. Open daily 10 a.m. to 5 p.m. Admission charge.

U.S.F. Constellation
Constellation Dock
Pier 1, Pratt Street
Baltimore, Maryland 21202
410-539-1797

The U.S.F. Constellation was the first commissioned warship of the United States Navy; it was launched in 1797. It is docked in Baltimore's Inner Harbor near the spot where her original planking was laid by Fells Point ship builder David Stodder. The oldest ship in the world continuously afloat, the Constellation has been restored and may be viewed at the Constellation Dock. Open daily. Admission charge.

■ MUSEUMS

**Babe Ruth Birthplace/
Baltimore Orioles Museum**
216 Emory Street
Baltimore, Maryland 21230
410-727-1539

Birthplace, February 6, 1895, of the "Sultan of Swat." Restored house and adjoining museum contain personal mementos, Orioles memorabilia, and a life-size figure of the Babe. Open daily winter, November 1 to March 31, 10 a.m. to 4 p.m.; summer, open daily 10 a.m. to 5 p.m. Admission charge.

**Baltimore City Fire Museum
at Old Engine House No. 6**
414 North Gay Street
Baltimore, Maryland 21202
410-727-2414

This magnificent structure, built in 1799, is one of the oldest fire stations in the nation devoted to fire-related activities. The Florentine bell tower was added in 1853. Collections include antique fire apparatus, fire memorabilia, and photographs. Open Sunday 1 p.m. to 4 p.m. Special tours by appointment. Free.

Baltimore Museum of Art
Art Museum Drive
Baltimore, Maryland 21218
410-396-7101

Browse through permanent and special exhibitions of art from old masters to contemporary. Open Tuesday, Wednesday, Friday, 10 a.m. to 4 p.m.; Thursday 10 a.m. to 7 p.m.; Saturday and Sunday, 11 a.m. to 6 p.m. Free on Thursdays; admission all other days.

Museums, cont.

Baltimore Museum of Industry
1415 Key Highway
Baltimore, Maryland 21230
410-727-4808

Located in the heart of industrial South Baltimore, this museum demonstrates the importance of the city in the industrial revolution. Inventors such as Ottmar Mergenthaler, who invented the linotype machine, lived and worked in Baltimore. The museum features working recreations of an antique machine shop, clothing factory, and print shop, along with displays and exhibits of Baltimore's present industries. Live demonstrations and films. Call for hours Monday through Friday, Saturday 10 a.m. to 5 p.m., Sunday noon to 5 p.m. Admission charge.

Baltimore Streetcar Museum
1901 Falls Road
Baltimore, Maryland 21211
410-547-0264

A rolling history of the Baltimore streetcars from 1860-1963. Climb aboard an antique streetcar and enjoy a ride along one-mile of reconstructed tracks. Exhibits history of rail transport in Baltimore. Open Sunday noon to 5 p.m.; Saturday noon to 4 p.m. June through October. Admission free; fares for rides.

Center for Urban Archeology
802 East Lombard Street
Baltimore, Maryland 21202
410-396-3156
410-396-3523
410-396-3279

The area known today as Baltimore City has been inhabited for 12,000 years. This center houses a fascinating display of artifacts spanning the period, from prehistoric Indian tools to pottery and glassware from 18th and 19th century homes, industries, and shops. Watch Baltimore archaeologists and volunteers at work. Seasonal hours. Admission charge.

Cloisters Children's Museum
10440 Falls Road
Brooklandville, Maryland 21022
410-823-2550

Offers changing exhibits, creative art experiences, perfor mances, and workshops. This restored "castle" also houses the historic Parker collection. Open Thursday 10 a.m. to 4:30 p.m.; Saturday and Sunday, noon to 4 p.m.. Thursday free; admission charge other days.

Edgar Allan Poe House and Museum
203 North Amity Street
Baltimore, Maryland 21223
410-396-7932

This is the tiny house where Poe began his career during 1832 through 1835. Contains period furniture, changing exhibits, and special performances. Poe lived here with members of the Clemm family. Open Wednesday and Saturday, 12 p.m. to 4 p.m.; July and August, open Saturday only, 12 p.m. to 4 p.m. Closed January through March and all holidays. Admission charge.

Museums, cont.

Flag House and 1812 Museum
844 East Pratt Street
Baltimore, Maryland 21202
410-837-1793

This is the 1793 home of Mary Pickersgill, who made the 30-by-42-foot flag of Ft. Henry during the War of 1812. Her handiwork inspired Francis Scott Key's "Star-Spangled Banner." Federal period furnishings and special exhibits. Open Monday through Saturday 10 a.m. to 4 p.m. Admission charge.

The Homewood Museum
3400 North Charles Street
Baltimore, Maryland 21202
410-338-5589

Peruse a beautifully restored mansion, an example of federal architecture. Built in 1801 by Charles Carroll, signer of the Declaration of Independence. Open Monday through Friday, 11 a.m. to 5 p.m., Sunday noon to 4 p.m. Admission charge.

Maryland Science Center
601 Light Street
Baltimore, Maryland 21202
410-685-5225

The Maryland Science Center is more than fun. It's "sciencesational." Explore three floors of exciting hands-on activities and exhibits. Thrill at the larger-than-life action on the five-story screen of the IMAX Theatre. Travel to other galaxies under the dome of the world-famous Davis Planetarium. Witness live science demonstrations—where you conduct the experiment. Open daily: Monday through Friday 10 a.m. to 5 p.m., Saturday 10 a.m. to 6 p.m., Sunday noon to 6 p.m.; closed New Year's, Thanksgiving, Christmas Eve, and Christmas Day. Admission charge.

**Museum and Library of
Maryland History**
The Maryland
Historical Society
201 West Monument Street
Baltimore, Maryland 21201
410-685-3750

Founded in 1844, this repository houses Maryland paintings, furniture, silver, and costumes in its galleries, as well as books, maps, manuscripts, and records in its library—all of which pertain to Maryland from its founding in 1634. Open Tuesday through Friday, 11 a.m. to 4:30 p.m.; Saturday 9 a.m. to 4:30 p.m.; and Sunday, 1 p.m. to 5 p.m. Admission charge.

The Peale Museum
225 Holliday Street
Baltimore, Maryland 21202
410-396-1149

Built in 1814 by the American portrait painter, Rembrandt Peale, this building is the oldest original museum building in the United States. It served as Baltimore's first city hall. Located just a half block north of the present city hall, it houses a fine collection of historical photographs of Baltimore; prints; paintings, including more than 40 by members of the Peale family; plus an intriguing exhibit on Baltimore's famous row houses. Open Tuesday through Saturday, 10 a.m. to 5 p.m.; and Sunday noon to 5 p.m. Admission charge.

In 1824, the first Egyptian mummy ever brought to the western hemisphere was exhibited at Baltimore's Peale Museum. Record numbers of people flocked to see this "curious relic of Antiquity." This ad appeared in the American & Commercial Daily Advertiser on June 16, 1824.

Museums, cont.

USS Torsk
Pier 4, Pratt Street
Baltimore, Maryland 21202
410-396-5528

Another great tourist attraction in the Inner Harbor is the submarine USS Torsk. The ship was put to sea on December 31, 1944. She sailed toward the Pacific war zone and had the distinction of firing the last torpedo and sinking the last Japanese combatant ships of World War II. She also won the Naval Commendation Medal for taking part in the Naval blockade of Cuba. In 1972, the Torsk became a floating museum and is now berthed in the Baltimore Harbor. Open daily except Tuesday and Wednesday. Admission charge.

■ PARKS AND GARDENS

The Baltimore Conservatory
Druid Hill Park
Gwynns Falls Parkway and
McCullogh Street
Baltimore, Maryland 21217
410-396-0180

Besides cultivating exotic, tropical greenery and flora, the passing of the local seasons is always celebrated at the conservatory. Open daily 10 a.m. to 4 p.m. Free.

Druid Hill Park
Druid Park Lake Drive
Baltimore, Maryland 21217
410-396-6106

The second-largest urban park in the country. Created in 1688, it is an idyllic spot for exploring, playing tennis, picnicking, and relaxing in the shade. Open daily until dark. Free.

The Maryland Vietnam Veterans Memorial Park
3301 Waterview Avenue
Baltimore, Maryland 21230
410-837-4636

This scenic area along the water's edge features a memorial to Maryland's Vietnam veterans. Free.

Patterson Park
2601A East Baltimore Street
Baltimore, Maryland 21224
410-396-9304

The pastoral park surrounds a shimmering lake (perfect for paper sailboats) and a unique pagoda tower. Free.

Sherwood Gardens Greenway
Baltimore, Maryland 21212
410-366-2572

Amid dogwoods, magnolias, wisteria, and azaleas grow 100,000 tulips. All are in breathtaking full bloom during late April and early May. Open daily dawn to dusk. Free.

Wortzberger Sculpture Garden
Art Museum Drive
Baltimore, Maryland 21218
410-396-7100

The Wortzberger Sculpture Garden is a wonderland of artistic expression. Within this gardenscape are graceful terraces and meandering walkways. Featured are 14 contemporary metal, bronze, and stone sculptures by internationally-known artists. Open Tuesday through Saturday, 10 a.m. to 4 p.m., open Sunday 10 a.m. to 6 p.m.

■ SEASONAL EVENTS

Baltimore Spirit Indoor Soccer
201 W. Baltimore Street
Baltimore, Maryland 21201
410-625-2320

The Spirits kick up a storm from October to April in regular season, with playoffs running to May. They play at home in the Baltimore Arena. Admission charge.

Baltimore Orioles Baseball
Oriole Park at Camden Yards
Baltimore, Maryland 21218
410-243-9800

The professional baseball season runs April through September. Don't miss "The Birds" exciting brand of baseball in their new stadium at Camden Yards. Admission charge.

Baltimore Thunder
201 Baltimore Street
Baltimore, Maryland 21201
410-347-2090

If you fancy the fast-moving game of lacrosse, the Baltimore Thunder go at it regularly in the Baltimore Arena from December to March during their regular season. Admission charge.

Preakness Celebration
Pimlico Race Course
Hayward and Winner Avenues
Baltimore, Maryland 21215
410-542-9400

What do bagpiping, antique airplanes, sailing kites, Italian sausage, and horse racing have in common? It's the Preakness Week, of course. Don your colors and get in the spirit as the Second Jewel of the Triple Crown of racing runs each year in mid-May. Admission charge.

Restaurants

Baltimore is famous for its neighborhoods. In Little Italy, you can indulge in delicious, old-world cuisine at a cluster of Italian restaurants that lure visitors and celebrities from around the world. Plan an evening meal in Fells Point and discover this handsome historic maritime community, founded in the 1700s. Browse, shop, and tavern-hop at Brown's Wharf.

■ DOWNTOWN

American Cafe
301 Light Street
Harborplace
Baltimore, Maryland 21202
410-962-8800

At the American Cafe, you will enjoy crayfish bisque, lobster and scallop pie, shrimp and crab pizza, grilled catch of the day, and if that is not enough, chocolate amaretto pate with toasted almonds and raspberry puree. Open for lunch and dinner. Credit cards: AE, D, DC, MC, and V.

Bamboo House
301 Light Street
Harborplace
Baltimore, Maryland 21202
410-625-1191

The city's only Chinese restaurant with a harbor view. Features traditional Chinese favorites and seasonal specialties. Voted by Baltimore Magazine as the best Chinese restaurant in the area. Open for lunch and dinner. Credit cards: AE, DC, MC, and V.

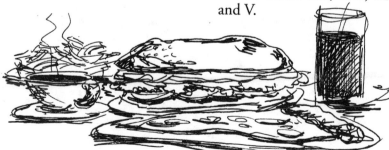

Restaurants, cont.

Bay Cafe
2809 Boston Street
Baltimore, Maryland 21224
410-522-3377

Sit out on the deck overlooking the water and beautiful bayside gardens. Inside, it's light and airy. This building once housed warehouses. Today you can enjoy large windows, fireplaces, and brick walls. Specialties include a raw bar, homemade soups, char-grilled all-beef burgers, individual gourmet pizzas, and overstuffed sandwiches. Entrees include jumbo lump crab imperial, chicken scampi, and New York strip steak. Open for lunch and dinner. Credit cards: AE, DC, MC, and V.

City Lights Restaurant
Harborplace
301 Light Street
Baltimore, Maryland 21202
410-244-8811

Share in the Baltimore tradition of fresh seafood, harborside tables, and good friends. Open for lunch and dinner. Credit cards: AE, D, DC, MC, and V.

Pier 5
711 Eastern Avenue
Baltimore, Maryland 21202
410-783-5553

Enjoy casual indoor elegance and spectacular harbor views while experiencing Maryland's finest tradition—picking fresh, steamed crabs. Or eat from the raw bar aboard an authentic Chesapeake "buy boat" anchored at the dock. Open for breakfast, lunch, and dinner. Credit cards: AE, MC, and V.

Haussner's
3242 Eastern Avenue
Baltimore, Maryland 21224
410-327-8365

Over 200 proficient employees weave their talents into the traditional fabric that is Haussner's. Their respect for customers and pride in their product, fostered over the decades, is evident in their professional approach. The main dining room seats 500. Everything is prepared to order. Haussner's has its own bakery. The restaurant is filled with a magnificent art collection. It is truly a masterpiece of art and dining. Open for lunch and dinner; closed Sundays and Mondays. Credit cards: AE, D, DC, MC, and V.

Lighthouse Restaurant
10 Park Avenue
Baltimore, Maryland 21201
410-727-3814

Steaks and seafood including crabcakes, surf & turf, stuffed softshell crabs, oysters, and homemade specialties. Open daily for breakfast, lunch, and dinner. Credit cards: AE, DC, MC, and V.

Restaurants, cont.

Obrycki's Crab House
1727 East Pratt Street
Baltimore, Maryland 21231
410-732-6399

The new Obrycki's Crab House was constructed on property that included a warehouse and parking lot. The windows came from a monastery dating back to 1927. They have been sandblasted and decorated by a local artist. The bar's oak top boards and all the door and window casings came from the same monastery. Your best reason for coming to Obrycki's though is the wonderful steamed crabs and their seafood seasoning. Open for lunch and dinner Tuesday through Saturday. Credit cards: AE, D, DC, MC, and V.

Phillips Harborplace
301 Light Street
Baltimore, Maryland 21202
410-685-2722
410-547-9060

This restaurant is decorated in the traditional Phillips style. Victorian Tiffany lamps, stained glass windows, and other period items are as much a part of the Phillips tradition as their steamed crabs, crab cakes, cream of crab soup, and creamy crab imperial. Open for lunch and dinner. Credit cards: AE, C, DC, MC, and V.

Rusty Scupper
402 Key Highway
Baltimore, Maryland 21230
410-727-3678

The Rusty Scupper is located opposite the National Aquarium. You will dine in a multi-levelled eatery whose generous portions are an important aspect of dining here. Greenery and glass enhance the restaurant. House specialties include shrimp teriyaki, clam chowder, smoked trout, shrimp and vegetable stir fry, and incredible soft shell crabs. Open for lunch, dinner, and Sunday brunch. Credit cards: AE, D, DC, MC, and V.

Windows Restaurant
202 East Pratt Street
Baltimore, Maryland 21202
410-685-8439

In a word, it's sensational. At Windows Restaurant, you'll be treated to stunning views of the Inner Harbor and the city in a relaxed, informal atmosphere where you can come as you are. The contemporary menu features luscious American dishes highlighted by fresh seafood specialties. Open for breakfast, lunch and dinner. Credit cards: AE, D, DC, MC, and V.

■ FELLS POINT

The Admiral Fell Inn
888 South Broadway
Baltimore, Maryland 21231
410-522-7377
800-BXB-INNS

House specialties include oysters three ways, flaky pastry triangles, baby crab cakes, quiche du jour, lemon tarragon chicken salad, and succulent Maine lobster. Open for lunch and dinner. Credit cards: AE, MC, and V.

Restaurants, 'cont.

Bertha's
734 South Broadway
Baltimore, Maryland 21231
410-327-5795

"Eat Bertha's mussels" is one of the best-known bumper stickers from Maryland. If you visit this Fells Point restaurant, be sure to sample an order. You can choose from a wonderful variety of preparations: mussels with melted butter; mussels with garlic butter and capers; mussels with anchovy, tomato, and garlic sauce; mussels with sour cream and scallions; and mussels with spinach, tarragon, and garlic sauce. Listen to live jazz while you feast on Bertha's mussels. Closed on major holidays. Open for lunch and dinner. Credit cards: MC, V.

■ LITTLE ITALY

Chiapparelli's Restaurant
237 South High Street
Baltimore, Maryland 21202
410-837-0309

Chiapparelli's is one of Little Italy's most popular restaurants. House specialties include hot antipasto, seafood, lasagna, eggplant, and veal. You can select from the long list of veal dinners, spaghetti, chicken parmigiana, and chicken cacciatore. Open for lunch and dinner. Credit cards: AE, CB, D, DC, MC, and V.

DaLesio's
829 Eastern Avenue
Baltimore, Maryland 21202
410-539-1965

Make reservations on the weekends to enjoy this three star restaurant specializing in Northern Italian cuisine. Look forward to such delights as duck ravioli and smoked mozzarella, along with an extensive wine list. Open for lunch and dinner. Credit cards: AE, MC, and V.

Da Mimmo
217 South High Street
Baltimore, Maryland 21202
410-727-6876

Da Mimmo's features superb Italian cuisine such as antipasti, zuppa, vegetali, pollo, and manzo. Open for lunch and dinner. Credit cards: MC and V.

De Nittis'
906 Trinity Street
Baltimore, Maryland 21202
410-685-5601

De Nittis' is a third-generation Italian restaurant established in 1950. Family-style dining is featured in a warm, cozy atmosphere. Serves Little Italy's best pizza as well as veal, pasta, chicken, and seafood dishes. Open for lunch and dinner. Credit cards: AE, CB, D, DC, MC, and V.

Luigi Petti
1002 Eastern Avenue
Baltimore, Maryland 21202
410-685-0055

Specialties at Luigi Petti's include homemade pasta, fresh seafood, veal, and chicken in an up-beat, art deco setting. Enjoy dining and drinking in the newly opened outdoor garden. Open for lunch and dinner. Credit cards: AE, MC, and V.

Restaurants, cont.

Sabatino's
901 Fawn Street
Baltimore, Maryland 21202
410-727-9414

Famous for its pasta. Specialties include tortellini, rigatoni, linguini, capellini, and baked rigatoni. Everyday Italian specials at Sabatino's include homemade ravioli, manicotti, lasagna, eggplant parmigiana, and fettuccine Alfredo. All meat, poultry, and seafood dishes are served with your choice of spaghetti with tomato sauce, French fries, or salad. Open for lunch and dinner. Credit cards: AE, MC and V.

Velleggia's Restaurant
829 East Pratt Street
Baltimore, Maryland 21202
410-685-2620

Since 1937, Velleggia's has been a Little Italy landmark. This third-generation, family-owned restaurant still serves dishes made from "Miss Mary's" original recipes. Enjoy veal, seafood, pasta, and chicken in this modern and attractive restaurant shaded by tidy gardens. Open for lunch and dinner. Credit cards: AE, DC, MC, and V.

Accommodations

■ HOTELS, MOTELS, AND INNS

Baltimore Marriott
Inner Harbor
110 South Eutaw Street
Baltimore, Maryland 21201
410-962-0202

Best Western Hallmark
Inner Harbor
8 North Howard Street
Baltimore, Maryland 21201
410-539-1188, 800-528-1234

Brookshire Hotel
120 East Lombard Street
Baltimore, Maryland 21202
410-625-1300

BWI Airport Marriott Hotel
1743 West Nursery Road
BWI Airport
Baltimore, Maryland 21240
410-859-8300

Clarion Inn
711 Eastern Avenue
Baltimore, Maryland 21202
410-783-5553,
800-CLARION

Comfort Inn
Mt. Vernon
24 West Franklin Street
Baltimore, Maryland 21201
410-727-2000

Days Inn
Inner Harbor
100 Hopkins Place
Baltimore, Maryland 21201
410-576-1000

Harbor City Inn
1701 Russell Street
Baltimore, Maryland 21230
410-727-3400,
800-528-1234

Harbor Court Hotel
550 Light Street
Baltimore, Maryland 21202
410-234-0550

Holiday Inn
BWI Airport
890 Elkridge Landing Road
Linthicum, Maryland 21090
410-859-8400

Holiday Inn
6510 Frankford Avenue
Baltimore, Maryland 21206
410-485-7900

Holiday Inn
Inner Harbor
301 West Lombard Street
Baltimore, Maryland 21201
410-685-3500

Hotels, Motels, and Inns cont.

Hyatt Regency
300 Light Street
Baltimore, Maryland 21202
410-528-1234

Schaefer Hotel
723 St. Paul Street
Baltimore, Maryland 21202
410-332-0405

Johns Hopkins Inn
400 North Broadway
Baltimore, Maryland 21231
410-675-6800

Sheraton Inner Harbor Hotel
300 South Charles Street
Baltimore, Maryland 21201
410-962-8300

Omni Inner Harbor Hotel
101 West Fayette Street
Baltimore, Maryland 21201
410-752-1100

Shoney's Inn
1401 Bloomfield Avenue
Baltimore, Maryland 21227
410-646-1700

Quality Inn East
5625 O'Donnell Street
Baltimore, Maryland 21224
410-633-9500

Society Hill Hopkins
3404 St. Paul Street
Baltimore, Maryland 21218
410-235-8600

Radisson Plaza Lord Baltimore
20-30 West Baltimore Street
Baltimore, Maryland 21201
410-539-8400

Stouffer Harborplace Hotel
202 East Pratt Street
Baltimore, Maryland 21202
410-547-1200

Ramada Hotel
1701 Belmont Avenue
Baltimore, Maryland 21207
410-265-1100

Tremont Hotel
222 St. Paul Place
Baltimore, Maryland 21202
410-576-1200

"When Captain John Smith sailed up the Patapsco, he failed to realize he was entering a complex river system, encompassing miles of shoreline and numerous creeks and tributaries. In a shallow draft vessel designed for exploring inland bodies of water, Smith sailed to within sight of the present Baltimore harbor basin. Finding no inhabitants or unusual developments, Smith left the area and later recorded his sightings in his journal."

■ BED AND BREAKFASTS

Admiral Fell Inn
888 South Broadway
Baltimore, Maryland 21231
410-522-7377

Ann Street Bed and Breakfast
804 South Ann Street
Baltimore, Maryland 21213
410-342-5883

Betsy's Bed and Breakfast
1428 Park Avenue
Baltimore, Maryland 21217
410-383-1274

Celie's Waterfront
Bed and Breakfast
1714 Thames Street
Baltimore, Maryland 21231
410-522-2323

Eagle's Mere Bed and Breakfast
103 East Montgomery Street
Baltimore, Maryland 21231
410-332-1618

Paulus Gasthaus
2406 Kentucky Avenue
Baltimore, Maryland 21213
410-244-0906

■ CAMPING:

Patapsco Valley State Park
8020 Baltimore National Pike
Ellicott City, Maryland 21043
410-461-5005

"The river basin, Baltimore's harbor is a two-pronged estuary of the Chesapeake. The basin is located on the Bay's western shore, 170 miles upstream from the Atlantic Ocean. Divided into the Northwest Harbor and the Middle Branch, the basin composes the larger body of water most people recognize as the Patapsco. Although water movement there is directed by the tidal changes in the Chesapeake Bay, the basin remains a part of the river system, extending the flow of its inland branches. The harbor's perimeters include the edge of Baltimore's downtown business and industrial districts and extend fourteen miles in a southeasterly direction to the Chesapeake Bay. At the point where the Patapsco meets the waters of the Bay, the river reaches its greatest width of approximately four miles, measuring from Fort Howard on the north bank to Fort Smallwood on the south bank.

From *The Patapsco, Baltimore's River of History* by Paul J. Travers.
Copyright © 1990 by Tidewater Publishers. Used by permission.

HAVRE DE GRACE

■ **BACKGROUND:** You'll enjoy a visit to historic Havre De Grace, a charming waterfront community where the Susquehanna River meets the Chesapeake Bay. The smooth-flowing Susquehanna, bringing water from the central Pennsylvania farmlands and forests, empties into the huge, flooded flatlands that locals call "the flats." The Bay is actually a "drowned" river valley of the Susquehanna. The name of Havre De Grace, "Harbor of Grace," comes compliments of General Lafayette. He admired the astonishing beauty of the spot. The War of 1812 had a devastating effect on Havre De Grace. During the early morning hours of May 3, 1813, the British fleet burned the town. Since then, the community has redeveloped, featuring tourism today, with a variety of marinas and other water recreation facilities.

Attractions

■ **VISITOR INFORMATION**

Harford County Tourism
220 South Main Street
Bel Air, Maryland 21014
410-838-6000

Havre De Grace Chamber of Commerce
P.O. Box 339
Havre De Grace, Maryland 21078
410-939-3303

■ **BOAT CRUISES**

Havre De Grace Sailing School Services
P.O. Box 441
Havre De Grace, Maryland21078
410-939-2869

If you do it right, learning to sail can be one of the happiest eperiences of your life. To do it right requires a fine boat and an instructor in whom you can really feel confident. You'll find both here. Private instruction on your own boat is also available. Fee.

398

■ **HISTORIC SITES:** The Havre De Grace Historic District claims about 800 structures. In order to simplify all these buildings, town literature divides them into six chronological groups: the early 1780s to 1830s, canal era, middle period, Victorian, late, and contemporary.

Christmas Candlelight Tour
Havre De Grace, Maryland
21078
410-939-3947
410-939-3303

Tour includes homes, businesses, lockhouse, decoy museum, and lighthouse. Mid-December. Admission charge.

Concord Point Lighthouse
Concord and Lafayette Streets
Havre De Grace, Maryland
21078
410-939-9040

The Concord Point Lighthouse was built in 1827. Your tour of "The City by the Bay" should begin with the most-photographed structure in the city. This lighthouse was one of the eight built by John Donahoo of Havre De Grace. It was part of the navigational improvement effort that enhanced the flow of goods down the Susquehanna River to the Port of Baltimore. The construction of these lighthouses coincided with the opening of the Chesapeake and Delaware Canal that linked the Chesapeake and Delaware Bays. Open to visitors May to October, Saturday, Sunday, and holidays, from 1 p.m. to 5 p.m. Free.

399

■ MISCELLANEOUS

Conowingo Hydroelectric Plant
Route 1
Conowingo, Maryland 21918
410-457-5011

This hydroelectric generating station is the one of four dams to span the Susquehanna River, and features a visitor's center, tours, field trips, a new fish lift, special programs, bird watching, fishing, and wild flowers. It is one of the largest hydro-electric plants in the country. Its enormous dam forms a 14-mile-long freshwater lake, and, until recently, blocked upstream fish movements into the 300 miles of the Susquehanna.

The first automatic fish lift (an elevator-like device) on a Susquehanna dam was opened here in April, 1991, and will allow the return of spawning American shad and herring upriver once fish passage ways are completed on the other dams within the next five years. Shad and herring have been sorted and transported upriver since 1974, but the new lift will automatically take all comers. Public tours of the lift take place April through May each year. Free.

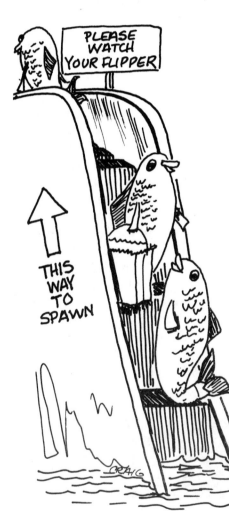

■ MUSEUMS

Havre De Grace Decoy Museum
Giles and Market Streets
Havre De Grace, Maryland 21078
410-939-3739

Havre De Grace bills itself as the decoy capital of the world. Celebrated here are the works of master decoy carvers. As you observe the decoys, keep in mind that the vast majority of the decoys here are working decoys—those that have actually been used for hunting, or created for that purpose. Wooden birds with each feather carved and painted to resemble the real birds are called decorative decoys, and are now considered an art form. Open daily, 11 a.m. to 4 p.m.; closed on major holidays. Admission charge.

Havre de Grace Maritime Museum
100 LaFayette Street
Havre de Grace, Maryland 21078
410-939-4800

The Havre de Grace Maritime Museum is dedicated to preserving the maritime heritage of the upper Chesapeake Bay. A part of that heritage has been preserved in the launching of the skipjack MARTHA LEWIS. This unique sailing vessel has recently been restored by the Museum and will be used for cruises and environmental education. While you're here walk "The Promenade," a new boardwalk that meanders along the waterfront from LaFayette Street to the Tydings Memorial Park.

Museums, cont.

Susquehanna Lockhouse Museum
Erie Street
Havre De Grace, Maryland 21078
410-939-2686
410-939-5780

The Susquehanna and Tidewater Canal was completed in 1830 and opened all of Central Pennsylvania to convenient two-way trade with Philadelphia and Baltimore. The museum is situated at the first lock on the Susquehanna and Tidewater Canal. It is furnished as an 1840 lockhouse. The bridge over the lock has been reconstructed and is operational. Open year 'round, Sunday 1 p.m. to 5 p.m. Free.

Tudor Hall Museum
Tudor Hall Lane
Bel Air, Maryland 21014
410-838-0466

Built in the 1800s by Junius Brutus Booth. The building was the birthplace of Edwin Thomas Booth, the great American Shakespearean actor, and his brother John Wilkes Booth, President Lincoln's assassin. House tours run Memorial Day to September 29, Sundays at 2 p.m. and 3 p.m. Admission charge.

SteppingStone Museum
461 Quaker Bottom Road
Havre De Grace, Maryland 21078
410-939-2299

Turn-of-the-century farm museum with stone farmhouse and supporting shops. Open May to early October, Saturday and Sunday, 1 p.m. to 5 p.m. Admission charge.

U.S. Army Ordnance Museum
Aberdeen Proving Grounds
Aberdeen, Maryland 21001
410-278-3602
410-278-2396

A couple of miles down the road from Havre De Grace, military buffs will be fascinated by rows of tanks, armored cars, and assorted military artillery. Also on exhibit is the first American tank from 1919. Another fascinating weapon is the 166,638 pound "atomic cannon." Open Tuesday to Friday, noon to 4:45 p.m. and Saturday and Sunday, 10 a.m. to 4:45 p.m. Closed on national holidays. Free.

■ PARKS AND GARDENS

Frank Hutchins Memorial Park
Market Street
Havre De Grace, Maryland 21078
410-939-1800

This mini-park is open for daytime use. Try your hand at fishing here. Free.

Gunpowder Falls State Park
P.O. Box 5032
Glen Arm, Maryland 21057
410-592-2897

This 11,000 acre park, laid in various locations along the Gunpowder River valley, attracts families for picnicking, hiking, biking, and wind surfing. There is a marina on Dundee Creek and a host of other facilities. No family camping. Best to call for the brochure listing extensive opportunities in Maryland's largest state park system. Some activities free; charges for others.

Parks and Gardens, cont.

Susquehanna State Park
Route 155
Havre De Grace, Maryland
21078
410-836-6735

Susquehanna State Park is located about 3 miles north of Havre De Grace and offers over 2,000 acres on the west bank of the Susquehanna River. Several main attractions include the Carter Mansion and Rock Run Mill, as well as the Jersey Toll House. Other features are a self-guided nature tour, bird sanctuary, picnic and camp sites, bicycle paths, and one of the best fishing holes on the East Coast. Free.

Tydings Memorial Park
Commerce Street
Havre de Grace, Maryland
21078
410-939-3303

The best view of the Susquehanna Flats is from the rolling hills of Tyding's Memorial Park. Along with river overlooks, a gazebo, boat launch and shaded picnic tables, are yours to enjoy. Open daily, dawn to dusk. Free.

■ SEASONAL EVENTS

Classic Boat Show
Frank Hutchins Park
(Congress Avenue)
Havre de Grace, Maryland
21078
410-939-4800
410-939-2155

Annual Maritime Festival
Formerly
The Antique & Classic
Boat Show

The boat show features antique and classic vessels—power and sail—in the water and on land, as well as plenty of live music, food, drinks, door prizes, artwork, various exhibits, bay authors, and activities just for children. Special attractions include a wooden boat building demonstration and a hands-on demonstration of knots and mechanical advantage. Held in late June, Saturday and Sunday, 10 a.m. to 5 p.m. Admission charge.

Harford County Seafood Festival
Tydings Memorial Park
Havre De Grace, Maryland
21078
410-838-0800
410-838-6000, ext. 339

It's worth coming to this one, just for the menu. Featured is a late summer menu written by nature herself, including steamed Maryland crabs, home-made crab cakes, homemade crab soup, fried fish, corn on the cob, cole slaw, potato salad, and watermelon. Continuous entertainment, arts and crafts, and historic tours will also keep you busy. Mid-August. Admission charge.

Havre De Grace Arts and Crafts Show
Tydings Memorial Park
Havre De Grace, Maryland
21078
410-939-3303
410-939-4440

Along the banks of the Susquehanna, hundreds of artisans exhibit their works in a beautiful park-like setting. Regional artists display their best. Mid August, 10 a.m. to 5 p.m. Free.

Havre De Grace Decoy Festival
P.O. Box A
Havre De Grace, Maryland
21078
410-939-3739

Since time immemorial, thousands of migrating waterfowl such as swans, Canada geese, and canvasbacks have passed annually through this area and have fed on the abundant beds of celery grass. Hunting for these waterfowl spawned the creation of decoys, devices first used by American Indians and then perfected by watermen. The Decoy Festival benefits the Decoy Museum and features decoys, paintings, carvings, refreshments, artists, and much more. Early May, three days, 10 a.m. to 5 p.m. Admission charge.

Restaurants

Baldwin's Crab House
525 Pulaski Highway
Joppa, Maryland 21058
410-679-0957

Exclusively seafood—steamed crabs, shrimp, clams, lobster, crab cake platters, excellent Maryland crab soup. Relax and eat in a large, open dining room. Family atmosphere, excellent service. Open April to November, daily for lunch and dinner. Credit cards: AE, MC.

The Crazy Swede
400 North Union Avenue
Havre De Grace, Maryland 21078
410-939-5440

Fresh seafood and beef. The warm glow of brass, wood and stained glass make for pleasant meals at the Crazy Swede. Open daily for lunch and dinner. Credit cards: AE, DC, MC, and V.

MacGregor's Restaurant and Tavern
331 Franklin Street
Havre De Grace, Maryland 21078
410-939-3003
410-575-7045

Cajun dishes, pastas, fresh seafood, prime ribs and steaks. Open daily for lunch and dinner. Credit Cards: AE, D, DC, MC, and V.

San Lin Garden Chinese Restaurant
913 Pulaski Highway
Havre De Grace, Maryland
21078
410-939-4696

Oriental culinary paradise. Superb cuisine selection of Szechuan, Hunan, and Mandarin entrees. Open daily for lunch and dinner. Credit cards: CB, DC, MC, and V.

Price's Seafood
Water Street
Havre de Grace, Maryland
21078
410-939-2782

Price's Seafood Restaurant is a popular seafood place that has been preparing great food since 1944. The attraction here is the delicious steamed crabs. Need more? Open daily dinner only.

Restaurants, cont.

Tidewater Grille
300 Franklin Street
Havre De Grace, Maryland
21078
410-939-5200

Fresh fish, great pastas, prime beef, new and traditional veal dishes. Two outdoor decks. Open daily for lunch and dinner. Credit cards: AE, MC, and V.

Vandiver Inn
301 South Union Avenue
Havre De Grace, Maryland
21078
410-939-5200

Sneak in for supper on this bed and breakfast's varied, a la carte menu. Start with butternut soup and move on to anything from poached salmon and crab cakes to grilled duck, veal and surf & turf. Open daily from 6 p.m. to 9 p.m.

Accommodations

■ BED AND BREAKFASTS

Spencer Silver Mansion
200 South Union Avenue
Havre De Grace, Maryland 21078
10-939-1097

Tudor Hall
Tudor Lane
Bel Air, Maryland 21414
410-838-0466

Vandiver Inn
301 South Union Avenue
Havre De Grace, Maryland 21078
410-939-5200

■ CAMPING:

Chesapeake View Campsites
P.O. Box 768
Perryville, Maryland 21918
410-642-6626

Riverside Ponderosa Pines
1435 Carpenter's Point Road
Perryville, Maryland 21903
410-642-3431

■ HOTELS, MOTELS, AND INNS

Comfort Inn
61 Heather Lane
Perryville, Maryland 21903
410-642-2282

El Capitan
5271 Pulaski Highway
Perryville, Maryland 21903
410-642-2282

TRAVELED THIS ROAD

NORTH EAST

■ **BACKGROUND:** The Upper Chesapeake Bay enjoys a rich history of maritime activity. Water-related industry and commerce have long played vital roles in the local economy. For hundreds of years, watermen have earned their livelihoods from the bounties of the Bay. Many local people view the Northeast River, rather than the Susquehanna, as the true head of the Chesapeake Bay. Today the area is also a busy boating center where fresh-air recreational opportunities abound. Lovely forests, beautiful parks, sandy shorelines, and open marshlands provide a wealth of natural wonder for the hiker, hunter, fisher, swimmer, birder, or just plain looker. The town of North East, Maryland, is located at the head of the Northeast River and was founded in 1658. North East, the geographic center of Cecil County, is 28 miles southeast of Wilmington, Delaware, and 45 miles northeast of Baltimore, Maryland.

Attractions

■ **VISITOR INFORMATION**

North East Chamber of Commerce
300 Cherry Street
North East, Maryland 21901
410-287-5801
410-287-5800

■ **MISCELLANEOUS**

Day Basket Factory
110 West High Street
North East, Maryland 21901
410-287-6100

Gilpin Falls Covered Bridge
Route 272
North East, Maryland 21901

The Day Basket Factory is Cecil County's oldest industry. Here you will find hand-woven white oak baskets that are made basically the same way as they were in 1897 when the factory was founded by the Day Brothers. A variety of baskets are available for purchase from the retail store. Open Monday through Friday, 8:30 a.m. to 4 p.m.; Saturday,10 a.m. to 4 p.m. Closed Sunday. Free.

North of town, on Route 272, stands one of the few remaining covered bridges of Maryland. Gilpin Falls Covered Bridge was built about 1860 and was recently renovated to its original splendor.

■ MUSEUMS

Upper Bay Museum
P.O. Box 275
Walnut Street
North East, Maryland 21901
410-287-5718
410-287-8428

On display is the rare, original swan decoy. It is part of the museum's comprehensive collection of early Susquehanna Flats working decoys. Handsome and functional, these carved waterfowl replicas have become a popular folk art. Today, the heritage of both the commercial hunters of the past and today's recreational hunter is preserved. The museum is located in two spacious buildings located at the head of the Northeast River. This unique museum houses an extensive collection of hunting, boating, and fishing artifacts native to the Upper Chesapeake. Open Sundays from Memorial Day through Labor Day, 9 a.m. to 4 p.m.; other hours by appointment. Free.

■ PARKS AND GARDENS

Elk Neck Demonstration Forest
130 McKinneytown
North East, Maryland 21901
410-287-5333

Here, hunting enthusiasts will enjoy seasonal camping (primitive only), equipped cabins, swimming, hunting, and fishing. Admission charge for some activities.

Elk Neck State Park
4395 Turkey Point Road
North East, Maryland 21901
410-287-5333

The Elk Neck State Park is located 10 miles south of town on Route 272. Its 2,000 acres lay between the Elk and Northeast Rivers. Visitors can enjoy such activities as swimming, fishing, boating, boat launching, row boat and canoe rentals, biking, and bird and wildlife study. Of note is the Turkey Point Lighthouse standing on the point of land that separates the Elk and North East Rivers. It is the only lighthouse in the Upper Chesapeake. Established in 1933, it still functions and is serviced by the US Coast Guard. Admission charge.

North East Park
Walnut and Cherry Streets
North East, Maryland 21901
410-287-5801

This waterfront park offers picnic pavilions and riverside fishing (requiring no licenses). Take a line along with your picnic basket, and you may even be able to grill a bass or trout for supper. Open from dawn to dusk daily. Admission charge.

Restaurants

River Watch Restaurant
200 Cherry Street
North East, Maryland 21901
410-287-8030

Enjoy a spectacular view of the Northeast River from a spacious window of any of the three dining rooms. A complete menu features seafood from the Chesapeake and many meat and fowl dishes. Open for breakfast, lunch, and dinner. Credit cards: AE, DC, MC, and V.

The Wharf Restaurant
One North Main Street
North East, Maryland 21901
410-287-6599

House specialties at The Wharf include pot roast, prime rib, top round, meat loaf, chicken and dumplings, and special Italian nights with pasta and lasagna. Open Sunday to Thursday from 6 a.m. to 8 p.m.; Saturday from 6 a.m. to 9 p.m.

Woody's Crab House
29 Main Street
North East, Maryland 21901
410-287-3541

Chef Paul Pierce takes pride in his crab imperial. It's one of the best the Bay has to offer other selection is the Wednesday night seafood special. "All the crab legs and shrimp you can seat." Open daily for dinner only. Credit cards: AE, DC, MC, and V.

Accommodations

■ BED AND BREAKFASTS

Chesapeake Lodge
Route 272
North East, Maryland 21901
410-287-5433

Mill House Bed and Breakfast
102 Mill Lane
North East, Maryland 21901
410-287-5433

■ CAMPING

Elk Neck State Forest
4395 Turkey Point Road
North East, Maryland 21901
410-287-5675

Elk Neck State Park
4395 Turkey Point Road
North East, Maryland 21901
410-287-5333

ELKTON

■ **BACKGROUND:** Elkton, originally named "Head of Elk," was a crossroads for major participants in the Revolutionary War. Lafayette embarked with his troops from Elkton to capture the traitor Benedict Arnold. Arnold evaded capture, later fighting with the English commander Cornwallis. Lafayette returned April 9, 1781, and began an overland march to Virginia on April 12. Other revolutionary heroes, Washington and Rochambeau, rested their combined forces in Elkton on September 6 and 7, 1781, on their way to Yorktown. There, Lafayette, Washington, and other American forces defeated Cornwallis—who had since sacked Arnold and sent him to England. A unique blend of historic attractions, time-honored events, and outdoor recreational activities make this county perfect for a getaway trip. Tucked away in Maryland's northeastern corner, Cecil County boasts of miles of rolling countryside, scenic rivers, and the Chesapeake Bay.

Attractions

■ **VISITOR INFORMATION**

Cecil County Chamber of Commerce
135 East Main Street
Elkton, Maryland 21921
410-392-3833

Cecil County Economic Development Office
Room 324
County Office Building
Elkton, Maryland 21921
410-398-0200

The Elkton Chamber of Commerce
101 E. Main Street
Elkton, MD 21921
410-398-1640

■ BOAT CRUISES

Captain Phineas McHenry, Ltd.
38 Oak Hill Lane
Elkton, Maryland 21921
410-287-2028

Sailing school, cruising course, wine and cheese cruise—take your choice. Catch a breeze, relax, and let Moon Shadow glide you through the Upper Chesapeake. Open daily from March 15 to November 15. Admission charge.

■ HUNTING/FISHING

Cecil County Clerk's Office
Room 109
County Office Building
Elkton, Maryland 21921
410-398-0200

Permits for both hunting and fishing can be obtained from licensed agents, at sporting goods stores, and here from the Cecil County Clerk's Office.

■ MISCELLANEOUS

Fair Hill Races
Fair Hill Grounds
Elkton, Maryland 21921
410-398-6565

Fair Hill Races are renowned as the only steeplechase races in the United States that permit pari-mutuel wagering. The races take place over rolling hills and fences, creating a breathtaking spectacle. Races take place near Labor Day and Memorial Day, and occasionally at other times. Admission charge.

Miscellaneous, cont.

Milburn Orchards
1495 Appleton Road
Elkton, Maryland 21921
410-398-1349

Milburn Orchards has been a family-owned farm since 1902. The family is now in its third and fourth generations of orchard operations. The farm market offers you high-quality fruit, vegetables, and family fun during ten months of the year. Among highlights at the farm are the cherry, apple, and peach seasons, honey and preserves, hayrides, craft shows, school tours, mums, and custom-made fruit baskets. The peaches here are among the most delicious in the world! Call for the orchard's seasonal brochure to time your visit. Open July 5 to December 24, Monday to Saturday, 8 a.m. to 8 p.m. After third Sunday in October, Sunday hours are 10 a.m. to 5 p.m. Free admission; charge for products.

Plumpton Park Zoological Gardens
1416 Telegraph Road
Rising Sun, Maryland 21911
410-658-6850

Plumpton Park is a portion of land granted from William Penn to James William and Mercer Brown in 1701. The 18th century structures and sites within the park were placed on the National Register of Historical Places in 1987. The Zoological Gardens feature exotic animals living in a country setting. Zoo hours are daily from 10 a.m. to 5 p.m. Admission charge.

Sinking Springs Herb Farm
234 Blair Shore Road
Elkton, Maryland 21921
410-398-5566

Any herb fancier will delight in the fragrant herbs of Sinking Springs. Take a guided tour of the secluded herb gardens, the colonial house, and the gift shop. Open Monday Through Saturday 9 a.m. to 4 p.m. Self-guided tours are free. Guided tours, admission charge.

■ PARKS AND GARDENS

Fair Hill Natural Resources Management Area
Routes 273 and 213
Fair Hill, Maryland 21921
410-398-1246

This natural area is the site of many major events, such as a steeplechase, Scottish games, and the Cecil County Fair. At the Fair Hill Nature and Environmental Center, which offers environmental education, members and public groups can learn about the area and the Chesapeake Bay. (By reservation only. Call 410-398-4909.)

Restaurants

The Chesapeake Restaurant
216 Bridge Street
Elkton, Maryland 21921
410-398-7990

Seafood and steak specials. Complete seafood market on premises. Open daily for lunch and dinner. Credit cards: AE, DC, MC, and V.

Howard House Tavern
101 West Main Street
Elkton, Maryland 21921
410-398-4646

Taste the Bay here, with crab and seafood specialties. Crabs featured year-round. Open daily for lunch and dinner. Credit cards: MC, V.

Swiss Inn
Route 40
Elkton, Maryland 21921
410-398-3252

Stop here for Chesapeake Bay specialties at reasonable prices. Homemade soups, pie, and ice cream. Open daily for lunch and dinner. Credit cards: AE, D, MC, and V.

Accommodations

■ **BED AND BREAKFASTS**

Garden Cottage at Sinking Springs
234 Blair Shore Road
Elkton, Maryland 21921
410-398-5566

■ **CAMPING**

Woodlands Camping Resort
265 Starkey Lane
Elkton, Maryland 21921
410-398-4414

■ HOTELS, MOTELS, AND INNS

Econo Lodge
I-95 and Route 279
Elkton, Maryland 21921
410-392-5010

Knights Inn
I-95 and Route 279
Elkton, Maryland 21921
410-392-6680

Elkton Inn
Route 40
Elkton, Maryland 21921
410-398-0530

Motel 6
223 Belle Hill Road
Elkton, Maryland 21921
410-398-5020

Elkton Lodge
I-95 and Route 279
Elkton, Maryland 21921
410-398-9400

Sutton Motel
405 East Pulaski Highway
Elkton, Maryland 21921
410-398-3830

INDEX

ATTRACTIONS

INDEX

INDEX

Historic Sites

INDEX

INDEX

Museums

INDEX

INDEX

Neighborhoods

Parks and Gardens

INDEX

INDEX

Seasonal Events

INDEX

Tours

RESTAURANTS

INDEX

INDEX

INDEX

INDEX

ACCOMMODATIONS

Bed and Breakfasts

INDEX

INDEX

Hotels, Motels, and Inns

INDEX

INDEX

INDEX

INDEX

For Other Readers

Alotta, Robert, *Sign Post & Settlers*. Bonus Books, 1992.

Duke, Maurice, *Chesapeake Bay Voice*. Dietz Press, 1993.

Shellenberger, William H., *Cruising the Chesapeake*. International Marine Publishing Company, 1990.

Sherwood, John, *Maryland's Vanishing Lives*. The Johns Hopkins University Press, 1994.

Rouse Jr., Parke, *The James*. Dietz Press, 1990.

Peters, Margaret T. *A Guidebook to Virginia's Historical Markers*. University Press of Virginia, 1985.

Robertson, James I., *Civil War Virginia*. University Press of Virginia.

Klingel, Gilbert, *The Bay*. The Johns Hopkins University Press, 1951.

Fox, Larry and Barbin-Radin-Fox, *Romantic Weekend Getaways*. Wiley, 1990.

Hatch, Charles E. *The First Seventeen Years of Virginia*. The University Press of Virginia, 1957.

Tilp, Fred and Fay, *Chesapeake, Fact, Fiction, Fun*. Heritage Books, Inc.

Mooney, Elizabeth, *Country Adventures*. The Washington Book Trading Co.

Smith, Jane Ockershausen, *One Day Trips to Beauty & Bounty*. EPM Publications, 1983.

Miles, Priscilla L. Miles, *Historic Baltimore*. Miles, 1987.

Sherwood, Arthur, *Understanding the Chesapeake*. Tidewater Publishers, 1973.

Hays, Anne, Hazleton, Harriet R., *Chesapeake Kaleidoscope*. Tidewater Publishers, 1975.

Niemeyer, Lucian, Meyer, Eugene, *Chesapeake Country*. Abbeville Press, 1990.

Whitehead III, John Hurt, *The Watermen of the Chesapeake.* Tidewater Publishers, 1979.

White, Dan, *Crosscurrents in Quiet Water.* Taylor Publishing Co., 1987.

Flemming, Kevin, *Annapolis.* Portfolio Press, 1988.

Bodine, Aubrey A., *Chesapeake Bay and Tidewater.* Bonanza Books, 1951.

Beitzell, Edward W., *Point Lookout Prison Camp for Confederates.* St. Mary's County Historical Society, 1983.

Burgess, Robert H., *This Was Chesapeake Bay.* Tidewater Publishers, 1963.

ACKNOWLEDGEMENTS

Linda Brudvig
Scott Brudvig
Clevie Clark
Crisfield Bill and Gracie
Leslie Dawson
Mike Dirham
Falls Camera
Jose Garnham
Dean Gore
Louise Jennings
Raymond McAlwee
New Bay Times
Pat Piper
Pica & Points Typography
Robin Quinn
Tab Distributing Co.
Tom Vernon

Cover Design by Denise McDonald

About the Author

Whitey Schmidt, a native Marylander who "lives on the Bay" is author of the popular culinary classic's *The Crab Cookbook* and the *Flavor of the Chesapeake Bay Cookbook*. Other Schmidt selections include, *A Guide to Chesapeake Seafood Dining* and the best selling *The Official Crab Eater's Guide*. The food writer's thoughts on fine dining and tempting meal preparations appear regularly in his syndicated cooking column "Schmidt's Hit's."

About the Illustrator:

Craig Robinson was reared in Baltimore, Maryland. His formal training was developed while attending the Maryland Institute College of Art. His work has appeared in *Scene* Magazine, *The New Bay Times* and *The Capital* Newspaper.

BOOK ORDER FORM

Chesapeake Books Make Excellent Gifts

THE CRAB COOKBOOK
Specialty dishes include:
- Crunchy Crab Nuggets
- New Orleans Crab Spread
- Baltimore Crab Soup
- G.W.'s She Crab Soup
- Crab Meat and Canteloupe Salad
- Chesapeake Bay Crab Salad
- Maryland Crab Cakes
- Oyster House Road Crab Cakes
- Deale Deviled Crab
- Northern Neck Stuffed Crab
- Soft Shell Crabs with Tarragon Sauce
- Spicy Stuffed Soft Shell Crab
- Miles River Crab Imperial
- Choptank Crab Fritters
- Sizzling Dungeness Crab Legs

BAYTRIPPER VOL. I / EASTERN SHORE

BAYTRIPPER VOL. II / WESTERN SHORE
Whitey gives you an insider's tour...town by town throughout the Western Shore of the Chesapeake Bay. Coverage extends to the Bay's Eastern Shore in Volume I. Bay trips, day trips, out-of-the-way trips...you'll find it all here in his two helpful, informative guides!

FLAVOR OF THE CHESAPEAKE BAY COOKBOOK

Whitey's exceptional recipes—some elegant, others informal—are combined with beautiful photographs by the region's foremost photographer, Marion E. Warren, along with historic anecdotes and relevant commentary. Browse through and experience the Chesapeake with pleasure. Or enjoy cooking these savory foods that are sure to delight. You and your guests are in for a flavorful treat!

ORDERED BY: _____

NAME   ADDRESS   CITY, STATE, AND ZIP

SHIP TO: _____

NAME   ADDRESS   CITY, STATE AND ZIP

ITEM NO.	QUANTITY	DESCRIPTION	PRICE	TOTAL	MAIL TO:
01		The Crab Cookbook	$12.95		MARIAN HARTNETT PRESS
02		Flavor of the Chesapeake Bay Cookbook	$13.95		Box 51
03		Baytripper / Eastern Shore	$12.95		Friendship Road
04		Baytripper / Western Shore	$14.95		Friendship, Maryland 20758
		TOTAL			
		Shipping for 1 to 3 books		1.75	
		Maryland Residents add 5% Sales Tax			
		TOTAL ENCLOSED			

For additional information on ordering books or discount schedule, write:

Marian Hartnett Press
Box 51
Friendship Road
Friendship, Maryland 20758